MOVIE MARKETING

OPENING THE PICTURE AND GIVING IT LEGS

TIIU LUKK

SILMAN-JAMES PRESS   **LOS ANGELES**

First Edition
10 9 8 7 6 5 4 3 2 1

Library of Congress Cataloging-in-Publication Data

Lukk, Tiiu.
Movie marketing : opening the picture and giving it legs /
by Tiiu Lukk. — 1st ed.
Includes bibliographical references.
1. Motion pictures—Marketing. 2. Motion pictures—Distribution.
I. Title.
PN1995.9.M29L85   1997
384'.8.0688—dc21   97-31744
                                               CIP

ISBN: 1-879505-38-X

Cover design by Wade Lageose, Art Hotel

Printed and Bound in the United States of America

Silman-James Press
1181 Angelo Drive
Beverly Hills, CA 90210

To my loving mother,
Aino Wain Lukk,
to the memory of my loving father,
Dr. Olaf Lukk,

to my precious family,
Mark, Michael and David,

and to my dear brothers,
Olaf and Ott.

CONTENTS

FOREWORD
by Mark Litwak

As anyone who peruses a newspaper, watches television or visits a McDonald's knows, movie marketing has pervaded our everyday existence. When a major studio releases an "event" film, the marketing campaign is tackled with the same zeal and methodical planning as a general preparing an invasion. Studio executives spend months agonizing over the best release dates and rollout patterns. Tens of millions of dollars in marketing funds are allocated among television, radio, billboard, and newspaper advertising. Publicists conceive news hooks and arrange celebrity interviews. Market research is used to gauge audience response and devise alternative advertising campaigns. Specialists are hired to cut trailers. By the time the film is released, a studio may have negotiated a multi-million-dollar cross-promotional deal with a fast-food giant, arranged for publication of a novelization, distribution of a soundtrack album, and licensed merchandising rights to hundreds of manufacturers. The outcome of this campaign is closely observed by the news media, which may second-guess the wisdom of every marketing decision and report widely on any mistakes. The success or failure of a movie has become news itself, with the media keeping a tally and reporting box-office statistics alongside baseball scores and stock market prices. It was not always this way.

In the days of the moguls, the so-called Studio Era, movies were often made with little attention paid to marketing preproduction. Upon completion of a film, marketing experts were brought in to figure out how to sell it. Nowadays, marketing executives at the major studios are involved in the earliest stages of development. If a story sounds promising, but the marketing department opines that it will be a difficult sell, the project may be shelved. The increasing clout of marketing executives is reflected in the hierarchy at many studios, where the head of marketing and distribution functions at the same level as the head of production.

One reason that marketing has become so critical is because the major studios increasingly aim to create blockbuster hits. Such films require enormous marketing expenditures to back up their wide release. As the cost of advertising has escalated, and as the marketplace has become increasingly crowded and competitive, marketing decisions have become critical. While a brilliant marketing campaign cannot save an awful picture, a good picture can be lost in the shuffle if it is not marketed well.

A basic knowledge of marketing has become important for creators of movies as well as those who aspire to work in studio marketing departments or ad agencies. A writer can waste a lot of time crafting a screenplay that will never obtain distribution because it is difficult to market. Filmmakers must understand how movies are sold to the public if they ever hope to market their projects to a distributor.

In order to understand how movies are marketed, one must recognize that the "movie industry" is actually comprised of a group of sub-industries that operate alongside one another. These industry segments release different types of films, and the manner in which they are marketed varies as well. The three major segments of the industry are 1) the major distributors, 2) the specialty distributors, and 3) the B-movie distributors.

The largest segment of the "movie industry" by far, as measured by box-office revenues, is that of the major distributors. The majors, such as Paramount, Warner Bros. and Universal, garner more than ninety-five percent of domestic box-office revenues. Ever since *Jaws* become a hit in 1975, these companies have focused their efforts on releasing movies that have the potential to become blockbuster hits. Such a film can generate hundreds of millions of dollars in box-office revenues, with additional millions derived from the home video and television media. The dream of major-studio executives is to hit a home run by creating not only a popular film but a new franchise. Movies like *Jurassic Park* and *The Lion King* can generate a billion-dollar revenue stream when one considers the sequel, television, toy and other merchandising, soundtrack album, and theme-park attractions that can be spun off the original movie. Although each studio may only have one or two blockbuster hits a year, the revenue generated from them can cover a great deal of studio overhead, development expenses, and losses from flops.

While the major studios occasionally release smaller pictures—often prestige projects that can garner critical acclaim and awards, projects that may cement relationships with important talent and/

or projects that can be made on modest budgets—their primary focus is on potential blockbusters. Of course, many blockbuster candidates do not realize their potential. To understand how skewed the market is, one need only examine each year's box-office grosses.

About 450 movies are released in movie theaters each year in the United States. Of these, approximately 150 are released as major-studio films, with the remainder released by independent distributors or specialty divisions of the major studios. Approximately a dozen films each year earn a domestic box-office gross above $100 million. Three dozen films or so have grosses over $50 million. The average cost of studio movies is $35 million or more, and another $17 million or more is spent on prints and advertising. Since about half of box-office gross is remitted to distributors (the rest remains with exhibitors as their share of revenues), most films do not earn their costs back from their domestic theatrical release. This would be a very risky business, indeed, if not for the substantial revenues earned from home video, television, and sales to foreign territories, revenues that today are far greater than those collected from the domestic box office. However, while most studio movies do not earn back their production and marketing costs from their domestic theatrical release, the advertising and promotion dollars spent here build public awareness of the film and enable the studio to earn substantial sums from the home video and television markets. In these so-called ancillary markets, studio marketing expenses are modest and revenues can be substantial.

Since studio movies are designed to be potential blockbusters, they are mass-marketed. Typically, they are released on 500 or more screens, sometimes opening on 2,000 to 3,000 screens. A wide release is backed with a national advertising campaign relying on television, radio, and full-page newspaper ads. A cross-promotional deal with Burger King can add millions more in advertising dollars.

A different type of picture is marketed by specialty distributors such as Sony Pictures Classics, Miramax, October Films, and Goldwyn. These films are not marketed with a mass audience in mind. The audience is primarily young urban professionals. Examples of such films are *sex, lies and videotape*, *Welcome to the Dollhouse*, and *The Brothers McMullen*. These pictures are often independently financed (i.e., not financed by the distributor) and produced on low budgets without big-name actors, or with big names willing to work for modest up-front compensation. Specialty films tend to be much more offbeat and quirky than major studio films. Specialty distributors handle American independent films and foreign films and an occasional documentary.

Specialty films are marketed with little, if any, television advertising. The distributor places much more reliance on benefit screenings, free publicity, festival showings, critical reviews, and other methods designed to spread positive word-of-mouth.

The difference between the majors and the specialty distributors is analogous to the difference between Sears Roebuck and a small clothing boutique. Both companies operate in the clothing industry but each sells different products marketed in a distinct manner. Sears Roebuck is a mass marketer. It is looking for clothing that will appeal to common tastes. Sears stocks clothes that will sell in Peoria, Illinois and their many other locations. It buys and sells in volume. The chain spends considerable sums on advertising. Sears does not stock avant-garde items for which there would be minimal demand among its customers.

The clothing boutique, on the other hand, selectively stocks product that will appeal to its clientele. Boutique customers are look-ing for something different, more offbeat, than what can be found in a chain department store. The boutique may sell fewer items, but overhead costs are lower and advertising expenses minimal. The bou-tique doesn't try to compete with Sears in volume of sales. The poly-ester leisure suit that is a Sears bestseller would never be stocked by the boutique.

The major movie distributors operate like Sears Roebuck. They are looking for films they can mass market. The specialty distribu-tors, on the other hand, are looking for something special that will appeal to their clientele. Of course, many specialty distributors are now subsidiaries of major studios, such as Miramax/Disney, Fine Line/Time Warner, Sony Classics/Sony, Fox Searchlight/20th Cen-tury Fox. As this book went to press, one of the last remaining in-dependents, October Films, was tentatively sold to Universal, while MGM announced that it would acquire Metromedia and its Goldwyn subsidiary. So perhaps a better analogy would be that the specialty distributor operates like the Calvin Klein section in a Macy's department store.

Filmmakers who don't understand the difference risk creating motion pictures that are neither fish nor fowl, films that don't sat-isfy the needs of either kind of distributor. Such a project, for ex-ample, might be a story about a lesbian cattle drive. This story may meet with great resistance at the major studios. Executives might feel that middle America is not ready to embrace a Western about lesbian cowgirls. While this movie might play well in New York, Los Angeles, and other large urban areas, it might fare poorly in smaller markets where there are fewer moviegoers wanting to see a gay-themed picture.

The specialty companies might reject this project, but for entirely different reasons. I can imagine a specialty executive exclaiming, "I love the lesbian angle, but lose the cattle. Do you have any idea how expensive it is to rent a herd of cattle?" Here the project is likely to be rejected because of its cost. Many specialty distributors do not fund production—they acquire finished films that have been independently financed. This hypothetical project would be difficult to finance from private investors. It is one thing to raise $800,000 from a group of dentists; it is quite another, and a much more difficult task, to raise the $10 million needed to make a period piece shot on numerous locations involving herds of wild animals.

Distributor classifications have become blurred as major distributors have acquired or established specialty divisions. These divisions operate somewhat autonomously, but their corporate parents provide financial backing, which allows them to tackle bigger projects. The specialty divisions are increasingly financing their own movies, rather than just acquiring independently made product, because the competition for the best independent films has become so intense.

The third major segment of the movie industry I will refer to as the B-movie companies. These companies handle low-budget genre movies, often stories with gratuitous sex or violence. Films like *Carnosaur* from Roger Corman or *Toxic Avengers* from Troma are examples. Today, few of these films will get much, if any, theatrical release in the United States. Many of these films, however, can make a profit on home video, television, and foreign sales. This market niche has been squeezed as the major studios have lost their inhibitions about releasing movies with a lot of sex or violence. Why should moviegoers buy a ticket to a low-budget horror film when they can see *Alien* and other films with much better production val-

ues? Moreover, with the demise of drive-in theaters, the venues for
B-pictures have declined.

• • •

While marketing has become critically important to the film business there is a remarkable absence of in-depth works on the subject.
The few books on the topic that I am aware of are either out-of-
date primers or academic treatises with impenetrable prose. Tiiu
Lukk's *Movie Marketing: Opening the Picture and Giving it Legs* admi-
rably fills the gap with an informative survey of how movies are
marketed today. She has written about a wide variety of films to
show the different ways that movies can be marketed. This book
not only reveals a great deal of inside information on distributor
strategies and their marketing expenditures, but does so in a highly
entertaining fashion, by writing about the people who market films.
It is rare to find a book like *Movie Marketing*, which covers the nuts
and bolts of a complex topic and is also enjoyable to read. This book
is destined to be a primer in film and business schools for many
years to come.

Mark Litwak

September 1997

[Mark Litwak is an entertainment attorney and producer's rep who
advises independent filmmakers on marketing and distribution. He
is the author of *Reel Power, Dealmaking in the Film and Television
Industry, Contracts for the Film and Television Industry,* and *Litwak's
Multimedia Producer's Handbook.*]

ACKNOWLEDGMENTS

I am profoundly grateful to a number of people for their assistance; without them, I could never have written this book. First and foremost, I am indebted to my husband, Mark, and our sons, David and Michael, whose love, support, encouragement, and forbearance has and will continue to sustain me. There are not enough thank-yous in the universe to shower on my parents, Aino and Dr. Olaf Lukk, for their sacrifice and priceless gifts. I will always be grateful to St. Olaf College, the Columbia University Graduate School of Journalism, the Alice Weel-Bigart Scholarship Fund, Mrs. Cecil Montgomery-Moore, and the family of Alice Weel-Bigart for their contribution to my growth as a journalist.

I would especially like to thank all the people who were kind enough to share their knowledge and insights with me and the readers of this book, especially Liz Manne, Ira Deutchman, Steve Flynn, David Dinerstein, Mark Gill, Alfa Tate-O'Neill, Mary Flatlie, Steve

James, Frederick Marx, John Iltis, Dave Sikich, Susan Missner, Melody Korenbrot, Ziggy Kozlowski, Leonard Klady, Anita Busch, Lauren De La Fuente, Tom Bernard, Michael Barker, Todd Solondz, Alex Kostich, Adam Simon, Jim Fredrick, Joe Berlinger, Chris Arnold, Bill Mechanic, Stuart Halperin, Bill Howard, Marty Brochstein, Mitchell Goldman, Dan Prince, Lynn M. Fava and Competitive Media Reporting, Marvin Antonowsky, Sid Ganis, Dan Michel, Julian Meyers, Arnold Fishman, John Jacobs, Joanne Watkins and Scott Wiseman. I owe special kudos to those who contributed behind the scenes in a thousand ways: Ryan Gawel and attorney Michael E. Morales ably and thoroughly assisted with the research; Amy Lee and Destiny McCune meticulously transcribed interview tapes; Liz Manne and others read early drafts of individual chapters; Jon Mostow, Grant Mitchell, Michael E. Morales, and Mark Litwak read and commented on early drafts of the book; Carol Erb gave her tireless support to our entire family. I am grateful to the Margaret Herrick Library of the Academy of Motion Picture Arts and Sciences and their librarians for their assistance and access to their research materials. Sincere thanks to Jim Fox and Gwen Feldman at Silman-James Press for guiding this book to publication.

● ● ●

When planning and executing their campaigns, movie marketers and advertisers need to know who is advertising, how often they're advertising, where they're advertising, and why they are advertising. In Hollywood, accurate information is very hard to come by, especially when it involves the expenditure of money. Competitive Media Reporting provides what they call "strategic advertising intelligence" to advertising agencies, advertisers, marketers, broadcasters, journalists, and publishers involved in the film industry. They gather this "intelligence" by tracking advertising occurrences and the creative executions of more than 750,000 "brands" across all media, including television, magazine, radio, outdoor, and the Internet.

Competitive Media Reporting (CMR) has generously offered to share their marketing intelligence on the advertising expenditures of the "brands," that is movies, that are the focus of this book. Hopefully, this intelligence will help readers put each movie's marketing strategy into dollars and cents.

CMR gathers this information through a sophisticated computer tracking system, supplemented by more traditional methods, including human beings clipping ads in newspapers. CMR also has relationships with broadcasters, advertising agencies, publishers and media buyers who supply them with rate card information. The company then develops advertising cost estimates and applies those estimates to the occurrence data to arrive at expenditure levels.

This information gives movie marketers valuable information when planning their campaigns, to make sure that they are getting the most effective use of their advertising dollars. Marketers and agencies use the data to track trends, to analyze their own expenditures, and to determine where their competitors' expenditures have been, so they can find the magic mix that will generate the greatest box-office.

Competitive Media Reporting expenditure reports have been included in each chapter.

PREFACE

When I first set out to write this book, I hoped to explain in a readable, entertaining fashion how movies are marketed. The news media often talks about box-office figures, but rarely delves into the strategy and specifics of how films are marketed. While marketing films does not require any genius, many marketing executives jealously guard the workings of their craft. This may be partially because they don't want their competitors to learn their marketing secrets, but also because marketing is an inexact science, and in many instances, the film does not succeed. Most marketing executives will concede that the most that they can accomplish is to get moviegoers to taste the movie the first week of its release. After that, word-of-mouth takes over. Ultimately, the quality of the story determines whether a film succeeds or fails. As one marketing executive said, "If the film succeeds, don't give me the credit; if it fails, don't give me the blame." Despite the marketing hype, word-of-mouth still depends on whether the writer/filmmaker did a good job of telling a story.

Nonetheless, in a world filled with media "clutter," a fine film *can* get lost in the shuffle, and numerous marketing executives, such as Michael Barker of Sony Pictures Classics, consider it their mission to see that these films have a chance to compete in the marketplace. I am grateful to Michael and the other marketers who took the time and had the patience to participate in lengthy interviews and share their marketing expertise with me and my readers. Some of the marketers, like David Dinerstein and Stuart Halperin, did so because they would have liked to have a book like this available to them when they were earning their graduate degrees. Many of those who participated did so out of sheer love of film, and I trust that readers will find their enthusiasm as infectious as I did.

When researching this book, I tried to focus on a cross-section of dramatic and documentary films in a range of budgets and genres, including romantic comedy, action-adventure, American independent, foreign, low-budget/B-movies, suspense thrillers, and science fiction. Rather than deliver a dry dissertation on the nuts and bolts of the marketing process, I took an anecdotal, case-study approach to the marketing of each of the films in an effort to describe how the marketing campaign evolved. In the process of compiling these case histories, I spoke to marketing strategists, ad agency executives, publicists, trailer producers, distribution executives, and to some of the filmmakers themselves. I've tried to present their perspectives on the creative process of planning and executing a marketing campaign and creating the posters, trailers, television and print ads, publicity and merchandising spinoffs that have such an impact on a film's bottom line. Because marketers and distributors speak their own language, I've chosen to let the experts speak in their own words as much as possible. In the interest of accuracy, every one of the interviews in this book was recorded. People deserve to be quoted accurately. However the interpretation of facts and events in this book are mine, and I take full responsibility for them.

Writing this book was a difficult task. Too many people in the film industry are not just reluctant to talk about what they do and how they do it, more often than not they are afraid to talk. It is understandable that marketers would not want to share proprietary information. What I encountered on the part of some prospective interviewees, however, was a palpable fear that if they shared information, someone would steal their magic. I also encountered a few misguided souls who apparently don't understand the difference between a journalist and a publicist, and assume that interviewees have a right to approve a journalists' copy—a right of approval no serious journalist in their right mind would ever give. In contrast, the most confident among the marketers realize that each movie is a "new business," requiring marketers to think on their feet and make quick decisions, that there is no *formula* you can steal, no substitute for good judgment. Many marketers recognize that personal connections often determine whether your trailer gets played and whether your campaign breaks through the clutter, and no one can steal a lifetime's worth of personal contacts.

From my perspective, every chapter in this book is incomplete, because it is a series of snapshots of a process that involves many people and many forces. It is not a 360-degree pan shot with a Steadicam. It is collection of "decisive moments," shot from various angles, with a perspective that is mine. It doesn't pretend to be the whole story. From my years as a journalist, I know full well that no two people ever see a story the same way. It is my hope that this book will still give readers a perspective on how films are marketed in Hollywood, and do so in an entertaining, informative way.

Tiiu Lukk

September, 1997

1
ROMANTIC COMEDY:
Four Weddings and a Funeral

Four Weddings and a Funeral is a stylish romantic comedy, starring Andie MacDowell (*sex, lies and videotape*) and Hugh Grant (*Remains of the Day*), set exclusively at four weddings and a funeral. It's a tale of eight friends, five priests, eleven wedding dresses, sixteen parents-in-law, 2,000 champagne glasses, and two people who belong together but may never be . . . Filled with fine breeding and bad language, beautiful churches and bawling bridesmaids, stylish receptions and appalling speeches, it is directed with astute perception by leading British filmmaker Mike Newell, who made the Oscar-nominated *Enchanted April* and the award-winning *Dance with a Stranger.*

That's how Steve Flynn and his team at Gramercy Pictures defined the appeal of their movie to audiences when they created the plan to market it. "We always write an executive summary of all the goals we are looking to reach," says Flynn, Senior Vice President of Marketing for Gramercy Pictures, which is a joint-venture distribution entity owned by Polygram Filmed Entertainment and Universal Pictures. Gramercy, a small company (twenty people, including the mail room) that has been in business since 1994, did an especially impressive job of marketing *Four Weddings and a Funeral*, taking the independent film to number one at the box office within six weeks of its release. "In this business," says Flynn, "if you're not the number one film the week you open, you usually never are number one, although you might make it to the top ten. You need a big push, a lot of money, a tremendous number of prints—usually 1,200-plus, and a good strong weekend to take the number one position. You spend so much money up front when you take a film out wide that you can never afford to spend that much money again." *Four Weddings and a Funeral* defied the odds by opening on ten screens, slowly platforming to other markets, and building unbeatable word-of-mouth. ("Platforming" is a release strategy that involves opening a film in one theater or a few theaters in key target cities, with the intention of building word-of-mouth, then widening the run to other cities, usually in phases.)

Gramercy distributes pictures in the $5 million to $10 million range that are produced by numerous production companies under the Polygram and Universal umbrellas. These include Propaganda Films, Working Title, ITC Entertainment, Egg Pictures (Jodie Foster's company), Def Productions (Def Jam Records' spinoff), Amblin Entertainment (Steven Spielberg), Alphaville, 40 Acres and a Mule Filmworks (Spike Lee), and Populist Pictures (Steven Soderberg). As a distributor of specialized films, Gramercy adopts more of a "stealth" strategy than a wide-release approach when it comes to leveraging its money and its talent for maximum box-office impact.

Marketing plans for *Four Weddings* began to take shape during the weekly Monday morning meetings of Gramercy's President, Russell Schwartz, and the department heads, a time to discuss release strategies and release dates. Schwartz and his management team, Steven Flynn (Senior Vice President of Marketing), Claudia Gray (Executive Vice President of Publicity), and Paul Rosenfeld (Senior Vice President of Distribution), determine release dates based on a number of factors: the date they receive a print from the production entity; how soon they can screen that print for media, such as magazines with long lead times; and how long it will take those long lead times to come to fruition. "Once we have it narrowed down to a couple of months, we look at the competition within those months and whether we can afford to buy media," explains Flynn. "We normally stay away from the summer, because it's just not affordable for us. You have to spend $11 million in prints and advertising to be noticed. We normally won't release films in June unless we are going to platform, so you'll find us pretty strong in January, February, and March, as well as in August, September, and October."

Avoiding the summer and holiday blockbuster seasons makes good sense for specialized film marketers. According to the Motion Picture Association of America (MPAA), the average production cost for a feature film (known as the "negative cost") is $34 million; the average cost for prints and advertising (known as P&A) has now climbed to $16 million per feature film.

Polygram originally intended to open *Four Weddings and a Funeral* in Great Britain, but those plans were changed when the film was selected to be the opening-night film at the Sundance Film Festival, a premiere festival for independent films. In preparation for the post-Sundance release in the United States, Gramercy did the type of market research and testing that is fairly standard throughout the industry. "The first testing that gets done on a film is to determine the pacing and whether there are any underlying themes of the film that weren't resolved by the end," says Flynn. "We also test to find out which scenes are the audience favorites, to determine our TV spots and trailers, and to find out which elements of the cast people fall in love with."

One of the most important decisions made in marketing a film is how to position it in the marketplace. "Positioning" is an advertising term that was defined by Al Ries and Jack Trout in their book, *Positioning: The Battle for Your Mind*, as follows: "Positioning starts with a product . . . But positioning is not what you do to a product. Positioning is what you do to the mind of the prospect. That is, you position the product in the mind of the prospect."

"Our primary positioning for this movie was Carrie and Charles' dilemma (*'two people who belong together but may never be'*); our secondary positioning was the humorous weddings with groups of friends, and the outcomes of those circumstances," says Flynn. Based on their research, Flynn and his team felt that fans of *Enchanted April* (which was directed by Mike Newell) would enjoy *Four Weddings and a Funeral*, but hard-core art-house fans might not. Thus, they decided to sell *Four Weddings* with a more commercial slant, as a "date" movie, and open the film on the east side of Manhattan rather than the west side, and at the AMC Century City in Los Angeles and Santa Monica.

Flynn has a thorough understanding of theatrical exhibition, which he gained from the ground up, beginning with his first job as a movie-theater usher, continuing with his sixteen-year tenure working for United Artists Theaters. He worked his way up to Senior Vice President of Marketing for UA Theaters, where he set marketing policy for the company's 2,700 screens, which represent ten percent of all the screens in the country. Flynn was the liaison between the United Artists chain and studios in matters involving newspaper directory ads in sixty markets, trailers of upcoming attractions, local promotions, and standees in the lobby (standees are large signs designed to literally stand in the lobby). His connections with theater owners paid off when he switched to distribution. With *Four Weddings and a Funeral*, Flynn personally contacted more than 100 theater owners and convinced them to run the trailer for the film. This type of personal contact is essential in an exhibition milieu that has a surfeit of trailers all competing for the same limited openings.

According to the marketing plan for *Four Weddings*, the target audience for this film was people eighteen to forty years old, with the primary core being the twenty-one to forty age group, appealing slightly more to women. The marketing team believed that eighteen-to-twenty-four-year-olds would see the film as "a comical look at the perils of being single." For the twenty-five-to-thirty-four-year-olds, the film would be seen as an English-humor romantic comedy, a high concept expressed as Monty Python meets *Sleepless in Seattle*. The thirty-five-plus segment of the audience would consider it an adult date movie, "a non-Shakespearean *Much Ado About Nothing*."

Their market research, conducted by the National Research Group, gave them valuable guidance in planning their advertising campaign. "Of the cast, Andie MacDowell was really the only star with some name recognition," says Flynn. "We figured that Hugh Grant had some rising recognition because he was simultaneously in *The Remains of the Day*, where he played alongside Anthony Hopkins and Emma Thompson, and also *Bitter Moon* and *Sirens*, which were coming out at that time. The research told us that even though Andie [MacDowell] and Hugh [Grant] were the two main characters, the ensemble meant a great deal to the audience. So the progression of the advertising in the newspaper went from originally Hugh and Andie as a two-shot, to the gradual introduction of additional cast members, until we ended up with the final cast shot. That process took place in the newspapers as we expanded into more theaters and more markets. We had five different print campaigns domestically."

The research findings also helped the marketing team finalize their plan to release the film on five screens in each of two markets (New York and Los Angeles). "Then we would continue to platform the film on a pretty fast, furious, consistent basis, but always watching our media dollars as we went along," says Flynn.

Many specialty distributors "platform" their films, that is, they initially open the film in just a few theaters in order to build awareness and word-of-mouth about a film, based on the hope that good news will spread from one market to another as the film is released more widely. In a *wide release*, commonly used in the distribution of big-budget studio films, a movie is launched with 1,000 to 2,000 prints. A wide release usually involves 100 theaters in Los Angeles and eighty theaters in New York, whereas a platform release will involve three to five theaters in both New York and Los Angeles. According to Entertainment Data, Inc., wide releases represent about three-quarters of total box-office revenue. Movies with large production budgets and extensive television advertising campaigns need to recoup their costs as soon as possible, which is one reason they rely on wide releases. Really bad movies are often released wide in order to make as much money as possible before bad word-of-mouth kills the film at the box office. Really wonderful small films need more time to build momentum, and a platform release gives them a chance to gain a following.

Distribution Plan: *Four Weddings and a Funeral*

- **Wave I Opening – March 11:**
  Tier I, Markets 1-2 on 5 Screens

- **Wave II Opening – March 18:**
  Tier II, Markets 3-10 on 19 screens

- **Wave III Opening – March 25:**
  Tier III, Markets 10-15 on 36 screens

- **Wave IV Opening – March 30:**
  Tier III, Markets 15-68 on 252 screens

- **Wave V Opening – April 8:**
  Tier III, Markets 68-162 on 545 screens

- **Wave VI Opening – April 15:**
  Tier III, Markets 162-212 on 721 screens

- **Wave VII Opening – April 25:**
  Tier III – Markets 212 – 240 on 900 screens

"We found that the film would readily play to a sophisticated audience, and we knew, looking at historical performances of films like *Father of the Bride, When Harry Met Sally, Sleepless in Seattle, Green*

Card, and *Enchanted April*, that those kinds of films played extremely well in New York and L.A. markets, and that was obviously the best bet," recalls Flynn.

"So after New York and L.A. opened, we were quite happy with the performance there, and we decided to launch an additional eight markets," says Flynn. "We looked at Chicago, Philadelphia, San Francisco, Miami, Washington, Baltimore, Detroit, Atlanta, and each of those markets would go out on a semi-exclusive basis, so that we had a single theater in each market."

Gramercy's distribution strategy built awareness of each opening, laid the groundwork for additional openings, and dictated the media that was bought for advertising. "We started off just buying what we would consider target media for New York and Los Angeles that would duplicate what we would do for the rest of the country without having to invest the $5 to $10 million in media expense that sometimes gets expended on launching a film," says Flynn. Gramercy bought local media, specifically local cable, targeted spot television and both metro and alternative newspapers, such as the *New York Times*, the *Los Angeles Times*, the *L.A. Weekly*, and *The Village Voice*, to create awareness of the platform opening in New York and Los Angeles. The company also did some out-of-home advertising, such as film kiosks in Manhattan and in L.A., bus shelters in L.A., wild posting, and Moviefone, which is the 777-FILM information number for filmgoers. ("Out-of-home" advertising is that advertising which literally reaches prospective moviegoers in locations outside of their homes.)

Gramercy placed local cable advertising in key zip-code areas to create awareness and "want-to-see" in the platform and exclusive markets. ("Want-to-see," also pronounced "wannasee," refers to the desire on the part of the audience to see the film.) Gramercy added national media, specifically national cable, three weeks before the expansion to ten markets in order to maintain awareness in the platform market, generate awareness for the exclusive opening in Markets 3 through 10, and expand "reach" to a national level for the expansion to markets 15 through 68. ("Reach" is a verb used as a noun in advertising lingo; it refers to the number of people reached by advertising in the effort to build an audience.) Local and national cable schedules were designed to reach the older segment of the eighteen-to-forty-nine audience through Lifetime, CNN/HLN, TNT, and USA; the educated, upscale audience through cultural programming on A&E, Bravo, and Discovery; and the music enthusiast through Nick at Nite, VH-1, and MTV.

Gramercy began aggressive spot television schedules two and a half weeks before the expansion to 252 screens in markets 15 through 68 on March 30, in hopes of expanding awareness among their target audience of adults eighteen to forty-nine. Savvy marketers recognize that spot television, which involves purchasing broadcast time on a market-by-market basis, can be a more efficient and effective advertising tool than network television for specialty films. Spot television gives marketers the opportunity to concentrate their advertising in the key markets that account for a majority of the national box office and to keep exhibitors happy by supporting their film on local screens. Gramercy's spot schedule included heavy concentration on prime dayparts, that is the early fringe period (5:00 – 7:00 P.M.) and prime access period (7:00 – 8:00 P.M.). ("Dayparts" refer to the time periods categorized for the purpose of determining the cost of advertising on radio or television broadcasts.)

The television schedules were designed to build reach by increasing the frequency of ads to generate the maximum awareness just before the March 30 expansion. Their psychographic target for this effort was "upscale, avid moviegoers," particularly English-comedy lovers.

Because Gramercy is a small company, Samantha Hart, their Vice President of Creative Advertising, usually farms out the creation and production of trailers and other advertising material. Flynn credits Hart, who came out of the record industry, for the visual appeal of Gramercy advertising campaigns. She is integrally involved in the positioning of the film and the selection of the best trailer house to execute that strategy. The entire marketing team works on the strategy for an advertising campaign. One of Flynn's responsibilities is to make sure that the TV spots are programmed with the appropriate TV buy. "I may look at it and say, 'This works well, but I need something that can actually air before 9:00 P.M.' Because it's really difficult to get spots on the air before 9:00 P.M. for R-rated films, sometimes you have to cut for a particularly soft spot. All those have to go through the MPAA and get their rating, and still go through the network and get those clearances. You really have to work together closely to make sure you're not wasting your efforts," says Flynn.

The bulk of the advertising budget for *Four Weddings* broke down as follows: newspaper 35.4%; spot television 23.3%; network television 23.3%; national cable 6.7%; Canada 2%; local cable 1%; out-of-home .5%; Moviefone .4%; promotions .3%.

Distribution Plan Media Support:
Four Weddings and a Funeral

Platform Opening: New York, Los Angeles (3/9)
- Local Cable
- Target Spot Television (Program Driven)
- Moviefone
- Phone Kiosk (New York & Los Angeles), Bus Shelters (Los Angeles)
- Metro and Alternative Newspaper

Exclusive Opening: Markets 1-10 (3/18)
- National Cable
- Local Cable
- Spot Television
- Moviefone: New York & Los Angeles
- Metro and Alternative Newspaper

Expansion Opening: Markets 1-59 (3/30)
- National Cable
- Spot Television (Markets 1-15)
- Moviefone (Eight markets)
- Metro and Alternative Newspaper

Publicity and promotions were an essential part of the marketing plan for *Four Weddings and a Funeral*. Research and common sense told the marketing team that Andie MacDowell had strong audience recognition, and a big name as a result of her performances in *sex, lies and videotape* and *Groundhog Day*, making her a natural choice for the focus of a publicity campaign. "We recognized that Hugh

Grant had the status of a rising star," says Flynn, "so we built the publicity campaign around the discovery of a new male romantic lead, and we were able to successfully pull that off."

Director Mike Newell already had a track record in the art-film circuit, so publicity about his contributions would be built on *Four Weddings and a Funeral* being a "break out" picture for him. "When you have directors that have done films before, you go back and look at critics or feature writers that have championed their earlier work," says Flynn. "Those are usually the first friendly critics that you bring in to screenings, and you usually do that very early on, to help you set your pace and also set up your positioning." The film's writer, Richard Curtis, is a major English comedy writer, so a publicity campaign was built around his established, long list of credits. Rowan Atkinson, who played the role of the hilariously bumbling but sincere priest in the film, had name recognition from the HBO *Mr. Bean* series. Gramercy publicists decided to build a publicity campaign around Atkinson's major scene, positioning it as "The Year's Funniest Five Minutes in Film."

Gramercy began press screenings for national print media in January, right after the film was delivered, cognizant of the fact that they would be premiering and launching the film at the opening night of the Sundance Film Festival on January 20, 1994. "The opening at Sundance was very important, because it gave a lot of recognition to both Gramercy and the film itself," says Flynn. "It was the first year Gramercy had participated in film festivals, and it marked our first full year of operation."

Media Targets: *Four Weddings and a Funeral*

National Print:

Glamour, Mademoiselle, Interview, Mirabella, Harper's Bazaar, Elle, Vanity Fair, Travel & Leisure, Paper Magazine, Premiere, U.S. Magazine, Vogue, USA Today, New York Times, Playboy, The New Yorker, Rolling Stone, Entertainment Weekly, Esquire, Redbook, Gentlemen's Quarterly, New York Magazine, New Woman, Lears, Ladies' Home Journal, McCall's, Family Circle.

National Television Outlets:

MTV News, Entertainment Tonight, W Magazine, The Today Show, CNN, E!, *CBS This Morning, Conan O'Brien, Good Day New York,* VH-1, WABC, *Weekend Today,* Fox Network, *KTLA Morning News,* Showtime/TMC, HBO, *BRAVO Champlin on Film, Good Morning America, Live at Five, Tonight Show, Letterman,* TNT, *Hollywood Insider, Hollywood Stars, Entertainment Report, Univision, Siskel & Ebert,* PBS, *Telemundo,* ABC Syndicate, NBC Newsfeed.

National Radio Outlets:

AP Radio, *J. Wolf's Hollywood,* SNN, *60 Second Preview,* Westwood One, *Entertainment Weekly,* ABC Radio, *Interview Factory.*

Andie MacDowell Satellite Junket (for 28 markets opening up after 3/15/94):

Chicago, Boston, Philadelphia, San Francisco, Washington, D.C., Miami, Tampa, Pittsburgh, Kansas City, Wyoming, Baltimore, Detroit, Atlanta, San Diego, Dallas, Houston, San Antonio, Hartford, Tucson, Minneapolis, Cleveland, Indianapolis, Phoenix, Denver, St. Louis, Portland, Cincinnati, Albuquerque.

Before the film was released, Flynn called on thirty advertising agencies in the field to coordinate a plethora of promotions that were designed to be implemented locally to reach both male and female upscale adults. The agencies were charged with finding promotional partners whose membership or customer bases matched Gramercy's target audience for this film. The promotions were supported with advertising and publicity, with the aim of generating additional word-of-mouth for the film. "We give the agencies a list of ten goals to meet, and each one tries to meet as many as they can," says Flynn.

The agencies planned to reach their target audiences using a database of women's groups, employers, and organizations established through promotions involving *A Home of Our Own* and *A Dangerous Woman*. They kicked off an extensive word-of-mouth screening program on Valentine's Day (Monday, February 14th) in the following markets: Chicago, Philadelphia, San Francisco, Boston, Washington, Dallas, Detroit, Houston, Atlanta, Minneapolis, St. Louis, Seattle, Cleveland, Miami, San Diego, Phoenix, Baltimore, Indianapolis, and Tampa. Promotional screenings were also arranged with Great Expectations (the dating service) and 1–800–Flowers. One of the agencies' mandates was to find a magazine to co-sponsor a contest that would give an award to the most unusual story in one of three topic areas: the funniest date you ever had, the most unusual way to meet people, or the strangest incident that happened at a wedding. Tie-ins with television stations offered awards for the best wedding videos in those categories. Winners of the story contest could win a dream date as a grand prize.

"We usually create a sweepstakes that can be executed on a national level so each of the local agencies can take the sweepstakes and sell it in," says Flynn. In the case of *Four Weddings and a Funeral*, Gramercy created a sweepstakes that teased their target audience with the line, "Did you hear about the person who went to *Four Weddings and a Funeral*, and won a trip to Tahiti?" Along with promotion partners AOM French Airlines and Tahiti Vacations, Gramercy offered filmgoers a chance to see the movie and win a trip to Tahiti. Gramercy sold this promotion to local candy companies, coffeehouses such as Starbucks, dating services such as Great Expectations, bridal shops, and florists such as 1-800-Flowers.

Gramercy had specific criteria for their promotional partners: they had to have a member/customer base that matched Gramercy's target audience, and they had to provide an in-store display opportunity, special events, and/or direct mail communications to support the promotion.

The "Just Say I Do" vacation sweepstakes was Gramercy's primary promotion for *Four Weddings and a Funeral*. The second-tier promotion was a tie-in with the publication of *Ten Poems by W.H. Auden*, which included the moving poem "Tell Me The Truth About Love," which was recited during one of the film's most poignant moments. Vintage Books, a division of Random House, created counter displays for bookstores carrying the poetry book and also published an audio version. The third-tier promotion consisted of the film's soundtrack.

One of the earliest promotions for the film consisted of the distribution of a commemorative alarm clock to the press at the Sundance Film Festival, a keepsake that referred to the leading man's amusing tendency to sleep through virtually any alarm clock, making him late for every event he attended. Another amusing promotion involved free admission to the movie to anyone dressed in a wedding gown, an effort that was rewarded with network and local television news coverage.

Flynn gives the Sundance Film Festival credit for helping to successfully launch the film. "The Festival attracted a considerable amount of press for us and really helped launch the New York and L.A. markets because we received really wonderful 'Calendar' pieces in both markets as a result of the festival," says Flynn ("Calendar" is the name of the Arts and Entertainment section of the *Los Angeles Times*). Gramercy also showcased the film in the Tarrytown, Miami, and Santa Barbara Film Festivals before the expansion at the end of March. "As we approached the expansion, we had twenty prints in the theaters and word-of-mouth had caught up with the film," says Flynn. "We were getting some wonderful press on it, so on April 8 we made the decision to give the film its first big boost, and that's when we took it from 200 prints to 600 prints. We found that word-of-mouth still held strong, that people wanted to come back and see this movie over and over, because the markets it was playing did not have a big fall-off. We followed our distribution plan, which was to increase the number of prints to 800 the following week, and to 1,200 the week after that. All of a sudden we ended up with the number one film in the marketplace, even though it was six weeks after we opened."

Gramercy executives were justifiably proud of taking a small, independent film with a modest production budget (negative costs were $5.5 million) and moving it up to a number one position within six weeks. For their efforts, their peers in the Film Information Council gave them the award for the Best Marketed Movie of the Month, an award that is rarely given to an independent film. "It was exciting, because we spent months and months and months working on this movie," says Flynn. "I think one of the good things about being in a small company is that every project has to be a number one project. We have to turn over every stone for every film we're working on." This thorough approach brought *Four Weddings and a Funeral* to the attention of the public, earning it $53 million at the domestic box office and $270 million total foreign and domestic. Expenditures for prints and advertising were $12 million.

The success of *Four Weddings and a Funeral* was just one of the marketing surprises Flynn has experienced during his tenure at Gramercy. *The Adventures of Priscilla, Queen of the Desert* was nominated for a ShoWest Award for being the top-grossing film in limited released (less than 200 prints) for 1994. Produced by Polygram in Australia, this film cost $2 million to produce and it grossed $11 million foreign and domestic at the box office. Gramercy decided to give it a limited release (192 screens at its maximum), and were confident that the film would create its own crossover market strictly by generating good word-of-mouth. "Polygram gave the film to Gramercy because of their expertise in marketing films with such 'unusual' content," says Flynn. *Priscilla, Queen of the Desert* was a film about three Sydney showgirls—with problems, as described in its production notes. "Felicia, Mitzi, and Bernadette are invited to play a cabaret engagement at a resort hotel in Alice Springs, in the middle of the Australian red desert. The prospect of traveling across the desert in a bus and leaving their troubles behind seems attractive at first. But getting there intact is another problem altogether. Our three beauties are not your usual strutters. Felicia and Mitzi are drag queens, and Bernadette is a transsexual. Meeting a man in a dress in the Outback is not a normal occurrence. The girls set off for the two-week trip with music blasting from the stereo, and the bus crammed with a gaudy assortment of frocks, stilettos, and an occasional padded bra. Their journey is more like a collision as they are continually swerving from a string of comic, bizarre, and sometimes dangerous situations. *Priscilla, Queen of the Desert* is a musical comedy road trip, and only when the weird get going does the going get mighty weird."

Another Gramercy success story, *Jason's Lyric*, described by Flynn as a "Romeo and Juliet love story" set in today's African-American culture, cost less than $6 million to produce and $7 million for prints and advertising, and it took in $21 million at the box office.

Flynn attributes the success of these niche films, in part, to publicity campaigns that carefully target genre publications. "There's always new magazines that are being published that you need to be in, and we cater to those publications," says Flynn. *Jason's Lyric*, for example, had a wonderful hip-hop soundtrack, so the Gramercy publicity department invited the top 50 hip-hop publications to a special press junket, confident that each publication, with a circulation of around 10,000 readers, had a large pass-along readership.

Gramercy has also had its marketing disappointments. *Back Beat*, a film about the Beatles before they became famous, never took off, despite top-drawer promotions with Volkswagen, who brought us the first Beetle automobile. "We gave away twenty Volkswagens," recalls Flynn. "We had strong corporate support on the film. We were everywhere. We had a huge outdoor campaign. We had everything except for an audience. I basically think people did not care about the story of the Beatles before they were the Beatles, because everyone knew the Beatles as those guys that were on the *Ed Sullivan Show* and went on to fame and fortune, and our film was basically everything before the *Ed Sullivan Show*. Other than the very limited art audience, it just had no mass appeal at all."

Computer networks have added another dimension to marketing, giving companies like Gramercy the opportunity to do online publicity junkets. Talent for a film gets on the Internet and answers questions from the audience for an hour or more. One of the other important ways marketing has changed, says Flynn, is the growing importance of national cable systems. "We now will launch a picture with national cable before we'll go in and buy local spots," says Flynn. "It's all targeted against the demographics that you're going after. You can always count on Viacom getting a proportionate share of the buy with Comedy Central, VH-1, and MTV. We still love working with Bravo, and the Fox Network, which is very promotion-minded."

Flynn enjoys the diversity of his job, particularly the ability to "embrace a film in all its aspects, including product placement, licensing and merchandising, field publicity and promotions, strategic planning and media." He has a realistic perspective about the strengths and limitations of marketing: "Marketing can get a film opened, and I think that's the best that marketing can offer," says Flynn. "Then it's based on the film. With *Forrest Gump*, marketing got that film opened, but the film's brilliant and the film is going to make as much money as it is, only because people continuously talk about it. It's not that Paramount is spending millions upon millions of dollars each week to add to the life of this film—the film sells itself. Now that's also the negative side of it. If the film doesn't open, if the marketing people don't get the audience in there, the film doesn't have good word-of-mouth, and the film is doomed because there is not enough momentum. If you don't get them in there the week that you open, you never go back and spend money against the film again. You just look to cut your losses and move on."

Flynn is always careful to avoid opening films on a crowded weekend against films with the same target demographics. "It gets harder and harder to pick those weekends, because there are so many films being released now," says Flynn. "You have Disney releasing one every week . . . it's tough to come up with a genre-free weekend. You don't want two films that go after the same young male audience going out on the same weekend, unless of course you have *Die Hard* or *Batman* and you just don't care. You just walk over them. But we can't afford to do that."

For now, Flynn and his team will focus on the wins and, hopefully, the upcoming winners. "We're now positioned with the exhibitors and recognized as a company that supplies them with good-quality films," says Flynn. Not only that, it supplies them with intelligent marketing and the tenacity to follow through on strategies that guarantee fine films don't get lost in the clutter of the marketplace.

Marketing Expenditures: *Four Weddings and a Funeral*
January '94 – December '95
$(000)★

Magazines	41.1
Sunday Magazines	0.6
Newspapers	4,879.3
Network Television	2,385.2
Spot Television	2,376.4
Cable TV Networks	655.3
Grand Total	10,337.9

★ All numbers in these reports of marketing expenditures from Competitive Media Reporting and Publishers Information Bureau are stated in thousands; for example, the figure of $41.1 in the above report represents an expenditure of $41,100.

© Copyright 1996 Competitive Media Reporting and Publishers Information Bureau.

2
AMERICAN INDEPENDENT FILMS: *Pulp Fiction* and *The Brothers McMullen*

At one of the first research screenings of *Pulp Fiction*, then-Miramax Marketing Vice President David Dinerstein first got an inkling of just how well the Quentin Tarantino film would eventually do at the box office. "Quentin was in the audience," recalls Dinerstein, "and tried to be sort of low-key because typically a filmmaker doesn't want to make a big deal of himself at a research screening, so it's not skewed one way or another. Some twenty-year-old moviegoers two rows in front of him turned their heads and one of them shouted, 'Quentin is God!' That said it all for us. That's when we knew we had something really special here. I think the biggest star in their eyes was Quentin. We knew that those two kids in that theater who were really tied into Quentin had two friends, who had two friends, who had two friends, and we felt that was the audience we would initially aim for: the eighteen-to-twenty-four-year-old male audience."

Even before the research screening, Dinerstein and his colleagues
at Miramax had an instinct about who would be attracted to this
film, based on Tarantino's track record with *Reservoir Dogs*. "When
you put a film in front of an audience, you typically have a feeling
for what type of audience is going to like the film," says Dinerstein.
"Whether it's going to be an upscale audience, a blue-collar audience, an ethnic audience. You can really project whether the film
will be more liked down south than it will be up north, so you can
break it down geographically, socio-economically. Now at that point,
Quentin had this film, *Reservoir Dogs*, that was a minor success at
the box office—it grossed about $3 million. But on video, *Reservoir
Dogs* went through the roof, so we knew that there was an entire
audience that tapped into that video, and we knew that with *Pulp
Fiction*, that audience would come back because there was something about Quentin Tarantino that that audience really admired.
At that first research screening, we had an audience that was comprised of different age groups. Along the way, we found that the
film was enjoyed not only by the eighteen-to-twenty-four-year-olds,
but also the twenty-five-to-thirty-four-year-olds and the thirty-five-
plus, urban audiences and ethnic audiences. Across the board, people
liked this film because it was different. I think if you would have
asked anyone what *Pulp Fiction* would have grossed when we originally got it, everyone would have been pretty far off. It really became a phenomenon, and a lot of it had to do with the way we
marketed the film, but at the same time, word-of-mouth on this
film was incredible. It was different. It was unique. It was incredibly
funny. It had action and a little bit of romance in it. There was something in it for everyone, and you either loved it or hated it. Very
few people were indifferent to the film."

David Ansen, reviewing *Pulp Fiction* for *Newsweek*, described it as "Set in today's L.A. but taking its spirit from forties' pulp magazines like *Black Mask*, this structurally audacious, two-and-a-half-hour movie unfolds separate but overlapping stories that start, stop, and jump about in time. Yet by the end the jumbled chronology falls into perfect, startling place. The stories start from pulp ground zero. Two hit men, Jules (Samuel L. Jackson) and Vincent (John Travolta) are sent to retrieve a stolen briefcase by their boss (Ving Rhames). . . . Vincent plays escort to the mobster's wife, Mia (Uma Thurman), knowing her husband once threw a man out a window for giving her a foot massage. . . . A boxer named Butch (Bruce Willis) is supposed to take a dive. He double-crosses the boss, takes the money and runs . . ."[1]

"*Pulp Fiction* was just very different," says Dinerstein. "It wasn't just another crime or caper movie, or a genre movie, it really had a sense of humor that caught a lot of people off-guard. Some people like the actual humor, some people don't find it funny whatsoever. But I think that's what made it into the phenomenon that it was. What Quentin was able to do with *Pulp Fiction* was push the violence so far that you had to laugh at it and you couldn't take it seriously. And he did that in a way that I felt worked. Some people may try doing that and fall flat on their face, but his dialogue, along with the other element, really captured people's attention."

When *Pulp Fiction* premiered at Cannes Film Festival and won top honors with the Palme d'Or award, a media frenzy ensued. "There was a lot of hype of the film—the response there was incredibly exciting," says Dinerstein. "We flew the whole cast there and a lot of the press championed the film. The heat was on: 'Why don't you go out with the film?' We really wanted to create an event, a must-see picture, and also felt there was potential for Academy Award nominations with this film. We decided that it would behoove the picture to wait until the fall to go with it, so we accepted the invitation to open the New York Film Festival [in 1994]. Miramax originally planned to open the film in New York and Los Angeles exclusively, but the tracking on the film was so strong, the want-to-see so intense, that they decided not to waste any time, and opened on October 14th on 1,338 screens around the country."

When *Pulp Fiction* was unveiled to the American audience at the opening night of the New York Film Festival, the marketers got yet another glimpse of just how viscerally moviegoers would react to this film. During one scene in *Pulp Fiction*, the Uma Thurman character overdoses on heroin, turning into a frothing, bleeding mess, the color draining out of her as she goes into cardiac arrest. The panicked John Travolta character grabs an enormous hypodermic needle filled with adrenaline and plunges it through Thurman's breastbone into her heart, causing her to bolt upright in a miraculous recovery. (N.B.: Paramedics say not to try this tactic with any addicts at home—the needle would snap off going through the bone.) Just as this scenario unwound on the screen, a gentleman in the audience had some sort of a seizure, and the house lights went on while he was given medical assistance. There were those in the audience who said that the episode was orchestrated by Miramax for publicity purposes, but Miramax executives say that was not the case.

When Miramax's marketing team first saw *Pulp Fiction*, Dinerstein says that they would have been ecstatic to reach a gross of $20 million. "We opened up to a phenomenal weekend, and we knew we had something big going on," says Dinerstein. The box-office gross for the opening weekend of *Pulp Fiction* was $9,311,882, for an average of $6,960 per screen. "It was a huge hit," says Dinerstein. "One thing that worked incredibly well with this film was that we had the cooperation of every actor, the director, the producer, everyone. It was a concerted effort to publicize and market this film, which is rare these days, very rare. Everyone felt they would do their duty and go on the evening talk shows, the morning shows, set up interviews, go to the press junket, and do as much as they could for the film while they had time."

The tracking reports before the opening, along with exit surveys collected once the film opened, served as a distant early warning signal that Miramax might have a hit on their hands. It's usually very difficult to track specialized films, because most of them don't open wide and don't have the far-reaching television advertising campaign that builds awareness for opening night. Most specialized films have a platform release, and the films don't seem to make even a blip on the tracking radar until they've expanded to 500 or 600 screens. But in the case of *Pulp Fiction*, early reports indicated that the film was tracking extraordinarily well, especially with young males, which Miramax saw as their core audience. The tracking showed that *Pulp Fiction* cast a much wider net and attracted a much bigger audience than their core target.

Dinerstein says Miramax positioned *Pulp Fiction* as "an outrageous film that was a comedy, if you will, that had Quentin's signature on it, his signature being defined on films like *Reservoir Dogs*, *True Romance* [which Tarantino wrote], and, to a lesser degree, *Natural Born Killers*. From day one, we positioned the film with a very funny trailer where audiences were laughing at what some people would perceive as the violence. It was so over-the-top that you had to laugh at it. It wasn't real. It was almost comic book-like." In early test

screenings, Miramax found that ethnic and urban audiences also responded well to *Pulp Fiction*, so they decided to create two different
trailers to target their different audiences. One was a red-band trailer,
which the MPAA only allows to play before R-rated or PG-rated
films, and the other was a green-band trailer, which the MPAA considers suitable for all audiences. "We created a red-band trailer that
we targeted and attached to the action and thriller films that were
out in the marketplace at that particular time," says Dinerstein. "So
there was an audience that may not have known Quentin Tarantino,
may not have typically gone to what everyone initially considered a
specialized film, but they were really interested in this. The
soundtrack for the film consisted of a lot of retro songs, songs that
probably the baby boomlet generation grew up on. There was a song
called 'Jungle Boogie' that was played in the film, and we put that
on both trailers, but really pumped it up for this action trailer, and
the audience just went wild for it.

"We also designed a poster that was very reminiscent of an old
pulp novel cover," says Dinerstein. "We set up a photo shoot with
Uma Thurman and really recreated that atmosphere. What we also
discovered with *Reservoir Dogs* was that five guys don't necessarily sell
a movie. As great as the *Reservoir Dogs* poster was, we felt we needed
an icon on this particular film, even though it was an ensemble piece,
so the icon ended up being Uma Thurman. The print ads, however,
involved an ensemble shot, which turned up on the cover of *Entertainment Weekly* as well as inside a lot of other magazines."

In planning media strategy when he was at Miramax, and now
as head of marketing for Fox Searchlight, Dinerstein prides himself
on "spending money intelligently . . . There are many different outlets you can spend money on, and some of them are measurable

and some aren't," says Dinerstein. "Some are egotistical and some aren't." Dinerstein's strategy for newspaper advertising with *Pulp Fiction* differed considerably from that of the major studios. Miramax took out a full-page ad in the *New York Times* three weeks prior to the opening of the movie. Studios are more likely to take a full-page ad on the Thursday before a movie opens, then take another full-page or double-truck ad (an ad with two adjacent full-pages) on the opening Friday. "We decided to jump the gun to really set the film up," says Dinerstein. "I feel the *New York Times* is a great launching pad because the Sunday edition is really a national paper that can position a film for regional audiences as well as critics. We feel the intelligentsia reads the Sunday *Times*. It was a gamble, because we were spending before we knew we had a big, big hit, but we thought it was a wise gamble."

At the head of the Miramax marketing team of "gamblers" are Harvey and Bob Weinstein, and their colleague Marcy Granata, who runs publicity for Miramax. According to Mark Gill, who eventually succeeded Dinerstein as Vice President of Marketing for Miramax, "Harvey, Bob, and Marcy are phenomenal angle-seekers. The idea of getting a cover for John Travolta with the tag line 'Welcome Back,' alluding to *Welcome Back Kotter* and to his comeback, is shrewd stuff. It's a tiny detail, but you would see that every step of the way. It's just a little more eye-catching, it's just a little more arresting, a little more unusual. All those things help you tremendously. Harvey and Bob are the two single best marketing people I've ever met, by far. They have extraordinary instincts, they have a real passion for movies, and they put more energy into it than anybody else does. Clearly, they are exceptionally astute about what makes people go to the movies. I think the reason for that is they started out as concert promoters, where you bet the house every time out. It's bankruptcy if you have a failure. What you're betting is that you can actually get people off their couches and into your arena seats. Bob recently said to me, 'You don't really understand until it's your money.' Now they happen to have help from Disney, but they're no less ferocious about it. Of course, two people can't do it all, and there's a department of thirty, thirty-five people. There's four or five of us who, on a regular basis, work with them to try to decide which way to go and how to go."

The Miramax marketing team made the decision to open *Pulp Fiction* on 1,338 screens, then expanded to 1,489 screens the second week. "We decided to immediately take on the world, if you will. We felt we had the movie, and with the per-screen average as high as it was [$6,960 per screen], we would continue to grow on that," says Dinerstein. Knowing where to open your film and how many screens to open on is the beginning of a juggling act required of every marketing executive. "Four months before your movie opens," says Dinerstein, "you have an idea of what's going on and you can put your pen to a piece of paper and jot down your numbers. But as you're approaching that particular launch date, things change and you have to react. For instance, with a film like *Pulp Fiction*, one may have thought that, like *Reservoir Dogs*, it was only going to be on 50 or 100 screens. But as you're approaching the opening, doing research on the film, and putting it in front of audiences, you realize that you have something greater on your hands. At that point, you have to make a decision. Do I take a greater risk and reap a greater benefit by putting it on 800 screens instead of 100 screens, and therefore have to spend five or eight times more than I anticipated spending? It's a very exciting time, but at the same time, those are decisions that have broken a lot of companies. So you have to be pretty sure of yourself."

While Miramax won't say what dollar amount they spent to market *Pulp Fiction*, Dinerstein will say that Miramax spent about sixty percent of their budget on television, and forty percent on newspaper advertising. He estimates that fifty percent of the television budget went to national buys, including national cable, although the cable buy was marginal. As the film moved further into its run, the television spending remained steady but the print buys diminished. Dinerstein is not a believer in billboards, because he doesn't feel they sell a movie. "I think a thirty-second spot on *Seinfeld*, or the NBA, if you're appealing to a male audience, sells a lot faster than a billboard a few hundred thousand people may pass during the life of the movie. It's not a great hit." However Dinerstein has bought ad space on New York subways because he feels that there's enough traffic on the trains to justify the ad buy. "On *The Crow*, I bought the New York subway because I feel that there you have a loyal audience that is using that as public transportation day in and day out," says Dinerstein.

Pulp Fiction so far has grossed $107 million domestically and more than $200 million worldwide. In the home video market, Miramax sold 715,000 units to the rental market and one million units to the sell-through market. (*Diehard With a Vengeance* broke the record for rental sales, shipping 735,000 units; *The Rock* later broke that record, shipping 830,000 units to rental.)

"When a film grosses over $100 million, typically it has crossed over and it has certainly broken the boundaries of the twenty-to-thirty-year-olds, or the eighteen-to-thirty-four-year-old demographic," says Dinerstein. "The film was really a phenomenon. I think audiences loved it—some people hated it—because it was so different. That's why I think the film really broke through. It wasn't linear, it wasn't what people were used to seeing. It reinvented cinema to some extent. In the old days, Charlie Chaplin, Buster Keaton, and some of the earlier filmmakers used music in a way where music was as important as the moving image. I think Quentin Tarantino, with *Pulp Fiction*, also used music as a real medium, not just as a background sound to go along with the picture, but to really move things and create a feeling. The soundtrack broke sales records—it was double platinum at the end of the day. [As of April 1997, the soundtrack sold 2,791,417 domestically.] And until recently, the *Pulp Fiction* video was the biggest presold video to the retail market out there. It did a tremendous amount of business. What we were really stressing in our marketing campaign was that *Pulp Fiction* was a fun night out and that people should be prepared for the roller-coaster ride of their life."

For many moviegoers, particularly those who hated the film, assertions by critics like Janet Maslin of the *New York Times* that *Pulp Fiction* is "a work of such depth, wit, and blazing originality that it places him [Tarantino] in the front ranks of American filmmakers"[2] are at best laughable. Indeed, there are those, like writer Donna Britt of the Washington Post Writers Group, who purposely avoided seeing *Pulp Fiction*, even though everyone was doing it. To quote Ms. Britt: "I had a great weekend. Friday night, before a wonderful dinner at a favorite restaurant, my husband and I didn't go see *Pulp Fiction*. It was wonderful, not discussing the rousing scene in which a gunshot sprays somebody's brains around a car interior, and not having our angel hair pasta remind us of it."[3] Said Britt's brother, who *did* see the movie, "It had really great moments, but after it was over, I was sitting in the dark, asking, 'Why am I learning so much about hit men and drug dealers? Does it enrich me to delve into their psyches?' Critics say, 'You have to see this!' But why is it so important to learn about depraved people?"[4]

Some film aficionados consider all the hoopla surrounding Tarantino as the cinematic equivalent of the emperor's new clothes. Among Tarantino's detractors is Mike White, a young documentary filmmaker who claims that Tarantino's acclaimed *Reservoir Dogs* is not just an homage to, but a rip-off of, Ringo Lam's *City on Fire*. White made an eleven-minute documentary, called *Who Do You Think You're Fooling?,* that juxtaposes scenes from *City of Fire* and *Reservoir Dogs*, showing striking similarities between parts of the two films. Tarantino's reported response to accusations of cinematic theft: "I steal from every single movie. If people don't like it, tough titty, don't go see it."[5]

While at Miramax, Dinerstein also worked on the marketing of the foreign-language film *Like Water for Chocolate*. "It was a quintessential story about how the youngest woman in a family, according to Mexican tradition, was responsible for taking care of her mother for the rest of her life and was forbidden to marry," says Dinerstein. "And of course, at a young age, she met the man of her dreams, whom she was not allowed to marry. The man she loved married her sister so that he could be near her for the rest of their lives. It was a beautiful, touching story that had people cheering and crying at the same time, reminiscent of Gabriel García Márquez or any of the Mexican magic-realist writers. This story had so much magic to it, and I don't think you see that in many films today."

Like Water for Chocolate did not present Dinerstein with an easy marketing equation, given its unknown cast, a relatively unknown director, and foreign-language (Spanish) dialogue with English sub-titles. Dinerstein says that the typical foreign-language film rarely makes more than $1 to $2 million, and *Like Water for Chocolate* became the largest grossing foreign-language film of all time, grossing nearly $22 million, until its box-office was surpassed by *Il Postino*. "It played for more than a year around the country because it was a universally appealing film," says Dinerstein. "It was a love story that centered around food and magical realism, directed by Alfonso Arau. This film really took on a life of its own, but we had something to do with it. We were able to publicize this film in many different ways because much of the plot of the film was concentrated in the kitchen, and based on food. We were able to get a lot of press to write about the food side and put out a recipe book based on the film. We had people doing travel articles about Mexico and where it was filmed. We sold it as a recipe for passion. We just had a lot of fun with it."

When David Dinerstein left Miramax in 1994, he went to work at the newly formed Fox Searchlight Pictures, which he describes as dedicated to filling the void in the specialized film marketplace with low-budget films. Their first foray into the marketplace was with *The Brothers McMullen*, a very low-budget film by a new film-maker, Ed Burns, which won the Grand Jury Prize at the Sundance Film Festival in 1995. "This film was made for about $20,000, shot in 16mm over an eight-month period because Edward Burns, the guy who made the film, had a passion, and his passion was to make a film about people he knew. He didn't recognize his people in any other films today. While it's about an Irish-American Catholic family, one doesn't have to be Irish-Catholic to see the characters in this film and say, 'Hey, I know those people,' or 'that's my family.'"

The challenges in marketing this film were numerous: "Every film in the past five or ten years that has won the Sundance Film Festival was a box-office failure," says Dinerstein. "So we had this jinx on us immediately. All of a sudden, people were saying, 'Uh-oh, will this film now fall into this black hole?' We were able to get beyond that. The things we had to work on, the things that were non-exploitable about the movie, were, first of all, the marquee value—not one of the actors in the film had ever been heard of before. The only one that had previous acting experience was one of the brothers that had been in *Porky's II*. Not typically our audience. Another difficult barrier we had to cross was the fact that this was a romantic comedy about guys. Very few comedies like that have ever worked. How do you get guys to see a romantic comedy about guys and about guys' problems? Another problem was that technically this film wasn't perfect. It was a film that was shot on 16mm, blown up to 35, shot over an eight-month period on weekends. There was no continuity in the lighting or in the sound. I think Eddie was able to really pull it off, but some of the hairstyles changed over that period of time, etc. Most of all, we wanted to stay away from being targeted as another Gen-X movie, because I've always felt that's a real stigma. This film didn't have a rock 'n' roll, Gen-X soundtrack, it had Irish folk music and a beautiful, haunting, end-credit song by Sara McLaughlin. The strengths of the film were that it won an award at a major American film festival, at least for the specialized movie market, and we were able to exploit that. Some very important critics were early champions of the film. Its greatest strength was that audiences really, really enjoyed the film. It's the most pleasing experience to sit in a crowded theater and, at the very end of a movie, watch people clap and talk about what they just saw, because it rarely happens these days. What's really exciting about working with a filmmaker like Ed is that his level of excitement and anticipation is just refreshing. For him, it's just so exciting to see his trailer playing in front of an audience and having people laugh, seeing his poster up in a movie theater. We have good expectations for this film. It's a very small film, but we're trying to cast the net and bring in a wider audience."

When Fox Searchlight first got involved with *The Brothers McMullen*, they gave Ed Burns finishing funds so that he could get the film into the Sundance Film Festival, in exchange for first rights to the film. Right before Sundance, Fox Searchlight bought the film, and eventually spent "about $150,000" to finish the film, according to Dinerstein. The film grossed more than $10 million, and was named the Number One Limited Release of 1995 by *Daily Variety* in the category of films that go out on less than 400 screens.

Dinerstein attributes the success of the film to the fact that "it was unexpected and it was very humble. Guys typically don't go to romantic comedies—a lot of people call them 'chick flicks'—and I think that's what made this film so special. Although *The Brothers McMullen* was made for $20,000, the story itself was a very commercial story. However, if it had been a Hollywood film made for $20 million, it probably wouldn't have been seen because it wouldn't have had that charm and flavor. I think the audiences really loved it because they were able to discover a film for themselves. The key to our marketing strategy was to continue to let the moviegoer discover this movie in much the same way the audience at the Sundance Film Festival discovered it. That's very difficult. After the Sundance Film Festival, there was an incredible amount of media attention on Eddie being the winner, and we had to downplay all of that. He was not only the director but the writer, the producer, and the star. In the old days, publicists used to want to get as much press for their clients as possible. Nowadays, publicists try to keep their clients out of the press at times, because the press has gotten so hungry for the entertainment business that it's sort of gotten a bit crazy. We wanted to make sure that people still have the opportunity to discover this film in their own theaters. That was our biggest challenge, and the way we went about this was to do a sort of whistlestop tour with Eddie. We sent Eddie around to about thirty cities around the country where he was the best spokesman for his film. He was able to really talk about his project, what it meant to him, and why he made it. He was really great at it!"

At the same time director Ed Burns was on his whistlestop tour, Fox Searchlight arranged a screening program to preview the film to audiences before its opening. They targeted the top twenty-five cities and promoted screenings in university areas through alternative publications and radio spots. The audience for those screenings turned out to be sixty-five percent women, thirty-five percent men. Screenings were held at the Museum of Fine Arts in Boston, the Producer's Club in Baltimore, and other venues that attracted film aficionados.

"Immediately after the Sundance Film Festival we did another deal with Ed to make a second film with him," says Dinerstein. "So we had a vested interest in Eddie. We wanted to make him part of our family, and we also felt he deserved to be recognized as a very up-and-coming and talented filmmaker. So one of the key strategies was not only to let people discover the film, but also to let people discover Eddie Burns and try to make Eddie Burns into a household name."

On this whistlestop tour, Burns didn't turn down any interviews. He spoke to entertainment critics and entertainment journalists, on radio and television stations, to museum groups, Irish clubs and bars, universities—as many venues as Burns could physically manage. Fox Searchlight also placed the film in other film festivals, including the San Francisco Film Festival and the Seattle Film Festival, downplaying the film's pedigree as a Sundance winner, giving those film festival audiences the same chance to discover the film as those who first saw it at Sundance.

The Brothers McMullen opened as a platform release on Wednesday, August 9, 1995, in New York, Los Angeles, and San Francisco. They chose a Wednesday opening because that summer there was a lot of traffic. On Friday, August 11, just a few days after *The Brothers McMullen* opened, there were at least another eight films opening. "Why should the film critic give us the space when, hypothetically, a movie by Kevin Costner or a much higher-profile film was opening?" asks Dinerstein. "We felt that in these key markets, the loyal readers of newspapers such as the *New York Times*, the *L.A. Times*, and the *San Francisco Chronicle* would still read the reviews if we opened on a Wednesday. We were hoping there would be good reviews. So we decided to open on a Wednesday so we could stand up alone, and knock on wood, we had rave reviews from each one of those papers."

Another reason Dinerstein wanted to open during the summer was because students are out of school, swelling the ranks of midweek moviegoers. "Typically, September has been a pretty difficult time for the box office," says Dinerstein. "We thought if we could build the momentum and get things going, not only would we get in a few weeks of summer play period, but we'd be able to get in

Labor Day, which is a holiday weekend. Then we would be able to build up some steam and play through the fall, and again, knock on wood, everything went according to plan.

"We did tremendous business in three cities that first weekend, opening on two screens in New York, three screens in Los Angeles, and one screen in San Francisco," says Dinerstein. On August 18, Fox Searchlight platformed the film to the top ten markets, with "exclusive engagements" at one or two theaters in each city. "At the same time, we went on a wide break in San Francisco, which was our way of testing the water and definitely a gamble for us," says Dinerstein. "We went on seventeen screens in the Bay Area with television, radio, and newspaper buys to complement it. We wanted to gauge, across the board, how different theaters and how different areas would embrace the film, and we got a fantastic read on it. From that test, we were able to determine if we were going to go on breaks, if we were going to widen this film out in a bigger way than we anticipated, and what types of theaters we should *not* play. The following week we expanded New York and Los Angeles with breaks similar to bigger Hollywood-type movie breaks. We were in about sixty to seventy screens in the tri-state New York area, and in about sixty screens out in the L.A. area, all in time for Labor Day weekend. Then we expanded another fifteen markets deep, so at that point we were in the top twenty-five or thirty markets."

Fox Searchlight launched *The Brothers McMullen* with a campaign of newspaper ads, cable ads including CNN, radio, and spot TV. "We bought the radio because it was a summer month and we were trying to appeal to the eighteen-to-twenty-four-year-olds," says Dinerstein. "I felt that at this particular time and at this particular place that it made a lot of sense. We bought the radio primarily on light FM stations. We were buying two prongs, which included a new type of programming that's referred to as "AAA" stations, which is alternative, eclectic rock, and we also bought what I call "Top-40" radio, which is primarily appealing to women eighteen to thirty-four."

The trailer for *The Brothers McMullen* was produced by Steve Werndorf, based on a scene from the film that Dinerstein says elicited a lot of laughs from the audience. "In this scene, Barry, played by Eddie Burns, was comparing man to a banana. It was sort of a two-edged sword. We loved the scene, but the MPAA didn't think it was a scene that was suitable for general audiences, and I tend to agree with them. So we had to intercut other footage with that particular scene and we had some fun. Because we had an unknown cast, unknown filmmaker, and low production values, one of our strategies was to lend credibility to the film by using quotes from critics. We had two big critics, Janet Maslin of the *New York Times* and Kenneth Turan of the *Los Angeles Times*, championing the film, so we put that on our trailer. One of the great things about being part of the Fox family is that we were able to attach the trailer to a movie called *Nine Months*, which got a tremendous amount of exposure and had a very good life in the theaters. It was one of the top ten films this year in terms of box-office. So we got the movie out to an audience that may not have normally been exposed to it, but who we knew would like it if they knew about it.

"We did the same thing with Spike Lee's new movie, *Girl Six*, by attaching it to the print of *Waiting to Exhale*," says Dinerstein. "Based on a Terry McMillan book, *Waiting to Exhale* is a film by first-time director Forest Whitaker, who starred in *The Crying Game*. There's a film the industry thought would maybe gross $20 million max, and it opened up to a $14 million weekend, and it's now up to $40 million and will probably do anywhere between $60 and $80 million. This is the first time any film has tapped into the black middle class in the way it has, and has crossed over to go beyond that box. All of a sudden, Hollywood is now realizing that there's another audience that they haven't tapped into, because *Waiting to Exhale* was considered a 'chick flick,' but now it's considered an African-American 'chick flick,' so it's even more of a niche."

Dinerstein first learned about niche marketing at Boston University, where he studied both film and business. When he got out of college, he went to work in the creative department of an ad agency, then quickly decided he'd rather work on the production side of the business. He went to work for a production company that made commercials and worked his way up from a production assistant to a commercial producer, then a music video producer. "I thought it was one of the best educational experiences I had in terms of learning the physical side of films, how one actually can make a film, even though it was a TV commercial that lasted thirty seconds," says Dinerstein. When he went to work for Miramax as a non-theatrical salesman, Miramax consisted of twelve people in a cramped New York office with a hallway bursting with desks and incredible energy. "A week later, I was putting on four different hats," says Dinerstein, and he made the move into marketing films. After his stint at Miramax, Dinerstein moved to Fox Searchlight, where he hopes to be part of a renaissance in the production and distribution of specialized films.

David Dinerstein is one of those marketing people who loves all of the permutations of his job: "What I find so satisfying is that I can work with a seed and really watch it grow. I have a passion for what I do. Not only do I love films, but I love promoting them. I love figuring out ways to get people in to see films they may not normally want to see. It's a real challenge. What I love about this, better than most businesses, is that you're launching a brand new business every time you go out there with a new film. The most satisfaction I get is watching audiences in movie theaters enjoy what they're seeing, and knowing that you're partially responsible for getting them in there. That's what I love about it. What I dislike about it is that it's a crazy business. The hours are miserable. You really have to love what you're doing."

Marketing Expenditures: *Pulp Fiction*
January '94 – December '95
$(000)

Magazines	67.8
Newspapers	5,618.3
Network Television	5,152.5
Spot Television	2,339.1
Syndicated Television	535.8
Cable TV Networks	343.8
National Spot Radio	340.6
Grand Total	14,397.9

© Copyright 1996 Competitive Media Reporting and Publishers Information Bureau.

Marketing Expenditures: *Like Water for Chocolate*

January '93 – December '94

$(000)

Magazines	18.1
Newspapers	1,119.0
Network Television	264.8
Spot Television	17.9
Cable TV Networks	178.6
National Spot Radio	18.9
Grand Total	1,617.3

Marketing Expenditures: *The Brothers McMullen*

January – December '95

$(000)

Magazines	23.6
Newspapers	2,802.2
Spot Television	473.4
Cable TV Networks	99.2
Grand Total	3,398.4

1. "The Redemption of Pulp Movies: The Crime Genre Gets a Shot of Adrenaline," David Ansen, *Newsweek*, October 10, 1994, p. 71.

2. "Quentin Tarantino's Wild Ride on a Dangerous Road," Janet Maslin, *New York Times*, September 23, 1994, pp. C1, C34.

3. "Money, Marketing Make for Movie Mayhem, Madness," Donna Britt, Washington Post Writers Group, *Houston Chronicle*, November 21, 1994.

4. Ibid.

5. "Stalking the Dog," David Bourgeois, *Film Threat Magazine*, October 1994.

3

ACTION-ADVENTURE:
GoldenEye

"The name is Bond, James Bond."

Imagine actor Pierce Brosnan practicing this line, getting the inflection just right, cognizant that his performance in the seventeenth James Bond film would help determine whether the industry's longest-lasting film franchise would rise like a phoenix from the ashes or turn into a parody of itself. While Brosnan was doing his homework, MGM/UA marketing executives were doing theirs, figuring out how to attract a new generation of moviegoers along with the aging Bond faithful to see *GoldenEye*, which MGM/UA was touting as "the event film of the holiday season" in 1995.

The Bond spy franchise had taken in more than $2 billion over thirty-three years before legal battles involving Eon, the company headed by Bond producer Albert "Cubby" Broccoli and United Artists, put the franchise temporarily out of commission in 1989. In the interim, action-adventure heroes such as Arnold Schwarzenegger,

Bruce Willis, and Sylvester Stallone supplanted Bond, winning over moviegoers with their distinctly ethnocentric blue-collar appeal, a sharp contrast to Bond's cosmopolitan, European sophistication.

MGM/UA pulled out all the marketing stops to reclaim Bond's place in the pantheon of action-adventure heroes, orchestrating a marketing campaign including a fast-paced, gadget-packed, high-tech trailer, upscale, high-profile promotional tie-ins with the likes of BMW, a pre-release sale of home videos from the Bond Library, and a broad-based advertising campaign designed to pull in the eighteen-through-forty-nine demographic. "Brosnan is a younger Bond, and coupled with the film's breathtaking action sequences, fantastic stunts, a beautiful villainess in Famke Janssen . . . and a story updated for the nineties, we believe the film is something the whole family can enjoy. It is good escapist entertainment," opined *GoldenEye* producer Michael Wilson on the occasion of the film's opening.[1]

MGM/UA Senior Vice President of Media Mary Flatlie says they faced one big question in designing their marketing campaign for *GoldenEye*: "Is Bond passé? What can we do to make sure that our new Bond film is current and hip and will appeal to a younger audience? Let's face it, the people who originally went to see *Dr. No* and *Goldfinger* and all those films are well into their forties and fifties now. That was our ongoing concern: how can we contemporize the campaign and make it appealing to younger people?"

Contemporizing a character that has been called an anachronism is no small task. Despite a public receptive to Brosnan, the newest James Bond film faced certain problems inherent in the series' formulaic storyline, which has always involved spectacular stunts, a stunning but dangerous villainess, and a megalomaniac in search of world domination. The actions of this British secret agent with a license to kill may have been dramatically justified by the threat of Russian communism during the Cold War of the sixties, but since then, communism has collapsed under the weight of its own incompetence, posing more of a threat to Russia's own survival than that of the free world. Part of the Bond formula was the characterization of Ian Fleming's secret agent as a promiscuous womanizer, behavior that isn't taken so lightly in the age of AIDS and common-sense safe sex. Another complication has been the ubiquitous presence of the so-called "Bond *girls*," whose main function in past Bond films seemed to be to service Bond and parade around in various forms of undress. Bond was also facing a marketplace where the competition threatened to out-do the world's longest-living secret agent in terms of stunts, special effects, computer graphics and explosions. *Lethal Weapon*, *Die Hard*, and *True Lies* have all upped the ante in action-adventure flicks, with the budget for *True Lies* almost twice that of the $50 million budget for *GoldenEye*.

For those on the marketing team, the long-running history of Bond films was both a tremendous strength and a weakness. "If people had perceived the whole idea of Bond as passé, it would have been a weakness," says Flatlie. "There was the question of how the women are going to be treated in the new Bond movie. Are they just objects or do they have minds of their own? It was a delicate balance. We knew that we had a good entertainment movie to work with and our early screenings went well. The special effects were fun and interesting. The locales—Monte Carlo, Switzerland, Puerto Rico, St. Petersburg, and the French Riviera—were interesting. Our one strength throughout the campaign was Pierce. There didn't seem to be any downside. First of all, he's drop-dead gorgeous. He has a certain suaveness, sophistication, caché that people think of in terms of Bond. And because he had already been accepted for the role many years prior, I think there was a built-in acceptance for him."

Pierce Brosnan, forty-two, had originally been selected to succeed Roger Moore as Bond in 1986, when he was starring in the NBC-TV series *Remington Steele*. At the time, NBC wouldn't release him from his contract, so Timothy Dalton played the Bond role instead. Previous Bonds have also included Sean Connery (the original movie Bond) and Roger Moore, who both played the character seven times, and George Lazenby, who played the role once. David Niven played the retired agent 007 in the spy spoof *Casino Royale*, and Leslie Nielsen played the aging secret agent "WD-40" in *Spy Hard*, a spy spoof that made fun of Bond films, *True Lies*, and other action adventure flicks.

"I think after Roger Moore, everybody was hungry for a permanent James Bond, and Pierce filled that role," says Flatlie. "Then we had the requisite gorgeous 'Bond girls,' two really new actresses, Famke Janssen and Izabella Scorupco. Some of the original Bond characters were back, with Dame Judi Dench playing M and Desmond Llewelyn playing Q, which lent some credibility to the whole project. Promotion and publicity was fairly easy for us because there seemed to be an inherent interest in the Bond project, and particularly publicity concerning Pierce, because he seemed to be so accessible to everyone."

Alfa Tate-O'Neill, General Manager of the southern California office of The Saatchi Entertainment Group, who worked with Flatlie on the marketing of *GoldenEye*, says they had some major obstacles to overcome: "The recent Bond films weren't as good as they could have been, they didn't successfully update the franchise, and they didn't pick the right people to play Bond, so the demographic kept getting older and that means your audience shrinks.

"If you only get one demographic into the theater" says Tate-O'Neill, "you can only achieve a certain level of success. The only way to ensure that a film has broad appeal is to break out and go beyond just the core audience. There are many configurations for broad-appeal films, those with a male emphasis, female emphasis, or kid emphasis. If *Toy Story* or the classic animated Disney films had been written specifically only for kids, then that's the only demographic which would have been targeted and, thus, the only universe the film would have attracted. The films are successful because they work on different levels. The music in most Disney films is Broadway-caliber, with rich scores and fabulous lyrics, so parents can enjoy the film on one level while the kids appreciate it on another. The net/net is that both groups walk away having enjoyed the movie. In terms of *GoldenEye*, it was the same thing. If it had been written in a very derivative, unimaginative, un-updated type of way, the Bond core audience (which is primarily men over twenty-five) may have turned out for the film, because the marketing campaign would have been skewed to reach them, and that would have been it. Women and younger males would have been disenfranchised, thus limiting the potential for the film."

In planning their strategy for a broad appeal film, the MGM/UA team also carefully considered the competitive landscape for the upcoming opening of *GoldenEye*. *The American President* was opening on the same day as *GoldenEye*, and the Jim Carrey film *Ace Ventura: When Nature Calls* would open a week earlier. "*The American President* was, in our mind, the consummate Saturday night date film. Jim Carrey had huge awareness and interest among young males," says Tate-O'Neill. "So with all this clutter, how are we going to make *GoldenEye* the biggest opening for any Bond adventure? We knew we had to get Pierce Brosnan out there and make sure that people could relate to him and appreciate him as Bond, that he is believable and has the insouciance the character has to have. Bond had a quality which appeals to men—men like the fact that he's the master of his own universe—but he must also appeal to women. Bond's appreciation for women has not changed over time, though the women themselves have. *Goldfinger's* Pussy Galore has become *GoldenEye's* Xenia Onatopp [a character described in press materials as "the lasciviously lethal assassin . . . who proves to be a formidable—albeit alluring—adversary for James Bond"]. This change obviously speaks to what has changed over time, in terms of the feminist movement and Bond's role in it. The fact that the filmmakers recognized this and wrote it into the script meant that we could target women as well. They updated the story and put in all the high-tech toys so we could also target younger males. I guess the overall limitation we had was interest by young females, but we knew that going in. It certainly wasn't a surprise."

Before *GoldenEye* ever hit the big screen, it received a substantial promotional boost from the re-introduction of home videos from the Bond Library, which is owned by MGM. Warner Home Video, which sells and distributes all MGM and UA artist titles, took eight of the best Bond films and put them on moratorium (which means they weren't available for sale) for several months before *GoldenEye* opened. They repackaged the eight films, added some extra value, such as original theatrical trailers, and launched the home videos of the movies right before *GoldenEye* went into theaters, generating extra publicity and creating awareness of the Bond franchise. MGM/

UA produced a half-hour, direct-response infomercial to promote *GoldenEye* and sell the Bond library videos—a clever way to produce advertising that pays for itself. TV infomercial viewers were offered the first video for $9.95, and the following seven videos for $14.95 each. The videos would be sent to their homes one at a time. Customers would receive a *Making of "Goldfinger"* tape and *Making of "Thunderball"* tape with their sixth video, and a copy of the script for *GoldenEye* with their eighth video. MGM bought syndication time all over the country to run the prepackaged infomercial, which focused on the lore and history of the Bond films and sold the Bond collection videos through an 800 number.

Traditionally, home video divisions of major studios don't get very involved with theatrical marketing. However, during the budgeting process for a theatrical movie, the home video division of a studio does estimate what the potential of the title is, in terms of revenue that can be derived from the exploitable revenue strains such as home video, cable, pay television, etc. They come up with a forecast based on a set of assumptions including a box-office number (stated in film rentals, which is roughly half of total box office), the cast (who is starring in it), credits (who is directing and producing), and genre. Certain genres perform better than others in an aftermarket like home video. For example, a $100 million action movie would sell a lot more copies and have a lot more rentals than a $100 million drama or romance. These calculations are essential for studios, who need the revenues from one production to finance subsequent productions. In many cases, the aftermarket revenues are necessary for the studios' continued survival, according to one home video executive: "These days it's very difficult to recoup from the theatrical run alone, because of the skyrocketing costs—the P&A

[prints and advertising] alone is $12 to $15 million. The negative cost of a film is so high today, it's difficult. There are different philosophies on how to cope with that. Warner Bros. has a philosophy of not trying to hit a ball out of the park with every release, unlike an Orion or some of these other studios that got into trouble when they tried to bank on huge, very expensive event releases every time, and it became difficult to make them all work. Warner's tries to hit a lot of singles and doubles and have a steady stream of movies that are profitable. It's such a crap shoot these days that the video marketplace is a guaranteed revenue source. We're to the point in the rental marketplace where you can look at a movie with an estimated box office and a certain cast and credit package, and pretty much guarantee what the video revenue and profitability is going to be, within plus or minus ten percent, if it hits that box office. So it becomes a less risky proposition these days because of the video marketplace. It's much easier to insure the down-side against it. Video is a big source of profits, but it's just one source. You also have pay-per-view, which comes right after us, pay cable, a network television purchase perhaps, and the HBOs of the world which are owned by Time Warner. There are other revenue strands, but video is the biggest. With feature films, even though you do recoup and make profits pretty quickly in the first year after your theatrical release, you have this asset—the video—which becomes an annuity that pays off year after year after year. At Warner and MGM, sales of back-catalog videos becomes an asset base that generates revenues that you then use to put back into production. That's why such upstart studios like Savoy and some of these new guys can't make the equation work: because they don't have the video asset base that continues to throw off cash year after year after year. A big studio has that asset that generates the money that pays for the productions, so you can afford to have a string of bad movies because you have the catalog that generates the cash to pay for it. I can tell you Warner Bros. tries to make every movie open big, they don't see movies as loss leaders for video. But what you realize is that you're willing to invest a little extra money and take a risk on the theatrical production because it's the engine that drives the train. If you don't recoup a big box office when it's in theaters, every other revenue stream is impacted."

The direct response infomercial for the marketing of the Bond Collection was the brainchild of Beth Bornhurst, MGM Home Entertainment Vice President of Market Development, who was looking for yet another way to lay the groundwork for boffo box office for *GoldenEye*. "Having done direct response in the past, I came up with the idea of using an infomercial to help build awareness of the product," says Bornhurst. "Obviously, a thirty-minute infomercial provides longer blocks of time than thirty-second campaigns, and people who are interested would really get into it. Our objectives were to increase awareness of *GoldenEye* on opening box-office weekend, and increase the awareness of the availability of the first sixteen James Bond movies, to let people know that they were coming to the marketplace in retail. We positioned and built the show around those goals. By just using emotion and reminding people how great these films were, we succeeded in meeting those goals. We also had a lot of behind-the-scenes footage that hadn't been released before for *GoldenEye*, so that would pique people's interest."

The infomercial was produced in an entertainment news format, with male and female co-hosts introducing clip packages about Bond, an interview with Pierce Brosnan about the new *GoldenEye*, two music-video clip packages set to the old Bond, testimonials from Bond fans at a fan convention, packages on the stunts done in the Bond films, a package on the women in Bond films, behind-the-scenes footage of *Thunderball* and *Goldfinger* that they had created for the special videotape collection, and an interview with actor Desmond Llewelyn, who has played spy-toy master Q in every Bond film since they began. The half-hour infomercial was produced by MGM in conjunction with Los Angeles-based In-Finn-Ity Direct.

MGM tested the infomercial the last week of August, 1995, ran it for a couple of weeks in September, then rolled it out on October 1st. They increased frequency through October until the movie opened on November 17th, then kept the infomercial on the air through the holiday season, in a continuing effort to drive people to the theaters. "We thought that it was real important to get the word out to remind people how much fun the James Bond films were, and it worked," says Bornhurst. "We had the biggest opening for a Bond film ever, and it's since set records for a Bond film. Our video sales went through the roof, and we had great activity at retail for the video. It really was successful."

According to one home video executive, Warner Home Video sold 400,000 units of the Bond collection videos nationally as a direct result of the infomercial. They also sold "several million" through their traditional distribution outlets, which include Wal-Mart, Kmart, Blockbuster, and Tower Records. While executives are reluctant to site exact numbers, one executive said that the number of videos sold through retail was about ten times the amount of videos of those same titles that had been sold in the previous five years. Bornhurst says that they've sold "close to five million" Bond videos as a result of the infomercial.

In a unique twist, the Bond collection videos were sold in retail outlets at the same time the infomercials were airing. Apparently, retailers were not upset that MGM/UA was going directly to consumers with an 800 number. They saw the direct-response effort as another way to promote the video in their stores. Retailers looked at the direct-response effort as one whose primary target was people who don't traditionally buy videos in stores, and therefore was not competitive with their retail sales.

GoldenEye was released on November 17, 1995. On May 21, 1996, it went to the video rental market, which means the distributor sells it wholesale for $60 to $65 to stores like Blockbuster Video, who rent it to consumers. The price per unit to the video rental market is high because the distributor wants to capture some of the rental revenues. Warner Home Video distributed 475,000 units of the video for the U.S. rental market, which one executive characterized as "about as much as you can get out of the marketplace today." Six months after the video is sold to the rental market, the sell-through video window opens for direct retail sales to consumers. In the case of *GoldenEye*, the video was re-priced at $19.98 for mass distribution through merchandisers like Wal-Mart, Kmart, Target, music stores like Sam Goody and Tower, and discount clubs like Price Club/Costco and Sam's Club. The distributors of *GoldenEye* timed the sell-through to coincide with the day that *Toy Story* came out for consumers. "Because Disney's *Toy Story* is going to be one of the biggest videos ever released, it will be driving the family audience into stores," said one home video executive. "We figure this is good counter-programming for adults—an adult action feature—so we will be having *GoldenEye* out in stores the same day that *Toy Story* hits, so that we get a nice bump from what they generate in stores." One executive estimated they would sell approximately a million and a half units of *GoldenEye* in the sell-through market. After the introduction of the first eight videos in the Bond collection during the theatrical release of *GoldenEye*, Warner Home Video brought out a second set of eight videos when *GoldenEye* went into the rental market in May, selling "several million units" of those, according to one home video executive.

Bornhurst is delighted with the results of her experiment with infomercials. "It was a tremendous success," says Bornhurst. "One, we achieved our objectives of getting a great opening and the sales of the video. Two, it launched a whole new way to market entertainment products through direct response, and we have since done two more shows, one for *Pee-wee's Playhouse* and another for *The Outer Limits*, a science-fiction show, and both have been successful. It has also encouraged other studios to look at this way of marketing in the course of normal business, versus something they would never do."

Bornhurst says that initially she ran into some resistance to the infomercial idea, and had to spend some time convincing people to come on board. Nonetheless, she says she couldn't have pulled off this coup if she didn't work in an environment that allowed her to take risks and exercise autonomy in producing the infomercial in the best way possible. There was also the need for follow-up to the infomercial. "This is not like a traditional marketing campaign, where you buy a bunch of ads in magazines and on television, and then you don't do anything about it," says Bornhurst. "In this case, I would say eighty percent of your work is done after the show airs. That means getting products to people, making sure someone is there to answer the telephone, doing all the back-end fulfillment operational stuff. We were about ninety percent prepared, but we got a few gray hairs for a couple of months over that ten percent we weren't prepared for."

If successful marketing of a picture involves "opening a picture and giving it legs," the marketing team did this one right. ("Giving it legs" means assuring its longevity in the marketplace, making sure the film stays in theaters for as long as possible.) *GoldenEye* opened on 2,600 screens on November 17, 1995, and took in $26.2 million on its opening weekend—the highest opening gross in MGM/UA's history. This success involved the collaborative efforts of numerous marketing people from MGM/UA, The Saatchi Entertainment Group and the National Research Group (which is a division of Saatchi), and creative "boutiques" such as Frankfurt Gips Balkind. *GoldenEye* was originally a UA film, brought under the MGM/UA banner after the two companies merged. Because MGM/UA is a relatively small studio, marketing strategy percolates from the top down, through Chairman and Chief Executive Officer Frank Mancuso, President of Worldwide Marketing Gerry Rich, and President of Worldwide Theatrical Distribution Larry Gleason.

"While a collaborative process, MGM/UA sets the overall strategy and guides the effort," says Tate-O'Neill. "We place the media buys, but in order to do that effectively and as targeted as possible, we have to be involved very early on in the marketing of any film, because so much money is at stake. We're experts in the media marketplace. We offer suggestions and ideas based on what the creative materials look like, what the promotional and publicity efforts will be and what the distribution pattern is. Oftentimes, from the beginning of a process like this, we would amend our campaign strategy thirty times, and that's normal for most studios. The leader of the whole effort—at MGM, Gerry Rich—keeps it all on track."

Signs that the revitalization of the Bond franchise was working came early, from the London set where much of the film was shot. "There was a tremendous amount of positive feedback from journalists, who were favorably disposed to the idea of having Pierce as James Bond because he handled himself well," says Tate-O'Neill.

With the publicity campaign in high gear, the marketing team began to concentrate on the advertising campaign. "We had to make sure we made our male franchise aware that *GoldenEye* was coming out at Thanksgiving," says Tate-O'Neill. "We measure our effectiveness in terms of awareness and interest. Creating awareness is an art, blending movie trailer placement with publicity, both of which are effective weapons to combat spiraling media costs. The final element, the consumer media schedule, comes in during the final phase of the overall marketing campaign and imparts a sense of urgency to the effort. We put together a very aggressive, smart, and tactical campaign to open this film. The first part was targeted to reaching our core audience, which we call boomer males." Tate-O'Neill describes "boomers" as people twenty-five through forty-nine, who came of age in the sixties and carried a lot of attitudes and buying clout with them into the nineties. "This is in juxtaposition to other demographic groups," Tate O'Neill says, "like fifty-plus, Generation X (people in their twenties), teens, and kids."

Tate-O'Neill says that the MGM/UA team formulated their strategy by dividing their audience into four quadrants, in this case males twenty-five-plus, females twenty-five-plus, males twenty-five-minus (under twenty-five), and females twenty-five-minus. "If you get every single boomer to see your film, the film will be a success," says Tate-O'Neill. "But that's not realistic. The best way to insure success is by reaching people outside the core group. In the case of

Bond, we got two other boxes. It was the combination of couples on dates and young males in groups that got the film to the level that it did—it had a record-breaking $25-million opening. It's the same marketing exercise for a film like *True Lies*—you go after the male coefficient. The good news, for *True Lies*, is that Arnold Schwarzenegger does have young male appeal, so it's easier for them to motivate the twenty-five-and-under box than it would be for us with Bond, but the fact that we did it right made it work. Also, with *True Lies*, they had Jamie Lee Curtis, who has a great women franchise. People respond very well to her and she's got great appeal. People think she's a smart, sexy heroine and can hold her own. It's a formula and it's the same thing for the *Die Hard* franchise. Luckily, that had Bruce Willis in it. It started out when he was hot, so it had tremendous appeal to young males. Obviously, they had to broaden it by expanding to the other boxes as well."

In the case of *GoldenEye*, Tate-O'Neill says they began the second phase of their campaign "by using creative materials which showcase humor and romance, and which were placed on television shows targeted to reaching women and younger viewers. While there was always action, emphasis was given to the exotic locales. When you think back on the history of the Bond films, you've been everywhere—Buenos Aires, the Caribbean, the Alps, tropical jungles, the Orient, the Soviet Union. When we entered this second phase, we felt comfortable, because of all the publicity and response to the video sales, and with the positive response to 'Bond Is Back.' We used what Bond is noted for, tongue-in-cheek humor. He's still well-groomed and drives fast cars and he's put in all these situations where he has to figure out how to overcome obstacles. There are the bad guys and women who aren't always what they appear to be. But

then, neither is Bond, because we were, perhaps, expecting someone else.

"The final phase of our campaign called for the broadening out
of the character to make him accessible to all moviegoers," says Tate-
O'Neill. "It became an event film for Thanksgiving. It was everything you want and need from Bond and more."

According to Tate-O'Neill, MGM/UA tried to take advantage
of the greater number of moviegoers during the summer months by
shipping its teaser-trailer to theaters by Memorial Day weekend. "Because the material was action-packed, high-tech, and fast-paced, with
a wry tweak by Brosnan ('You were expecting someone else?' he
asked), the trailer played consistently during a summer of blockbusters, reaching many moviegoers, especially adventure buffs," says Tate-
O'Neill. "The teaser was then paid off when the final trailer hit the
screens in fall, two months before the film opened."

Tate-O'Neill worked closely with Mary Flatlie, MGM/UA Senior Vice President, Media, to formulate media strategy for
GoldenEye. At MGM/UA, Flatlie's role is to decide which media
vehicle is best to reach a particular audience: "For Bond, for example, the target audience is pretty broad. We're not segmenting a
tiny portion of the population. We're really going after adults eighteen to forty-five and we want to make sure we reach men. We had
a fabulous teaser trailer, and our A-V [audio-visual] materials were
outstanding—the television buys flowed out from there."

As with most movies that open broadly, the bulk of the
GoldenEye media expenditures were used to place ads on network
television. Television accounts for two-thirds of the average movie
advertising budget, and network TV expenditures per film average
as much as all other broadcast media combined.[2] MGM/UA execu-

tives wouldn't say exactly how much was spent on various media for the *GoldenEye* marketing campaign, but the trade paper *Variety* said the spending was "about average for an A-list picture." According to Competitive Media Reporting, MGM/UA spent close to $24 million to market *GoldenEye*.

According to *Variety*, tie-ins with promotional partners such as BMW, Omega watches, and Yves Saint Laurent added "as much as $50 million in extra exposure for *GoldenEye*"; BMW's contribution alone involved a $20- to $30-million ad buy for its new Z3 roadster, with commercials featuring the sports car in scenes from the film.

Flatlie says that the advertising expenditures for *GoldenEye* were comparable to those of other action films, perhaps even lower because of the advertising dollars contributed by the promotional partners. According to *The Hollywood Reporter*, the typical studio film costs more than $15 million to advertise, and that includes ads only, not the cost of prints.[3] The cost of advertising a movie has increased fifty percent since 1990.[4] These escalating costs put heavy pressure on movies not just to perform, but to perform big-time at the box office on opening weekend. If the film's opening weekend is weak, the film will be taken off the screen and replaced by the next competitor. And a film's success at the domestic box office has a direct impact on foreign, video, and TV revenues, so the dollars spent on opening a film have a multiple impact throughout the life of the film.

"With this kind of big event film opening at Thanksgiving, the meat of the campaign is television," says Tate-O'Neill. "We needed to get eighty to ninety percent awareness nationally. So even though our three-pronged attack segmented various demographics, ultimately we used a variety of broad-reaching network television shows

and dayparts to showcase *GoldenEye* against the overall target of
people eighteen through forty-nine. *NYPD*, sports, and late-night
could help speak to males, shows like *Seinfeld* and *ER* helped reach
women. Having seeded the campaign nationally, the effort closer to
opening would be bolstered by media placement of television schedules in selected local markets. This activity may have been preceded
by outdoor advertising in local markets, as well as local market promotions, handled by MGM/UA promotions people and field agencies strategically located in key markets across the country." ("Outdoor" advertising refers to poster-size advertising that is literally
placed outdoors, on billboards and bus shelters. "Dayparts" refers to
the daily time periods categorized for the purpose of determining
the cost of advertising on radio or television broadcasts.)

Tate-O'Neill summarized the advertising campaign as follows:

"Phase 1: Reach the core target of Males eighteen through forty-
nine:

A) Use high-profile national television programming, which
included college football, World Series, NFL, and new-
season primetime premieres.

B) Use creative advertising spots on television that are long
length (sixty-second and thirty-second spots) with a 'teaser'
look.

Phase 2: Reach all Adults eighteen through forty-nine:

A) Use high-profile network shows in a variety of dayparts,
which included *Good Morning America*, *The Today Show*, *Seinfeld*,
Murder One, *ER*, *Letterman*, *The Tonight Show*.

B) Use shows such as *Lois & Clark*, *Married . . . With Children*,
and *X-Files* to tap into the younger end of the broader
demographic.

C) Include national cable targeted to reach the demographic with CNN, ESPN for older males, MTV and Comedy Central to reach younger males, and A&E and E! to reach females.

D) Post outdoor in key markets to reinforce the Bond look.

Phase 3: The Close:

A) Keep emphasizing national media, but now include local market efforts to bring a 'call to action' close to opening.

B) Include spot television in those dayparts not covered by network, such as late news, prime access (those time periods immediately preceding primetime), and late fringe; buy local college sports and use local sports interconnects.

C) Use a mix of thirty-second and fifteen-second spots to give frequency to the message.

D) Run large-space newspaper ads in advance of opening, and support subsequent week with directory toppers, a co-op effort with the theater chains.

E) Use 'pay-off' creative that fulfills raised expectations and emphasizes 'Bond Is Back.'"

"Overall, the broad reach of network television was the workhorse medium," says Tate-O'Neill, "but because those costs continue to climb, it was necessary to use other media vehicles and secure active promotional partners to stretch the ad budgets."

"Because we were having a very wide-release film, in 2,000 theaters, you're basically national," says Flatlie. "What I wanted to do was to maximize the amount of network television, and that's a reflection of the theater base. In spot television, what I tried to do was use those areas that you cannot buy in network television, for example, the late news and local sports. So here in Los Angeles, for example, I would try to buy the USC or the UCLA football games.

Then I would heavy up in my major markets with spot. By 'heavy up,' I mean buy additional primetime, late fringe, the areas where there is an appeal for this type of movie."

Every year, in May, Flatlie makes what's called an "up-front television buy," basically a deal with each network to spend "x" amount of money, based on what she thinks her release schedule is going to be for the coming year. The up-front buy in May purchases programming for the period of September through August. "I don't even know what the movies are at that point," says Flatlie, but I go in and buy programming based on what I know our slate to be. I know I have to be in programming that's going to appeal to a movie-going audience. I can't go wrong with NBC on Thursday night, for example, because that's *Seinfeld* and *ER* and *Friends*. Thursday night is the night before most movies open, so you want to make sure that you have a lot of presence on a Thursday night. By the time my movie's opening, I don't go to buy programming, I go to rearrange what I already own."

"With *GoldenEye*, we were looking at adults eighteen through forty-nine, with an eye to men," says Flatlie, "so I would analyze each show based on that particular audience delivery. We rarely go just for households—we look at whatever demographic we're trying to reach. In a wide-release, big-event film like a *GoldenEye*, or any action film like an 'Arnold,' you are going to look for reach numbers that are in the nineties."

Broad-reach network television advertising is very expensive, and the costs keep climbing. In 1995, the major distributors spent $1.92 billion domestically on advertising; more than $1 billion of those advertising dollars went to television.[5] Advertisers who coveted NBC's winning Thursday night line-up faced a price increase of ten to twelve percent in the fall of 1995. "The cost of buying television time has increased every year," says Flatlie. "In a year like 1996, for example, it takes a bigger jump than normal because of the election and the Olympics. It's all supply and demand, so as there is more demand on the time, the price rises. Every four years when you have the Olympics and the elections, you usually see double-digit inflation on the networks, which is a very healthy increase. It's a real problem, because we can't have the cost of our advertising just going up double digits every year. We can't afford it, so we have to look for other ways to market films."

Some alternatives to network advertising that MGM marketers have tried include running less primetime in favor of various daypart mixes. "Primetime is your most expensive daypart, so we try to use primetime really judiciously," says Flatlie. "Depending on the film, we may heavy up in the late-night areas, or heavy up in the early morning. It didn't apply to *GoldenEye*, but *The First Wives Club*, for example, could run a lot of their spots in daytime, which is a much less expensive daypart than primetime. Their audience was women." Another way studios have tried to save money on television advertising is to use fifteen-second commercials rather than thirty-second commercials. Making these spots work creatively is difficult, because it's difficult to tell a story in fifteen seconds.

Newspaper advertising for *GoldenEye* involved large ads when the film opened, and increasing use of newspapers as a directory as the run went on. Most of the newspaper advertising was co-op advertising with the theaters. MGM/UA didn't put a lot of resources into magazine advertising, since that was an area that BMW covered, running everything from *Gentleman's Quarterly* to automobile publications to the *New York Times Magazine*.

The film opened to what Tate-O'Neill characterized as "tremendous reviews," including a two thumbs up from Siskel and Ebert. Of course, not all the reviews were uniformly glowing. Anthony Lane, writing for *The New Yorker*, was one of the disenchanted, saying, "To complain that Bond pictures are daft is beside the point, because 007 has grown, by some freak of fiction, into a hero; that is to say, he is now a name plus a myth, and doesn't need to bother with the dreary business of being a person. . . . *GoldenEye* is the first Bond film openly to address this peculiar state of affairs, so we shouldn't be surprised that it trembles with schizophrenia . . . the movie wants both to honor and to trash the tradition of 007 (and of his native country). He is scorned for his cheap one-liners, but the film supplies them regardless; it kicks off as a knowing parody of all preceding Bond pictures, but it ends up, two hours later, as a mindless one. As for whether Bond himself is a jerk or a jolly good fellow, well, nobody in this production has a clue."[6] Film reviewer Roger Ebert wistfully lamented Bond's loss of innocence in his syndicated newspaper review, noting that "in an important way, this James Bond adventure marks the passing of an era. This is the first Bond film that is self-aware, that has lost its innocence and the simplicity of its world view, and has some understanding of the absurdity and sadness of its hero. . . . Watching the film I got caught up in the special effects and the neat stunts, and I observed with a certain satisfaction Bond's belated entry into a more modern world. I had a good enough time, I guess, although I never really got involved. I was shaken but not stirred."[7]

Ignoring the occasional detractors, the marketing team used the positive reviews to pursue the adult segment of their target audience, and continue their aggressive efforts toward young males. "At that point the Jim Carrey movie had already opened in the market-place," says Tate-O'Neill. "We know that young males are repeat moviegoers, so it was a time when they could get the Jim Carrey thing out of their systems and then come and watch our film. We could carry all of that through to Thanksgiving, which is a very big moviegoing time of year."

Helping *GoldenEye* break through the marketing clutter were a reported $50 million worth of ad buys and promotions from BMW, Omega watches, Yves Saint Laurent, and others. BMW alone was reported to spend "a figure comparable to its normal investment in the launch of any new product—estimated at $20 to $30 million" to promote the launch of the car and the film, according to BMW "reps."[8] BMW tied the launch of their Z3 roadster to the opening of *GoldenEye*, positioning the two-seat convertible as James Bond's new "company car," replacing the Aston Martin that has served as Bond's preferred form of conveyance in past Bond films. One BMW commercial, titled "Lords," featured a fictional British House of Lords spellbound by the announcement that "Britain's most famous secret agent" was giving up his Aston Martin and now driving a BMW "on the wrong side of the road." Cut to scenes from *GoldenEye*, with the BMW Z3 roadster in chase scenes that "capture the thrill of adventure and the driving excitement that is the new BMW road-ster," in the words of BMW marketers.[9] When the tie-in campaign began, Jim McDowell, Vice President of Marketing for BMW of North America, said, "The new Z3 commercials are designed to establish the BMW roadster as a fun, exciting automobile that em-bodies the feelings of freedom, romance, and adventure. The link with James Bond, the most recognizable secret agent of all time, personifies these values and makes them come to life."[10]

Tate-O'Neill describes the tie-in as a win–win situation: the studio received the advantage of the BMW promotions linking the car to the film, and "it gave BMW a tremendous association with a very classy, sexy, exotic franchise that already existed in the marketplace." Print advertising for the roadster continued the James Bond theme, with the roadster escaping fiery explosions without a scratch, and readers urged to "see *GoldenEye* and see the BMW that made James Bond switch." BMW began running the Z3 spots in select regional markets on October 28, then expanded to national advertising on October 30, with TV spots running on NBC, Fox, and in late-night.

Other companies involved in tie-in campaigns included Yves Saint Laurent, which sponsored a retail promotion at 145 stores across the country; the oil company Citgo, which ran a point-of-purchase promotion in more than 9,000 stores, supporting it with TV advertising; and the watchmaker Omega, which supported the opening of the film with an ad campaign in upscale magazines. When cable Superstation TBS ran its yearly *13 Days of 007* retrospective, MGM/ UA tied into the film marathon by giving away a BMW Z3 roadster, an Omega watch, and other Bond-flavored travel packages. "All of these activities served as important parts of the closing effort of the advertising and marketing campaign," says Tate-O'Neill.

At this point in the campaign, the *GoldenEye* soundtrack was also in the stores. The *GoldenEye* title song, performed by Tina Turner and written by U2's Bono and The Edge, was released by Virgin Movie Music, and a music video to promote the single was distributed to video channels and retail stores.

GoldenEye opened on 2,667 screens on November 17, 1995, and took in $26.2 million on its opening weekend—the highest opening of any of the previous Bond films and the highest opening gross in MGM/UA's history. In the first ten days of its release, *GoldenEye* surpassed the total domestic gross of each of the last three James Bond movies: *Licence to Kill* ($34.6 million), *The Living Daylights* ($51.2 million), and *A View to a Kill* ($50.3 million).

GoldenEye opened big and kept going, the performance of a film that definitely had legs. "We kept going with a broad campaign which ran through Christmas and New Year's," says Tate-O'Neill. "We had good reviews and there was nothing in the genre to take us out of the marketplace. We were lucky that *Mission: Impossible* moved from Christmas to the summer. Both films would have done well because they had star power and lots of action. But they would have cannibalized each other had they been in the marketplace at the same time."

When the film finally opened, Pierce Brosnan proved to be a *mensch* as well as a movie star. The film's premiere, through the Permanent Charities Committee of the Entertainment Industries, raised more than $500,000 for the Norris Comprehensive Cancer Center for Ovarian Research, where Brosnan's late wife, Cassie, was a patient. Brosnan later boycotted the French premiere of *GoldenEye*, forcing its cancellation, in support of Greenpeace protests against French nuclear testing in the South Pacific.

Not only was *GoldenEye* a winner at the box office, but the excellence of the marketing campaign created by the MGM/UA team was recognized by their peers when *GoldenEye* was named the best-marketed film of 1995 by the Film Information Council, an organization of marketing, publicity, and promotion executives. Marketing mavens consider this annual award, named after the late Charles Powell, as the equivalent of an Academy Award in their field. It's given to the studio in recognition of outstanding efforts in the areas of advertising, publicity, promotions, and international marketing. In presenting the award, the Film Information Council spokesperson said that FIC "members were impressed by MGM/UA's ability to stimulate international box office interest in the 007 franchise in the face of two major obstacles: Bond's absence from theatrical screens for six years and a steady decline in ticket sales for Bond films over a twelve-year period." Aspects of the campaign that FIC members deemed praiseworthy included MGM/UA's introduction of the new Bond, Pierce Brosnan, at an open media day last January; the film's in-theater teaser trailer; and promotional tie-ins, including the tie-in with BMW, maker of the new Bond car.[11]

Ultimately, *GoldenEye* grossed more than $100 million domestic and more than $300 million worldwide. As the studio tallies its final take from *GoldenEye*, James Bond is getting ready to save the world from another power-hungry megalomaniac in the next installment of the Bond odyssey. The marketers will be there, too, making certain that the Bond franchise continues to entertain—and turn a profit.

Marketing Expenditures: *GoldenEye*

January '95 – September '96

($000)

Magazines	67.1
Newspapers	8,471.3
National Newspapers	37.4
Outdoor	53.7
Network Television	9,881.9
Spot Television	4,276.9
Syndicated Television	131.7
Cable TV Networks	754.5
Grand Total	23,674.5

© Copyright 1996 Competitive Media Reporting and Publishers Information Bureau.

1. "*GoldenEye* Opening with an Onslaught," *The Hollywood Reporter*, November 2, 1995.

2. *The Hollywood Reporter* Movies and the Media Special Issue, May 30, 1995, p. S-16.

3. "Going for Broke: When Distributors Go Into Overdrive to Launch a Movie, It's Like Marketing During Wartime," *The Hollywood Reporter* Movies and the Media Special Issue, June 18, 1996, p. S-14.

4. Ibid., S-4.

5. Ibid., S-4.

6. *The New Yorker*, November 17, 1995.

7. "This Bond Has Some Issues," Roger Ebert, *Long Beach Press Telegram*, November 17, 1995.

8. *The Hollywood Reporter*, November 2, 1995, pp. 1, 18.

9. "BMW Debuts New Television and Print Advertising for 7 Series and All New Z3 Roadster," BMW Press Releases, October 10, 1996. [source: Internet].

10. Ibid.

11. *Variety*, January 2, 1996.

4
DOCUMENTARY FILM:
Hoop Dreams

It was the closing night of the New York Film Festival and Avery Fisher Hall was packed. The audience of 2,800 sat transfixed for the duration of the picture, which ran for nearly three hours. At the end of the movie, in the tradition of the New York Film Festival, the spotlights focused on the box where the stars were sitting. The stars, in this case, were real people: the two young men whose *Hoop Dreams* had brought them to this unlikely place, the extended families who had nurtured them, and the filmmakers who documented their struggles over a seven-year period. The applause swelled as they were given a standing ovation. "It was the single most emotional moment of my movie career, and certainly the most emotional reaction I've ever seen at a New York Film Festival screening of any film," says Ira Deutchman, the President of Fine Line Features, which eventually became the film's distributor.

Deutchman first saw *Hoop Dreams* at the Sundance Film Festival, on the recommendation of Fine Line Features' marketing executive Liz Manne and John Iltis, a Chicago publicist who was acting as the producers' rep for the film. "The audience response to *Hoop Dreams* was extraordinary," recalls Deutchman. "It was unlike anything I had ever seen for a documentary before. I needed to make a very important phone call in the middle of the film, but I was riveted to the screen, and couldn't find an appropriate moment to run out. Finally I ran out and made the call, and ran right back into the theater again. It is a testament to the film that I didn't bag it at that point. When the film was over, I had my doubts about whether or not it was really commercial. The running time would be a problem. I had heard that the filmmakers were not willing to cut it down, and understood that point of view. It would be very difficult to edit it down without destroying what was so powerful about the movie. I left the screening room feeling like I wanted to talk to the filmmakers, but not sure whether I wanted to pursue it aggressively."

Fine Line Features' Senior Vice President of Marketing, Liz Manne also saw *Hoop Dreams* at Sundance. A basketball fan, she figured that she would never see the movie, a documentary, at her local cineplex, so she made plans to watch two hours of the three-hour movie before meeting a colleague. After two hours, she ran out of the theater with tears in her eyes, told her waiting colleague, "This is one of the best movies I've ever seen in my whole life, I'm watching the whole thing," and dashed back into the theater, loath to miss another second of the most compelling documentary of the year.

Manne was "passionately moved" by this story of two young basketball players who dream of playing in the NBA (National Basketball Association) to escape a dead-end life in the ghettos of Chicago. She sat teary-eyed through most of the picture, mesmerized by the true-life story of two young men who were plucked from inner-city playgrounds and put on the basketball career track before they were even in high school. "My marketer's instincts after I saw it were this movie's impossible for anybody to sell, any distribution company would be crazy to pick it up,'" says Manne. By the end of the festival, says Manne, "nobody was thinking of it in terms of the deal, everybody was talking about how it reached their heart and soul, that it communicated with them and made them think and feel things on a level they had never, ever experienced."

In a world of wheeler-dealers, where many people devote their lives to catering to people's baser instincts, *Hoop Dreams* was a true oddity—a film that appealed to people's finer instincts. The film touched so many people that it won the Audience Award for Best Documentary at Sundance in 1994. By the time Sundance was over, a number of distributors had expressed interest in distributing it.

"At the Sundance closing-night party, I had a conversation with John Iltis and Dave Sikich, the producers' reps," recalls Deutchman, "I expressed my wild enthusiasm for the film and my thoughts about whether it was something we could place. They told me they weren't rushing to make a deal. They wanted to hear from distributors what their plans might be. I was pleased to hear they didn't have outrageously unrealistic expectations of this movie, and that made me more interested in the film." Ultimately, Deutchman came to the conclusion that *Hoop Dreams* did have a shot in the marketplace, after seeing the other films that were available at Sundance and after gauging press and audience reaction to the film.

Despite the reaction at Sundance, this was no overnight success. Three filmmakers—Steve James, Frederick Marx, and Peter Gilbert—had spent seven years of their lives bringing this film to the screen. It started out in 1986 as a half-hour documentary film on the culture of the basketball "street game" in Chicago. Steve James and Frederick Marx had brought the project to Gordon Quinn of Kartemquin Films, the Chicago documentary production company that produced the film. At Kartemquin, Marx and James met Peter Gilbert, a cameraman who had shot Barbara Kopple's Academy Award-winning documentary *American Dream*. He joined the team just as the project began. They made the decision to expand the documentary when they found the two players who became the "stars" of their film. Coach Gene Pingatore of St. Joseph's High School of suburban Chicago introduced the filmmakers to Earl Smith, a high-school talent scout, who led them to Arthur Agee. Both Agee and William Gates, the other "star" of the film, whom the filmmakers met at a basketball camp, were considered hot basketball prospects when they were only in eighth grade. The film that began as a short look at the game on the streets evolved into a real-life drama about what happens when kids use their basketball hoop dreams to try to leave the streets.

Production on *Hoop Dreams* began in July 1987, with the filmmakers following Arthur and William through their high school careers for the next four and a half years. The public television station KTCA in St. Paul/Minneapolis became a co-producer with Kartemquin in 1990. After shooting more than 250 hours of footage on videotape, the filmmakers began postproduction, which was completed in January 1994. Their finished film was a true-life epic, with more than forty speaking participants, including Bobby Knight, Isiah Thomas, Dick Vitale, and Spike Lee.

By the time the filmmakers arrived at Sundance in 1994, they had spent close to one-third of their adult lives working on *Hoop*

Dreams. While they were savvy filmmakers, they were novices when it came to distribution. PBS had a three-year window for first television broadcast rights by virtue of their role as a funder of the film. Working on their own, the filmmakers had also booked the film into the Film Forum in New York for its theatrical release, scheduled for March of 1994.

When the filmmakers met producers' reps John Iltis and Dave Sikich of Iltis Sikich Associates at an Independent Feature Project seminar, the reps convinced them that they could secure a theatrical distribution deal for *Hoop Dreams*, and devised a strategy to market the film to distributors. Their first step was to decide on how to position the film to maximize the level of awareness and "want-to-see" among this first, crucial target audience. They positioned the film as an epic that was seven years in the making, a one-of-a-kind, real-life drama about two inner-city teenagers who dream of making it to the NBA. Despite the compelling nature of the film, they knew that they had some big obstacles to overcome. It was a documentary, a form that has rarely brought Americans flocking to theaters; it was three hours long, and had been shot in video; and its current financial arrangements with PBS removed the first television window.

Dave Sikich wrote a press kit complete with an announcement about the film's debut at Sundance. It included a list of forty "characters," credits, a synopsis of the film, background information about the production, biographical notes about the filmmakers, and information about the producers and the soundtrack. The press kit was sent to the top acquisitions executives around the country in preparation for Sundance.

Meanwhile, Iltis and Sikich called Larry Dieckhaus, the executive producer for *Siskel & Ebert*, the show that featured two of the highest-rated film reviewers on television in the country, in an effort to get Siskel and Ebert to review *Hoop Dreams* before it was screened at Sundance. Although Iltis and Sikich were good friends with Siskel and Ebert, they felt they would be lucky if the reviewers agreed to see it, considering that it had no distributor, no theatrical opening date, and no publicity going for it whatsoever up to this point. "It was one week before the Sundance Film Festival scheduled for January 1994," recalled Iltis. "I told Larry that they would be the first reviewers to see the film, but more important, I told him it was like no other film they had ever seen . . . this one is amazing."

"Siskel and Ebert have had a history of discovering independent movies and getting behind movies like *My Dinner With Andre* and *Roger & Me*," says Sikich. "We figured this was going to be a review-driven, publicity-driven film. By allowing them the opportunity to discover it, we felt we had a good chance of having Ebert write a Sunday piece (in the *Chicago Sun-Times*), of their going coast to coast and doing clips . . ."

Their prayers were answered when Siskel and Ebert reviewed the film immediately, giving it an enthusiastic "two thumbs up" after heaping it with praise:

ROGER EBERT: This is one of the best films about American life that I have ever seen. And for three hours I was just totally absorbed by the story of these two families, really . . . it's not just the kids, but their families. And you know, we get so many images in the movies of black inner-city characters with guns and drugs and gangs. Here are families that are struggling to make it. You don't hear all the four-letter words or the twelve-letter words, you see dinner on the table at night. You see kids getting up before dawn in order to take an hour and a half commute . . . to go to school. You see them trying to study, and then at the same time you see the way their basketball skills are really manipulated, even at the high school level. Before they ever get to college, by people who want to make use of those skills.

GENE SISKEL: Right.

ROGER: It's a movie that just raises so many questions and has so many insights.

GENE: And on the movie level, these are two characters . . . I know there are people who, when they hear "documentary," they back off. You're going to find these guys more interesting . . . and fully written in the ways that we're always knocking pictures for being underwritten. Here are two exciting characters.

The Critics' Joint Comments from the Summary Portion of the Program:

GENE: And finally two very enthusiastic thumbs up for *Hoop Dreams*, an epic documentary about a couple of inner-city kids who dream of becoming basketball stars. Through their eyes we see an unforgettable portrait of American urban reality. The film debuts this week at the Sundance Film Festival.

Ebert's opinion that this was "one of the best films about American life" he had ever seen became an integral part of the *Hoop Dreams* marketing campaign, and was ultimately used on the film's poster when it was released.

In addition to winning the Audience Award for best documentary, *Hoop Dreams* received great critical acclaim at Sundance. During the festival, the filmmakers and the producers' reps met with reporters from *Daily Variety*, the *Hollywood Reporter*, the *New York Times*, *Entertainment Weekly*, *Premiere*, *Time*, *Newsweek*, CNN, *Showbiz Today*, *Entertainment Tonight*, *Rolling Stone*, the *Los Angeles Times*, and National Public Radio. In the weeks and months following Sundance, these news outlets all ran stories about the film. Kenneth Turan of the *Los Angeles Times* called it "a landmark of American documentary film." Amy Taubin of *The Village Voice* also extolled it: "The richest film I saw at Sundance . . . was *Hoop Dreams* . . . . [it] has the potential to cross over into the mass market."

Todd McCarthy of the trade paper *Variety* said, "*Hoop Dreams* is a documentary slam dunk. . . . A dual approach of screenings at fests and for specially targeted urban audiences would trigger plenty of start-up word-of-mouth, and limited theatrical runs would seem warranted in advance of broadcast on public TV, where it could easily be positioned as a major event." "*Hoop Dreams* Team May See Some Fulfilled," wrote *New York Times* reporter Glenn Collins in an article about the negotiations that were already taking place between the filmmakers and potential distributors.

Following the film's success at Sundance, the filmmakers asked New York's Film Forum to delay the world theatrical premiere that had been scheduled for March 2 and they graciously agreed, but made the filmmakers guarantee that Film Forum would be one of the venues where *Hoop Dreams* played when it opened in New York.

Glenn Collins' *New York Times* article reported that *Hoop Dreams* cost $750,000 to make, and that the producers' representatives, Iltis and Sikich, were asking for $1.5 to $2 million for distribution rights to the film. In asking for this sum, the producers' reps had been influenced by the $3 million advance that Warner Bros. had given to the director of *Roger & Me*. The rights they were selling included North American distribution rights, worldwide distribution rights, and merchandising rights and remake rights. The following companies expressed interest in some or all of these rights: The Samuel Goldwyn Company, October Films, Disney/Miramax Films, Warner Bros., Universal/Gramercy Pictures, Sony Classics, Orion, and Fine Line Features. Miramax and Maverick Productions (Madonna's company) were solely interested in the remake rights, that is, rights to the dramatic recreation of the documentary.

After seven years of hard, loving labor, the filmmakers enjoyed being wined, dined, and courted at Sundance. *Hoop Dreams* director, co-producer, and co-editor Steve James, in his journal of the festival, recalled one particularly heady evening: "We were at dinner last night with some people from a major studio. Various company dignitaries are stopping by to chat and press the flesh. The head of a subsidiary company walks up to us, shakes our hands, and says, 'Guys, I haven't had a chance to see your film yet. But I just want to tell you: It smells good. It smells like something we're going to want to do.' He was serious." (This loquacious fellow's company never made an offer for the film.)

By the end of the Sundance Film Festival, Fine Line Features President Ira Deutchman was sold on the potential of the film, and decided to put on a full-court press to strike a distribution deal with the filmmakers of *Hoop Dreams*. Back in New York, Deutchman's instincts were confirmed when he arranged an afternoon screening of the film for New Line and Fine Line staff, and the screening was packed. After the film ended, he saw many in the audience with tears in their eyes, and asked what they thought of it. They all really liked it, but were dubious about its commercial potential. All of them thought the film was too long, but when Deutchman asked them individually what they would cut out, all the women in the room said they would cut down the basketball scenes and all the men in the room said they would cut down the family scenes, evidence that the filmmakers had struck the right balance.

When the smoke cleared, Fine Line was one of three companies seriously vying for *Hoop Dreams*; the other two were Orion and The Samuel Goldwyn Company.

Deutchman brought a lifetime of experience to the negotiations. He has been marketing motion pictures in various capacities for more than twenty-one years at United Artists Classics, Cinema 5 Ltd., and Films, Incorporated. He was a founder of Cinecom Entertainment Group, which distributed *A Room with a View* and *El Norte*, and his firm, The Deutchman Company, provided marketing consulting services on such films as *sex, lies and videotape*, *Straight Out of Brooklyn*, *To Sleep With Anger*, and *Metropolitan*. As the founder and President of Fine Line Features, he acquired and released Jane Campion's *An Angel at My Table*, Robert Altman's *The Player* and *Short Cuts*, Gus Van Sant's *My Own Private Idaho*, and many others. Deutchman and Manne had worked together for years. They met when Manne was earning her MBA in marketing at New York University and she went to work as an intern at Cinecom. After Deutchman started his independent production and marketing consulting company, The Deutchman Company, she continued to work with him. When Deutchman was recruited by New Line Cinema to start a specialized film division, Manne joined him in the creation of Fine Line Features.

When Deutchman and Manne set off for Chicago to woo the *Hoop Dreams* filmmakers, they knew that they had to build their marketing campaign around the playability of the film itself and the incredible word-of-mouth it generated. "We were crazy about the picture. We really wanted it and we wanted to make it work," recalled Manne. During the flight, Deutchman had worked up an entire marketing campaign that stressed the synergies inherent in New Line's recent purchase by Turner Broadcasting.

In Chicago, Manne and Deutchman met with the filmmakers, Frederick Marx, Steve James, and Peter Gilbert, and their representatives, John Iltis and Dave Sikich. The filmmakers had some firm ideas about how they wanted the film to be marketed beyond the standard theatrical and home video releases. They were interested in sounding out Fine Line about their openness to some of the things they wanted to do. Specifically, the filmmakers wanted a distributor willing to use a non-standard, grassroots approach to promote the film to inner-city community groups, as well as reaching for the standard art-house audience that would be drawn to this film. The filmmakers had been working with the Center for the Study of Sport in Society for two years, developing a curriculum guide for schools that would use the film as a departure point for inner-city schoolchildren to discuss athletic and academic dreams, practical goals, and how to achieve them. (The Center for the Study of Sport in Society is a well-respected organization, run out of Northeastern University in Boston, which helps student athletes weather the transitions in their careers, regardless of the level of success they may reach, and assists student athletes in earning their college degrees.) "We laid out our marketing plan and gave the entire pitch about why we were the best people to distribute their film," says Deutchman. "When it came down to talking about the deal, I said, 'what we want to know is that you believe we are the best company to handle this movie. If you feel that way, then come back to us and we'll try to match any offer that's on the table.' And that's exactly how I left it with them.' "

Fine Line had competition for the movie. Orion had already done an admirable job in trying to convince the filmmakers that they were capitalized and looking for product to fill the pipeline, even though they had emerged from bankruptcy just months earlier. The filmmakers were also impressed with the proposal from The Samuel Goldwyn Company.

According to filmmaker James, Orion flew the filmmakers and the producers' reps to Los Angeles first class, and offered them $800,000 for the rights to the movie. "While they did have a good presentation, we decided the best offer was not necessarily *financially* the best offer," says James. "We considered the best offer in terms of what a distributor could do for us creatively." The filmmakers were attracted by Fine Line's Turner connection. Fine Line also satisfied their comfort level in terms of solvency, and convinced the filmmakers that they would do a better job in terms of grassroots marketing. "There was a feeling that Fine Line was more politically in tune, more on our wavelength in terms of their sensibility and the kinds of films they do," says James. The filmmakers eventually decided to go with Fine Line Features, because "we recognized them to be fair, honest, and dependable," says Frederick Marx. "They approached us with an impressive plan to break the film out beyond the art-film market, and convinced us they were the best company to take the film out beyond a general conservative platform release, to get it out quicker to the general black and general film audience, more suburban malls and broader markets, to lovers of sport and beyond. Fine Line seemed like they had the means to do that; it was not just talk. They, and their parent company, New Line Cinema, had just been bought by Turner Broadcasting. This presented interesting possibilities to us, because of all the money behind the Turner empire."

"We were sympathetic to a lot of their points of view," recalls Manne of the negotiations, "and we had a lot of things to bring to the table, being part of the Turner family." Deutchman and Manne weren't certain just what "synergistic opportunities" would be available, given that Turner had only acquired New Line Cinema in January 1994, shortly before the Sundance Film Festival. But their entrepreneurial minds could dream, and dream they did. "We can't guarantee it, we don't know how it's going to work exactly," they told the filmmakers, "but we're part of this family." The plan Deutchman presented had included their new-found connections to TNT and Turner Broadcasting System (TBS), which broadcasts a lot of the NBA games; a publishing wing (Turner Publishing); Cable News Network; and the Atlanta Hawks (owned by Ted Turner). "There were all these sorts of possibilities we could keep floating: maybe we could get free trailer time on the air, maybe it would mean ad time, maybe it would mean cross-promotional opportunities for the basketball games—that whole piece of the puzzle, which was very amorphous, nothing we could put a dollar figure on or guarantee, was something that we could bring to the table that nobody else could bring," says Manne. "The other thing we brought to the table was obviously our undying passion for the film itself. It was very important to the filmmakers that this film be seen by inner-city kids, that it somehow be brought to the youth of America. You know that any documentary filmmaker is not in documentary filmmaking for the money. They're in it because of their social consciousness and their beliefs and commitments, on a moral, ethical, and sociological level. I think they felt the people at Fine Line were like-minded, in terms of our political orientation, and they also knew that our job is to make money for our shareholders. Their motivation, which is not necessarily to make money, but to have this picture be seen by the most people possible, happens to dovetail nicely with the motivation of profit-earning. What we said was, 'Hey, our vision of this picture is not just that it's a documentary art-film for white do-gooder liberals, who are going to see it in their local art-house theater. We're also going to make all these efforts to get it to inner-city audiences, especially youth.' We figured it would get a PG-13, so we could market it to kids thirteen and older."

When Deutchman went to Los Angeles for the American Film Market, he sat down with the filmmakers and their attorney for three and a half hours of "horse trading" and hammered out a deal. According to Deutchman, the deal involved an advance of around $400,000 and participation in the gross profits, which meant the producers would share in profits from day one, before expenses were deducted. Part of the deal included an agreement on the part of PBS to delay their broadcast of the film until a full year after its theatrical release. "In recent years, PBS has come to realize that a theatrical release before a PBS broadcast benefits PBS by raising the profile of the film," says James. "The PBS audience gets to see a TV premiere. When *Hoop Dreams* did appear on PBS, it drew twice the normal viewership for that time slot. It ended up a win-win situation for everybody."

Once they'd made the deal, Fine Line had to make good on their promises. Deutchman and Manne realized full well that the primary audience for any documentary would fit certain demographics: an upscale, educated, sophisticated, urban-dwelling, university/

city audience in the top ten movie markets. They knew they had to spend their marketing money on this core audience, because they knew that was where they would get a return on their investment. "The normal sophisticated art-film audience is in the habit of going to movies and dramatic subject matter isn't a turnoff to them," says Manne. "They've probably seen one or two documentaries in their life, and they're a literate group of people who read the newspapers and read the critics. We knew that we would have the critics on our side—we had to believe that our core audience would respond to those critics."

While they would concentrate their initial efforts on reaching that core audience, Fine Line was equally committed to reaching the secondary audience of inner-city youth that was so important to the filmmakers. Before they began their marketing campaign for *Hoop Dreams*, Fine Line held a research screening for inner-city kids at New York's Thalia Theater. "We recruited young black kids off the streets," says Deutchman, "and by the end of the screening, the theater was virtually empty. They really hated the movie and were sort of angry at us for presenting it to them in a way in which the film looked like it was some sort of *real* movie. They were walking out saying, 'This is a documentary, it isn't a movie.' It reinforced in our minds that we had a very difficult *overcome* with that audience, even though we all felt very strongly that we wanted to try to get inner-city youths to see the film. It was crystal clear that if we set it up as a real movie, which was the way we wanted to sell it to a more general audience, they would be upset with us because that audience had no history of having a theatrical experience with a documentary movie." ("Overcome" is a verb used as a noun; it is movie-marketing lingo for "a difficult obstacle to overcome.") Manne recalls that of those who stayed for the duration of the Thalia screening, many were "blown away by the film" and loved it.

At another screening for inner-city youth, filmmaker Steve James queried kids who left before the movie was over, and was told, "This is PBS stuff. I didn't think it was a documentary, I don't want to see a documentary." Others told him, "Things like this hit too close to home. I see this kind of thing all the time. I don't want to go to the movies and see this stuff." "It really got to them," says James. "Even if it's good, they don't want it." James estimates that sixty percent of the test-screening audience stayed until the end of the film, and reported universally excellent responses to the film.

Fine Line also attached a *Hoop Dreams* trailer to the print of a New Line film called *Above the Rim*. Moviegoers who responded to the commercial sell of the trailer were also angry when they went to see *Hoop Dreams* and realized that it was a documentary. However, when Fine Line screened the movie for the same inner-city youth audience in an educational setting, they really liked the movie.

"Inner-city youth audiences are a wonderful moviegoing audience, but you normally have to spend a lot of money to get those audiences, through a more wide-release pattern," says Manne. "You have to spend millions and millions of dollars in television advertising and open in every neighborhood theater. We knew we were never going to have a multimillion-dollar prints and advertising budget to open this picture, so we thought of other ways to get to this other audience. That's one of the things we pitched to the filmmakers in that first meeting."

Finding another avenue for reaching the secondary audience was essential. While the average P&A budget for a major Hollywood movie is $17.7 million or more, according to the MPAA, Fine Line originally budgeted $1 million for prints and advertising of *Hoop Dreams* for an estimated run of two months in sixty theaters. When the release period expanded to eight months using 250 prints, the cost of prints and advertising grew to around $3 million, including publicity, travel, film festivals, and parties, according to Deutchman. Fine Line spent the extra $2 million primarily on weekly newspaper advertising once the film had established itself as a hit.

The release of the film was scheduled for October 19, 1994, to coincide with the beginning of the NBA season. The release date itself required negotiations among all the parties involved. When the filmmakers first made their deal with Fine Line, they wanted the film to be released in the spring to coincide with March Madness and the NBA Playoffs. The filmmakers originally aimed for a spring release, because they had wanted to make sure that *Hoop Dreams* had a full theatrical and video release before the PBS window started. Fine Line was concerned that a spring release date wouldn't give the distributor enough time to exploit the vast array of promotional opportunities available to them. It also cut into the time they needed to make a 35mm blowup of the original video and to remix the entire soundtrack in Dolby stereo to add to the impact of the film— commitments Fine Line had made as part of the distribution deal. "In our minds, the most appropriate thing to do—and we had to convince the filmmakers of this—would be to put off the release until the fall, and use the New York Film Festival as a launching pad to create some excitement," says Deutchman. "An October release would give us time to finish all this stuff, and would coincide with the beginning of the NBA season rather than the end of the NBA season." Once Deutchman's team convinced the filmmakers that an October release was preferable, they arranged a meeting with the

PBS people in Chicago and convinced them it was worthwhile to push back their release date another six months to allow the film to fully exploit its theatrical and video windows. This also gave the filmmakers a chance to go back and cut an additional eight minutes out of the version that had shown at Sundance. "Psychologically it was important because we were able to go back to the press and talk about the fact that the film had been trimmed since Sundance, and it was much closer to two and a half hours," says Deutchman.

With the PBS airing delayed, Fine Line had nearly seven months lead time to prep the film and create a corporate sponsorship campaign not unlike the Olympics. To facilitate the community-outreach efforts, Fine Line called in Susan Missner, a Chicago-based sponsorship marketing consultant who had worked with Nike, Nutrasweet, Sears, and other large corporations. Missner is recognized for her special expertise in the corporate sponsorship world.

"We hired her the same way we hired all our outside vendors on this film," says Manne. "We said, 'See the picture, then call us.' They see the movie and lose their minds, because it's the most wonderful picture they've ever seen. Then we say, 'Okay everyone, it's a labor of love, everyone's working for bare minimums. We're going to build in bonuses, so if this movie makes any money at all, you'll get your normal fees. If it doesn't work commercially, at least you can have the satisfaction of having worked on an amazing movie.' Happily, at the end of the day, everyone got their bonuses."

In May of 1994, Missner joined the Fine Line team in a meeting with the filmmakers, PBS, and foundation supporters (The MacArthur Foundation) of the film in Chicago, where together they outlined their objectives. The team came away with a big wish list, which included obtaining corporate financial sponsorship for the film's community-outreach effort, so it would reach "the kids who wouldn't be caught dead in a documentary, and the average Joe who goes to Knicks games. We all felt there was strong educational value to this film," says Missner, "the question was how to present it without making kids feel like it was medicine." One of the objectives was to obtain the support and endorsement of the basketball hierarchy, "from prep to pro," including the state high school coaches association, the black coaches association, the NCAA (National Collegiate Athletic Association), and the NBA. This was not an easy task, given the sensitivity of these organizations to criticism of their operating procedures, and the film's candid, but not always flattering, look at the sports machine and how it operates. They faced another dilemma, says Deutchman: "We had a movie that was perceived of as small, and we were going after promotional partners who are normally concerned about how big the project is going to be—that's a major factor in deciding if they want to be on board."

Manne and Fine Line's Vice President of Publicity, Marian Koltai-Levine, coordinated the efforts of two public relations firms— Clein + White in New York and Block-Korenbrot in Los Angeles—to get the *Hoop Dreams* story into the entertainment press, the African-American press, and onto the national sports pages throughout the country. The country was divvied up, with local markets taken care of by field public-relations firms under contract to Fine Line. The public relations firms went after the film press; Missner pursued the sports press. Together they succeeded in placing an article on the front page of the Arts & Leisure section of the *New York Times*, as well as major stories on National Public Radio, in the *Chicago Tribune*, the *Miami Herald*, the *Los Angeles Times*, *Sports Illustrated for Kids*, and numerous sports talk radio shows.

Missner arranged screenings around the country for targeted sports associations, and based on the laundry list from the group meeting, compiled a list of things Fine Line wanted the organizations to do, including publicizing the film in their newsletters. She gave the organizations free passes when the film opened in their market and free curriculum guides so they would publicize the film in a favorable light. "These are powerful organizations," says Missner, "so there's a reason what happened in the film happened. They take the kids and mesmerize the parents. They have a whole way of operating that is difficult to infiltrate." Her efforts paid off with inside sports-world publicity such as the cover story about *Hoop Dreams'* William Gates in *NCAA News*, an *Inside Stuff* story, and the endorsement of one of the coaches organizations, which said, "We would recommend that every high school coach see this film."

Nike became involved in supporting the film after their western Regional Marketing Manager, Lauren de la Fuente, having heard about *Hoop Dreams* after Sundance, screened a videocassette of the film. Deutchman and Missner met with de la Fuente in Los Angeles, and asked her if Nike would underwrite a grassroots effort to get inner-city kids to come see the film. Deutchman says that Nike's interest in the movie stemmed from the fact that "the movie's message was something they felt they could get behind, and Nike was savvy enough to realize that because Nike is explicitly criticized in the film, it would be good public relations for them to be involved with the movie to undercut that criticism."

To their credit, Nike did agree to fund the film's major community-outreach efforts. The athletic footwear company did not shy away from the film that showed the good and bad sides of the sports establishment, which has become the repository for many kids' dreams of stardom. According to NCAA statistics gathered in 1992, each year more than 516,000 boys play high school basketball; the two young players in *Hoop Dreams* represent the 13,000 young men who play basketball at the college level each year. They face the nearly impossible odds of becoming one of the sixty-four professional rookies who join the NBA each year. (There are thirty teams in the NBA, with twelve players per team, for a total of 350 players.)

"Nike took a very responsible position about the film," says Missner. "It said, 'Here's a problem. Let's get kids to see this film, let's get them to talk about this in school, so kids understand the difference between dreams and reality,'" says Missner.

"We saw *Hoop Dreams* and really believed in the message of the film," said de la Fuente, the western regional marketing manager for Nike. "It's about hope and spirit and about sport and family."[1] Nike brought in their advertising partners, *Sports Illustrated* and Gannett Outdoor (the billboard advertising company), to bolster advertising efforts. The Nike promotional campaign included the creation of the *Hoop Dreams* Hotline, a twenty-four-hour-a-day 800-number underwritten by Nike that gave information about where the film was playing and group sales. Nike also underwrote the cost of the Gold Group, a specialized firm that Fine Line hired to handle the logistics of the group-sales efforts and a direct-mail effort. *Sports Illustrated* paid for the printing of the direct-mail pieces, and Nike paid the mailing costs for the campaign that targeted 30,000 schools, teams, basketball coaches, parent groups, Boys & Girls Clubs of America, churches, fraternal groups, and midnight basketball leagues to reach the audience of inner-city youth so important to the filmmakers.

Every group that went to see the film was given the study guides created by the Center for the Study of Sport in Society and under-

written by Nike. *Sports Illustrated* paid for the printing of the teach-
ers and students study guides, which were distributed to thousands
of secondary schools, youth groups, community groups, and church
groups throughout the country. *Sports Illustrated* and *Entertainment
Weekly* ran free ads for the Nike/*Sports Illustrated* program—not for
the movie itself, but for the 800-number for group sales and the
study guide information. Nike also brought in Gannett Outdoor
advertising, which gave the marketers all their empty billboard space
in the inner city and also put up free posters advertising the 800-
number in Los Angeles, New York, Chicago, and San Francisco.

Nike was also helpful in arranging radio promotions in the top
ten national markets, giving Fine Line promotional time that Nike
had accrued as a result of extensive advertising in that medium. The
radio promotion, called the "Win a Hoop Heroes Package," involved
the giveaway of tickets to see *Hoop Dreams*, CDs of the soundtrack
contributed by GRP Records, and Nike shoes.

For Missner, one of the surprises of working on a promotion
connected to a film was the film distribution system itself, which
could offer corporate sponsors no guarantee that the film they were
tying into would be around from one week to the next. "From the
corporation's point of view," says Missner, "their whole game is local target marketing. So it was extremely challenging and frustrat-
ing to try to coordinate corporate interest in the film tie-in with a
platform release."

Deutchman and Fine Line's Vice President of Advertising, Brian
Caldwell, took Fine Line's dog-and-pony show on the road to Atlanta, holding a screening for all the Turner divisions, then meeting
with the marketing heads of those divisions to figure out how they
could work together. The Turner Publishing Group had already been

negotiating for rights to the novelization of the film, and the Turner Networks wanted to know what was in it for them to promote the film. Deutchman repositioned his pitch, from the pitch he would normally make when looking for co-promotion partners, to more of a non-profit type of pitch, emphasizing the larger goals, the inner city, and the connection with Nike. By the end of the meeting, almost all of the Turner divisions had made some commitment to support the promotional effort.

The key meeting during the Atlanta trip was one with the Atlanta Hawks, an NBA team that was a Turner Division. "I knew that I had to walk away from that meeting with some kind of a commitment from them, because if I couldn't convince the Atlanta Hawks they should get on board, being our own company, there was no chance in hell we were going to get any other NBA team to come on board," says Deutchman. "We had already been warned by many people, Susan Missner included, that the NBA was going to be a really tough nut to crack, that they don't like getting into business with small things. They are also an organization that was implicitly criticized in the film, so we knew that was going to be really tough. When I walked in the door, this really hard-assed guy shook my hand and said, 'Thanks for coming, how much money are you spending on P&A on this film?' I said, 'No, no, no, you don't understand, that's not the issue, the issue here is'—and I launched into my pitch, which was what the movie was all about, what the Nike/ *Sports Illustrated* program was all about, what we were trying to accomplish with it. By the end he said, 'Oh, I get this, maybe we can underwrite a couple of those screenings for inner-city students, and certainly at the very least we can throw your trailer up on our scoreboard and maybe we can give out flyers.' These ideas were flowing from him. At that point I knew we had scored, because once we had them aboard, the next step was to go after the NBA."

When Deutchman returned to New York, he and the filmmakers' attorney, John Sloss (who also represents the New Jersey Nets), had a meeting with David Stern, the commissioner of basketball for the NBA, who was already familiar with the movie and understood its objectives. Deutchman told Stern about their arrangement with the Atlanta Hawks, then told him he would like to get local promotions going with as many of the NBA franchises as possible. "Stern said he would arrange for the national NBA office to E-mail all of the national franchises and say that the NBA approved of them getting into business with Fine Line on a promotional basis on the film," says Deutchman. "That was as close to an endorsement from the league that you're ever going to get."

After the meeting, Missner followed up with phone calls to encourage in-arena promotions of the film as it opened in each NBA market. Eventually, eighty percent of the NBA teams contributed to word-of-mouth by running the *Hoop Dreams* video on the jumbotron (the large scoreboard device that hangs from the center of the auditorium), and by flashing information about group ticket sales along with the 800-number on the running billboard outside of the auditorium. With the permission of the NBA and Turner Broadcasting, which broadcasts the NBA games, all of the play announcers received tapes of *Hoop Dreams* and were free to talk it up on the air, if they wished.

As Fine Line had hoped, the filmmakers and the movie benefited in numerous ways from the Turner connection. In addition to the in-game programming, the film received comp time for broadcast of the trailer during the Turner-owned Atlanta Hawks games. This was coverage in outlets that have strictly sports-oriented viewerships, which aren't easily accessible to the public relations firms that ordinarily publicize films.

The promotional machine was already in place when the film was released on October 19, 1994, timed to coincide with the beginning of the NBA preseason, as well as the New York Film Festival. *Hoop Dreams* opened in three major markets, on three screens in New York, three screens in Los Angeles, and twenty-four screens in Chicago. One of the theaters it opened at in New York was the Film Forum, which eventually profited from its early support of the film.

The resounding standing ovation at the New York Film Festival had already served to launch the film into the marketplace. Fine Line received an unprecedented and highly useful shot of publicity when the *New York Times* published a full-color, half-page photo with an article on the front page of the Arts & Leisure section the day of the opening. The story in the Arts & Leisure section was actually written by a *Times* sports columnist, Ira Berkow. After some cajoling from Fine Line, the *Times* ran their review of the film on the Friday prior to the Sunday evening New York Film Festival screening, ensuring that the review was not buried in the back pages of the Sunday Metro section.

"We had a very different approach in Chicago than in the other two cities," says Deutchman. "Our feeling was that with all of the press that Siskel and Ebert had already given the film, and all of the likely press that was going to continue to happen there because of the hometown-boys angle, that Chicago was the one shot we had from the get-go, of it playing like a commercial movie and crossing over to a larger audience. So we opened the film in every kind of neighborhood: black, white, upscale, downscale, middlebrow, suburban, inner-city, etc. We spent an enormous amount of advertising money on the opening, relatively speaking, in order to make it look like a big, commercial release."

The opening in Chicago was attended by celebrities as well as friends and families of the "stars," and was covered by all the local media. Nonetheless, Deutchman found the results of the opening "incredibly disappointing." In Chicago, the film did reasonable business on the upscale art-house screens, but poorly in black neighborhoods. New York results were "better than a disaster, but not a whole lot better than a disaster," says Deutchman. "That only reinforced a lot of the information we were already pulling in from the results in Los Angeles, and the research we were doing. It was going to be a more difficult job than we thought." Dave Sikich was outspoken in his view that Fine Line needed to spend more money marketing the film, according to Deutchman. "There wasn't evidence that that was our problem," says Deutchman. "There's always this temptation to say, 'No, no, no, you have to spend more money, you have to go out wider,' and we would look at Chicago and say, 'What's the evidence here?' We've done it and it didn't work. The one thing that we miscalculated was what an enormous overcome we were facing with the documentary, the subject matter, and the length of the film. Even though we'd had so much positive press and positive word-of-mouth, we realized the only way we were going to get people into the theater in numbers was that we were going to have to wear people down.

"After the opening, we regrouped very quickly and realized that the only way we could make this film work was through longevity, and we rearranged our entire release schedule, the way we spent money, every aspect of our marketing campaign, towards the goal of staying in the theaters as long as possible," says Deutchman. "This was against the pressure that was coming from the filmmakers at the time, although eventually they came around to our point of view, and pressure from our corporate parent as well, who also didn't understand the concept of leaving the film alone. From their perspective as a pseudo-studio at that point, they only know one way of marketing a movie, which is to push it out as wide and as fast as possible, and spend as much money as possible."

"This is a classic example of a movie that has very high playability and very low marketability," says Manne. "When that's what you've got, you're driven to a long, slow, rollout type of campaign. In fact, what the movie proved to be was a long, burning, slow, word-of-mouth sensation. For it to ultimately reach the more commercial audiences, it took five months of work, critic awards, and the Academy brouhaha."

Filmmaker Steve James says he has "nothing but incredible respect and appreciation" for Deutchman and Manne, whom he says "believed in the film and worked tirelessly on it. Everyone was trying to achieve the same thing. Along the way, people have different ideas about what will work and what will not work. Some things get done, others don't." Ironically, it was in the area of marketing to inner-city youths that James feels that Fine Line fell short. "Some of the reasons it didn't do well in black neighborhoods, in our view, was that Fine Line never really adequately marketed it properly to a black audience. They never really had a totally coordinated grassroots campaign to reach inner-city audiences." James felt that for the film's Chicago opening, Fine Line should have picked neighborhood theaters that were in crossover parts of town, where blacks and whites attend movies together, and should have reached out to more grassroots community organizations like churches. "We suggested they go to prominent black sports, political, and education leaders, get endorsements, and run them in ads in community newspapers. Jesse Jackson said he loved the film, he said, 'You guys have done something extremely important in the black community.' A quote like that when the film came out would have meant a lot to the black community."

The filmmakers also battled with Fine Line over the poster. "We thought the poster was way too boring of an image for the film— we wanted something much more dynamic and exciting," says James. "Did the poster hurt attendance? I doubt it." James is philosophical about these differences with the marketers, cognizant that marketing "is a process—there's not always agreement about this stuff. Ultimately someone makes a decision."

Manne points out that eventually Fine Line did reach the inner-city youth market through home video: "You don't get to 120,000 units subsequently in sell-through if you're not in a very mass-market type of situation. We were also able to get to a lot of those kids through the screening program."

Two weeks after opening, the film platformed to other major markets, with the number of screens growing to sixty by December. The plan was to expand at the right moment. Right before the Academy Award nominations, in February, Fine Line expanded the release to 250 screens. The decision to go out wider came about organically, as a result of the extraordinary crescendo of year-end and pre-Oscar publicity, according to Manne. "We thought, 'Okay, the heat's here! The time's right!'"

Hoop Dreams ran in theaters for nearly eight months, until April 1995, when the home video was released. Fine Line had projected a

North American box office gross of $3 million, with "pie in the sky" hopes for $5 million. By August 1995, *Hoop Dreams* had grossed $7.83 million in the U.S. and Canada, with $7.79 million of that earned in the U.S. New Line Home Video sold 140,000 units to video stores for rental and 120,000 units to the video sell-through (sales directly to customers) market in November 1995. *Hoop Dreams* became the highest-grossing non-music documentary in history. The home video sold more copies than Madonna's *Truth or Dare*, making it the bestselling documentary of all time in the home video market.

By the opening date, Fine Line had already "screened the heck out of it for the press," according to Manne, and press attention escalated. One NBA team ran a seven-minute halftime special about the film, and NBC anchorman Tom Brokaw did a piece on *Dateline NBC*. The Brokaw piece required extended negotiations to ensure that NBC didn't give away the entire story. Oprah even covered it. Roger Ebert and Gene Siskel, early champions of the film, continued to sing its praises, on their own show and during guest appearances on the Letterman show. "We got more press on this picture than on any picture I've ever worked on," says Manne.

The publicity came in three waves. The first wave was the normal magazine and pre-opening support it received in the general press. The second wave was the sports publicity it received via *Sports Illustrated*, *Sports Illustrated for Kids*, and other sports media outlets. The third wave of publicity began at the end of the year, when the Oscar handicapping lists came out. *Hoop Dreams* was recognized as an underdog candidate for best picture, and certainly considered by many to be a shoo-in for best documentary. "By January 1995, it was building up a head of steam," says Manne. The film was voted the Best Documentary by the Los Angeles Film Critics Circle, the

National Board of Review, the New York Critics Circle. It was named Best Picture (beating out *Forrest Gump* and *Pulp Fiction*) by the Chicago Film Critics Circle, and was listed on more than 100 critics' "Ten Best" lists. It was also named Best Picture of the Year by numerous critics, including the film's indefatigable boosters Roger Ebert and Gene Siskel, and also by Kenneth Turan of the *Los Angeles Times*.

"When we reoriented our release strategy to be more towards the long, slow burn, we knew that in order for the strategy to work we really needed to get the year-end awards and accolades," says Manne. "Each of those accolades was going to add more and more fuel to help drive us towards the Academy, which is the ultimate fuel, which would ultimately move it into the largest possible gross situation. This is part of wearing people down, a really aggressive awards campaign, so people would say, 'Geez, how can I *not* see this movie, it's been out for six months, everyone's talking about it, and here it got twenty-nine awards, I guess I better go see it finally.'"

"Part of the lesson we learned by how difficult that overcome turned out to be, was that we really had to get the press's help in reorienting the film away from that whole documentary thing in people's minds," says Deutchman. "We started pitching journalists at the end of the year. Liz and Marian and I had a critical lunch with Kenny Turan of the *L.A. Times*, in which we pitched him on the idea that *Hoop Dreams* should be considered for Best Picture, not for Best Documentary. He picked it as his number one film of the year, as did Siskel and Ebert. As our pitch began to work, and we started to see more and more people picking up on it, we actually started to believe that we had a shot at best picture."

"Anybody who's been watching this business for a while knows that the Best Documentary category for the Academy had a history of ignoring the most successful of the documentaries," says Manne. "Knowing that, we took a calculated risk when we went after Best Picture, because it was such a sensitive documentary nominating committee at that time. We knew that if we started going out in print positioning us for Best Picture, we were going to piss them off, and that they would be even more likely to tell us to go take a hike by not nominating us for Best Documentary."

In an effort to get the members of the Academy of Motion Pictures Arts and Sciences (who vote on the Academy Awards) to give their film serious consideration, Fine Line employees, including Deutchman, labored past midnight, without overtime pay, to pack, ship, and mail 5,000 copies to the entire Academy membership.

"We wanted to go wider the week before the Oscar nominations, because no matter what, we were in a win-win situation," says Manne. "If we got a Best Picture nomination, it would be unprecedented. We'd be one of the five Best Picture nominees, which always boosts your gross. If that scenario took place, we were there to exploit it. Second, if we got Best Documentary nomination, which is what most people thought was the likeliest scenario, it's still a great Academy Award nomination, and we still get featured well in the press. And the third possibility was we don't get either nomination. Those of us on the inside knew that that was a distinct possibility, given the Academy's history in terms of their documentary nomination procedures, and what they've done in the past. If this happens, people will be so outraged that we'll get more press than God. And in fact, possibility three is what happened. Nonetheless, we were quite thrilled to receive the editing nomination, because the truth is, it was a Herculean editing task."

After four years of shooting and two and a half years of editing, the filmmakers were understandably disappointed. Many other supporters of the film were outraged, and called for an investigation of the documentary nominating committee, which had a track record of passing over numerous fine documentaries over the years, including *A Brief History of Time*, *The Thin Blue Line*, *Roger & Me*, and others. Jack Garner of Gannett newspapers called the exclusion of *Hoop Dreams* from the best documentary race "the bonehead move of the Academy season." The only consolation was that *Hoop Dreams* did, indeed, receive more press than God, and Academy President Arthur Hiller ultimately acknowledged that reform was needed in the way the documentary committee operated.

"Another silver lining, from the point of view of those of us who are fans of documentary film," says Manne, "is that if these more accessible movies can finally be given the Academy accolades, which of course are the most influential of them all, it will only help broaden the audience for documentary films. *Hoop Dreams* became the straw that broke the camel's back. On the other hand, this furor helped increase the visibility of *Hoop Dreams*, and our grosses went up—we continued to do $600,000 a week and we were just climbing. We benefited financially from the controversy, no question about it."

Ironically, being passed over by the Academy gave *Hoop Dreams* the status of an iconic underdog, a status that was recognized by comedian David Letterman when he emceed the Academy Awards. After Academy President Arthur Hiller walked off stage, Letterman said, "Arthur, I think there's a couple of guys in the parking lot who want to speak to you about *Hoop Dreams*." He mentioned the film again later, during his recitation of "You Know You're Not Going to get an Academy Award when . . . Number Six, You make an excellent, well-meaning documentary about inner-city youths playing basketball." "You know you've made it when David Letterman is making jokes about you," says Manne.

The Academy of Motion Picture Arts and Sciences, which administers the Academy Awards, did finally change the rules for judging full-length documentary films, largely as a result of the furor surrounding the omission of *Hoop Dreams* from the documentary awards in 1995. The changes involve the creation of three panels, one in New York and two in Los Angeles, to share the judging of the documentaries. In the old days, because the single committee had to see all the films, they would reduce their workload by flashing little pen lights during the screening to indicate they wanted to stop a film and go on to the next one (known as the infamous "red light procedure"). Now, because each of the three panels only has to view one-third of all the films, they are required to watch them all the way through. The new rules also require documentaries to be shown for seven days in theaters in Los Angeles or Manhattan, not just film festivals, before they can be considered for an academy award nomination. Manne considers the changes both good news and bad news, applauding the bicoastal judging panel, fearing that the seven-day screening requirement will close the door to new filmmakers who haven't found distributors. In the case of *Hoop Dreams*, for example, if the filmmakers had gone ahead with their original plan to open their film at Film Forum before they went to Sundance, Manne says Fine Line would have been less interested in opening the film in New York, or picking it up for distribution at all.

Manne gives a lot of credit to what she calls "the professional sports machine in this country" for not running away from *Hoop Dreams* but embracing it. "It's not a Hallmark card to them, but neither is it a total damnation. The movie didn't say sports is good for kids or sports is bad for kids. It said, 'This is part of what the NBA dream is, this is part of what the sports dream machine sells you.' The reality is, it's virtually a million-in-one shot for a high school athlete to get into the NBA. What does having that dream do for you that's positive? It keeps these disenfranchised, urban kids in school, keeps them focused on their studies, and gets them college educations. If you can keep kids off the streets for eight years, through high school and college, in a program that requires concentration and discipline, chances are they can make it out the other end as a twenty-one-year-old man, with their head screwed on right and a college degree. That is an achievement. Even if the classic NBA dream—the hoop dream of being an Isiah Thomas or a Michael Jordan—is ultimately a pipe dream, it's gotten them to this point where they are miles ahead of where they might otherwise have been," says Manne.

Deutchman says that Nike and organizations like the NBA should be given a lot of credit because they understood the potential of the film to educate, and didn't shy away from it, even though it was critical of their organizations: "They were savvy enough to realize that by being involved in this movie, that the finger couldn't be pointed at them." Adds Manne, "They realized it would help undercut the criticism that they experience quite often as being part of this basketball dream machine that manufactures pipe dreams that really harm kids."

The *Hoop Dreams* story, like life, goes on and on. Fans of the film can hope that the filmmakers go back to their subjects in another few years, and give us an update on their lives, à la the ongoing British documentary, *35 UP* by Michael Apted, which followed a group of British children from childhood to adulthood with documentary installments shot every seven years. Moviegoers have seen one update, a thirty-minute program including a documentary segment and interviews with family members, that was aired after the PBS broadcast in November 1995. The sequel was produced by Kartemquin Films of Chicago and KTCA-TV of Minneapolis.

Both Arthur Agee and William Gates have about a year of coursework to finish before they receive their college degrees, since both of them took time off during their college years to go on speaking engagements and otherwise benefit from their involvement in *Hoop Dreams*. As of January 1997, Arthur Agee was still pursuing his hoop dreams. He played for the Long Island franchise of the United States Basketball League during the summer of 1995. At the beginning of 1997, he was moving to Phoenix to work with the Harlem Globetrotters, either as a player or in an administrative capacity, whichever works out. Agee is the father of two children who live with their respective mothers in Chicago and whom Agee helps support. Agee and his parents recently pooled their resources and purchased a house in Berwyn, Illinois, a suburb of Chicago, a move that has brought a great deal of joy to their lives.

William Gates is working as an Assistant Park Director for Oak Park Township, a suburb on the west side of Chicago, while he finishes his college degree in Chicago. He also volunteers his time as a gang intervention counselor. Gates has also worked with the Harlem Globetrotters, serving as an emcee for the team's tour of southern black colleges, which was sponsored by Apple Computers. He also gives speeches about the film and his experiences as a student athlete. Gates is married and the father of a son and a daughter. He recently moved back to the inner city of Chicago, and is encouraging his friends to do the same.

The filmmakers, in an unprecedented move, shared the profits from the film with Agee, Gates, and their families once the young players' collegiate eligibility had expired. Gates and Agee each get the same share of profits as each of the filmmakers; in addition, Gates' and Agee's families get a certain percentage of profits. "We didn't want to compromise their eligibility and their scholarships," says James. "The ethical and right thing to do, once that was no longer an issue, was to include them in the profits." In an unprecedented gesture in the documentary world, the filmmakers also set up a profit participation fund for thirty-seven "supporting participants," with percentages based on screen time.

The administration of St. Joseph's, the private high school that originally recruited both Gates and Agee, did not feel that the school was accurately depicted in the film and felt they deserved a share of the film's profits, so they sued the filmmakers. The lawsuit was settled out of court. One of the stipulations of the settlement was that the settlement money awarded to St. Joseph's would go toward scholarship funds for inner-city students, without being tied to achievement in sports. The filmmakers also voluntarily donated scholarship funds to Marshall High School (Arthur Agee's alma mater) to help students leaving Marshall go to college.

Filmmakers Steve James (director) and Peter Gilbert (producer) have completed a dramatic feature, *Prefontaine*, a biopic about Steve Prefontaine, a sixties distance runner who raised the profile of distance running in the United States until his untimely death in a car accident. The film was produced for Hollywood Pictures, a division of Disney. It premiered at Sundance in 1997, then opened in theaters in January of 1997. James wrote and directed the film, Gilbert produced and shot it. They have also raised part of the funding for a documentary series about immigrants, *The New Americans*. Filmmaker Frederick Marx is at work on a *Skaggs*, a documentary about media hoax artist Joey Skaggs, and has received partial funding from the NEA for production of an erotic drama, *Night Man*.

Those involved in the marketing of *Hoop Dreams* reflect on their experience with awe and satisfaction. "When we started with the roots of it more than eight years ago, who'da thunk?" says Manne. "Who'da thunk that we'd be Letterman's opening joke at the Academy Awards, with billions of people watching it worldwide? Who'da thunk that Arthur Agee would end up playing basketball with Bill Clinton during the NCAA finals? And who would have ever imagined that 2,800 mostly white people in New York City would be standing on their seats and giving a standing ovation that was longer and more dramatic than any standing ovation in the memories of the programmers of the New York Film Festival? That's a testament to how great a movie it is, but it's also a testament to what the swell of the PR and the marketing were over the course of the release."

Deutchman, who has since moved back to independent production under the banner of his company, Redeemable Features, says that "without tooting my own horn, I'm incredibly proud of the marketing of *Hoop Dreams*, given the challenges of the film. I didn't think it would beat out *Roger & Me*, it had so many strikes against it. I consider that a triumph of marketing. As good as the film is, how many great movies get lost in the shuffle, especially with all the competitiveness in the marketplace? *Hoop Dreams* was a personal mission for me and for everyone at Fine Line. It was that enthusiasm that bred it in others. Every time someone said to me, 'This project is impossible,' the more it fired me up to do it."

Hoop Dreams Media Coverage
(National, New York, Los Angeles)

Television: *WNBC 11 O'Clock News/Live at Five, America's Talking/R&R with Roger Rose*, BRAVO, *CBS This Morning*, CBS-TV, *The Charlie Rose Show*, Cinemax, *CNN Morning News, Dateline NBC, Day in Rock* (MTV), E! Channel, *Entertainment Tonight, Extra Entertainment* (syndicated), *Extra, Flix* (VH-1), *FX/Under Scrutiny With Jane Wallace, Good Day L.A., Good Day New York, Good Morning America, Inside Stuff* (NBA show on NBC), KCOP, KTLA, *The Jon Stewart Show, KTTV News, Last Call* (CBS), *The Late Late Show with Tom Snyder, Life and Times* (KCET-PBS), *Live at Five, McCreary Report* (Fox), *The Mike and Maty Show, MTV News*, N.I.T. Semi-Final Basketball Game, NBC's *The Today Show, NBC Nightly News*, NBC Sports, *New Sport Television, New York One, News at Five* (WCBS), *Nightline, The Oprah Winfrey Show, Showbiz Today* (CNN), *Siskel & Ebert, Sneak Previews*, Sports News Satellite, *Sportsnight* (ESPN2), *Talk Live* (CNBC), *Week in Rock* (MTV), World Television Network.

Radio: 1010 WINS Radio, Bernard White's AM Show (WBAI), Bill Bergoli (Westwood One), Bill Diehl (ABC), Bloomberg News Radio/Annie Bergen, CRN Radio Network and American Movie Classics, Ed Coleman's Show (WFAN), Entertainment Report (Mutual Broadcasting System), Entertainment Weekly Radio, Fresh Air (NPR), Mike and the Mad Dog (WFAN), Mike Reynolds (AP), New York and Company (WOR), Newsweek on Air, Sportsbox (WLIB), Studio A (WKCR-FM), Voice of Broadway (WKDM-AM), WABC Radio, Weekend Morning Edition (NPR).

Magazines: *Consumer Reports, Details, Elle, Entertainment Weekly, Esquire, The Film Journal, Filmmaker Magazine, Frontiers, GQ, Harpers*

Bazaar, IFP West Newsletter, The Independent Film and Video Monthly, International, Interview, L'Italo Americano, Los Angeles Magazine, MBA Style, Movieline, National Black Monitor, New York, The New Yorker, Newsweek, Out, Paper, Penthouse, People, Playboy, Premiere, Right On!, Rip City, Rolling Stone, Sassy, Scope, Sisters In Style, Slam, Source, Spin, Sports Illustrated, Sports Illustrated for Kids, Tart, Time, Troika, US, Vibe, Word Up, YSB.

Newspapers: Associated Press, *Carib News, Christian Science Monitor, Daily Breeze, Entertainment Today, Korea Times, Los Angeles Daily News, Los Angeles Reader, Los Angeles Sentinel, Los Angeles Times, Los Angeles Village View, L.A. Weekly, New York Daily News, New York Newsday, New York Post, New York Times, New Youth Connection,* Newhouse News Service/Bob Campbell, *Next, Orange County Register, San Pedro Pilot, Santa Monica Outlook, USA Today, USA Weekend, The Village Voice, The Wall Street Journal.*

Film Industry Trade Newspapers: *The Hollywood Reporter, Variety.*

Interactive Media: America OnLine, Compuserve, Electronic Mail Networks, Internet, Prodigy.

Special Events, Festivals, Screenings: Liberty Hill Foundation benefit premiere, New York City Schools Student Screening, WBET and "The Untouchables" benefit premiere, New York Film Festival, Sundance Film Festival, Toronto Film Festival, Regional Film Festivals (Boston, Denver, Mill Valley, New Orleans, Heart of Film Festival/Austin, Texas).

Field Press and Promotions: Feature pieces in newspapers in: Atlanta, Boston, Chicago, Cleveland, Denver, Detroit, Dallas, Houston, Miami, Washington, D.C., Seattle, San Francisco, Portland, Minneapolis, San Diego.

Oscar controversy pieces in newspapers in: Albany, Austin, Atlanta, Baltimore, Boston, Chicago, Dallas, Denver, Detroit, Ft. Lauderdale, Houston, Kansas City, Las Vegas, Miami, Minneapolis, Oklahoma City, Oakland, Orlando, Palm Beach, Philadelphia, Phoenix, Portland, Rochester, San Francisco, Seattle, St. Louis, St. Paul, Syracuse, Tacoma, Tampa, Washington, D.C.

Promotions: Radio- and print-promoted screenings held in all markets; community outreach to schools, churches, basketball teams and groups accomplished in all markets.

National Promotions:

Gannett: Gannett Outdoor provided bus shelter advertising in New York, Los Angeles and billboard advertising in Chicago and San Francisco free of charge.

NBA: Teams that participated in individual promotions: Cleveland Cavaliers, San Antonio Spurs, Orlando Magic, Denver Nuggets, Seattle Supersonics, Golden State Warriors, Los Angeles Lakers, Miami Heat, Philadelphia 76ers, Sacramento Kings, Boston Celtics, Atlanta Hawks, Detroit Pistons, New York Knicks, Minnesota Timberwolves.

Nike: Money was provided by Nike for special screenings for Boys and Girls Clubs in selected NBA markets; Nike sent tapes of television spot to local cable stations and assisted in getting air time; Nike purchased time on urban contemporary radio in ten major markets to promote 2,000 "Hoop Heroes Package" giveaways—package consisted of a pair of Nike shoes, CD of soundtrack album, and a pair of ROE passes.

Nike/*Sports Illustrated*: Nike and *Sports Illustrated* underwrote a program for group ticket sales. Program included a direct-mail piece sent to 50,000 homes and an 800 number on all advertising, which included newspapers, magazines, television and bus shelters, and billboards from Gannett. Over 50,000 people attended screenings through this program. An Educational Guide prepared by The Center for The Study of Sport in Society was provided to all school groups that attended via this program.

Turner: Ran *Hoop Dreams* trailer on Turner Networks.

Turner Sports: Turner Sports aired a piece on the film on TNT during halftime of one of the NBA games and on TBS during pregame shows.

Marketing Expenditures: *Hoop Dreams*
January '94 – December '95
$(000)

Newspapers	1,880.4
Spot Television	51.8
Cable TV Networks	530.5
Network Spot Radio	11.0
Grand Total	2,473.7

© Copyright 1996 Competitive Media Reporting and Publishers Information Bureau.

1. *New York Times*, Nov. 7, 1994.

5
MORE AMERICAN INDEPENDENT AND FOREIGN FILMS:
Welcome to the Dollhouse, Howards End, Crumb

In years past, the American intelligentsia looked to Godard, Truffaut, Bergman, and other foreign filmmakers for interesting, eclectic, offbeat films. Now young Americans and other selective moviegoers patronize American independent films to get their intellectual fix. Demand for independent films has grown because major studios, in their efforts to produce blockbusters, are putting out an increasingly homogenized product. The major studios have traditionally put their energies and resources into producing and marketing films that appeal to mainstream tastes, films that will sell in middle America. Since there's less diversity among the product that the major studios offer, specialty distributors like Sony Pictures Classics have moved to meet the demand for films that don't fulfill the formulas of the major studios. Distributors like Sony Pictures Classics operate semi-autonomously, even though they are technically owned by larger parent companies. In the last few years, most of the independent distributors have been acquired by corporate parents with deep pockets, as in the case of Miramax (Disney), Fine Line and New Line (Turner/Time Warner), Fox Searchlight (Twentieth Century Fox), Gramercy (Polygram), Sony Pictures Classics (Sony), and, most recently, October Films (Universal). The parent companies allow the subsidiaries to operate fairly independently because they realize that the teams running these companies have an expertise that marketers in the larger corporate parent may not have. The team at Sony Pictures Classics is one that has a track record of recognizing new talent and nurturing it.

"There's a new kind of cinema going on out there," says Tom Bernard, co-president of Sony Pictures Classics. "The new talent, the new voice is coming from American independent directors that have great storytelling skills and great ideas. These are people that bring a certain rawness and newness to their storytelling style, because they're not polished, slick, Hollywood film or TV commercial directors. There's a creativity in the way they tell their stories, because of the limitations of the budgets for their films, and it's captured the attention of America. The stories they tell are unique. They're not about great social causes, they're very personal. They're about themselves, about little things that happen in your life—going to get a cheeseburger, riding a school bus home. They're stories about moments, about people going to a restaurant, talking to someone about ordering a cappuccino. It's about a guy meeting a guy on the street corner and saying, 'Hey, what's going on?' In *The Brothers McMullen*, there's a couple of brothers talking about their girlfriends, cooking spaghetti at home, doing their chores. It's not movies on a grand scope. You don't see many American independent films where the headline is 'See the Grand Scope of This Story.'"

"Independent filmmakers tend to take a lot more creative risks than major studios," says Mark Litwak, entertainment attorney and producer's rep for independent filmmakers. "They're not trying to compete in the same arena. Obviously if you're a low-budget, independent filmmaker making a film for $400,000, you can't expect to dazzle people with the same kind of special effects that Paramount can afford. You can't afford a lot of things that the major studios can afford to do. You have to eliminate anything that's potentially expensive: herds of wild animals, films that require lots of expensive costumes or locations, films that require a lot of outdoor shooting, where it might be subject to inclement weather, films that involve young children or scenes on water. That's why a lot of low-budget, independent films tend to be shot at a limited number of locations, often a contemporary story, where there's a lot of scenes of people talking to each other. That kind of film is cheap to shoot. It's a real challenge to create something with limited locations that is entertaining.

"Some independent films succeed, but many fail. The usual reason for failure is the lack of an entertaining story," says Litwak. "*Welcome to the Dollhouse*, which was the winner of the Sundance Film Festival in 1995, succeeded. The year before that, Ed Burns, director of *The Brothers McMullen*, had a hit. Every year there's a handful of these low-budget films by unknown filmmakers that come out of nowhere, break through, and get great critical acclaim."

Welcome to the Dollhouse, a comedy about a female teenage nerd's experience in middle school, began to break through on its way to the Toronto Film Festival. Before he left for Toronto, Tom Bernard of Sony Pictures Classics got a tip from Cara White, formerly the head publicist at the public relations firm Clein + White in New York, who said that she'd heard the film was very good and suggested Bernhard and his partners see it in Toronto. Bernhard went to the screening at the Cumberland Theater in Toronto with his partners, Michael Barker and Marcie Bloom, who work as a team to make acquisition and deal decisions for Sony Pictures Classics. (Bloom is the point person on acquisitions and business affairs for the company; Michael Barker and Tom Bernard are the point people on marketing and distribution). Miramax, October Films, Fine Line Features, Gramercy, and other Sony competitors also attended the screening. "The audience's reaction was nervous laughter," recalls Tom Bernard. "We were in love with the film. We said, 'This is a hit.' Then we pursued the director, Todd Solondz, and the acquisition of the film with a vengeance. We don't know how many people were competing for the film—we don't feel there were many. We acquired the film for a very small sum, under a half-million dollars. We promised the director that the way we do business is to form a partnership with the director when we acquire a film. We say, 'If the picture does business and performs in the marketplace, you're certainly going to get overage checks from us.' On a movie like *Orlando*, we sent over $1 million in overage checks to the producers. Then we got into a discussion of how we felt we could market the film, and who the audience was for the film. We gave the director a strategy which he seemed to like and they chose to sell us the film while we were in Toronto."

Barker and Bernard quickly proceeded to develop a marketing strategy for the film. "Michael Barker and I thought that the film was a little rough around the edges," said Bernard. It's not your traditional happy-ending teenage adolescent movie. But we felt it would touch a chord in just about anyone's heart who saw the film. It would bring up their personal experiences with junior high, because everyone has a story about junior high. When we saw it in the first screening in Toronto, people came out of the theater and were stumbling over each other to tell the person next to them their junior high school experience and how it related to the movie. From that moment on, we knew we had a picture that would have tremendous word-of-mouth. People were going to talk about this film."

During the initial screenings in Toronto and for the press, Barker noticed widely contrasting reactions to the film, depending on how many people were in the audience. "When there was a substantial audience," says Barker, "the audience viewed the film in a kind of communal spirit and the black comedy of the film really came out. When there were very few people in the audience, the picture was viewed as a very dark, depressing, bleak movie that wasn't very funny at all. So we immediately came to the conclusion that this is a picture that needs to be seen with a large group of people. We knew we would have fewer press screenings where the room would be relatively filled, and invite the press to screenings that involved promotions with radio stations, MTV, *Entertainment Weekly*, and *The Village Voice*. Then, by opening the picture in screens that do not have too many seats, we would be guaranteed the kind of crowd that would enjoy it as a group."

Finding the appropriate venue for a film like *Welcome to the Dollhouse* has become easier since the proliferation of multiplexes, which offer a number of different capacity theaters on the same site. "The development of multiplexes has made it easier for independent films, because the exhibitor doesn't have to put all his eggs in one basket and just pick one film to show," says Litwak. "Multiplexes have allowed exhibitors to spread their risk over different types of pictures. Instead of just selecting just one mass-appeal picture to fill up a 2,000-seat theater, they now have a variety of different venues to fill, some of which are pretty small. They have more flexibility. They can take a chance on something that's unproven and risky subject matter. If it doesn't work out real well, it's not the only film that they're showing. Also, if a film doesn't prove to be that popular, they can move it to one of the smaller theaters. So multiplexes have helped encourage diversity of programming.

"In looking to market independent films," says Litwak, "distributors like Sony Classics look for one or more of the following elements: cast, reviews and festival honors. Basically, distributors of independently made films sell them on the basis of either the cast or occasionally a name director like Spike Lee or Quentin Tarantino; on the basis of winning film festivals, especially the important ones like Sundance, Toronto, or Cannes; and on the basis of critical reviews from important media outlets like the *New York Times*, the *Los Angeles Times*, and the trade papers. If an independent film does not have at least one of the aforementioned marketing hooks, the film is unlikely to interest most distributors."

Bernard and Barker realized *Welcome to the Dollhouse* would not fare well if it was opened right after Toronto, and that it needed a distinct profile in the marketplace. "When we met the director, it was apparent he was a very media-savvy guy who was a great interview—very entertaining and very smart," says Bernard. "We knew he was certainly going to be able to be part of our marketing campaign. We then decided that the best way to create a profile for the film would be through a series of film festivals leading up to a summer release for the film. Jeffrey Gilmore, the director of the Sundance Film Festival, had already invited the director to bring the film to Sundance when it was showing in Toronto. We felt that we had a good chance to win a prize at Sundance. We didn't know what prize—audience, director, actress, but we felt it had a chance to gain a profile in Sundance.

"The Sundance Film Festival is one of the highest-profile events in the U.S. for the youth market," says Bernard. "It's covered by the media more than any other North American event because there are so many Hollywood types from the studios and talent agencies out there, looking for new people to direct Hollywood movies. That's the excitement. It's sort of the lottery for someone with an independent film and a dream to not only get the film picked up, but then to get a job directing for studios, which you see many, many times. The next film for the guy who did *Clerks* is *Mall Rats* for Universal. It may not be the right move for the director, but that's their dream."

"Sundance has become the paramount festival in the United States," says Litwak. "Other important festivals in the United States are Seattle, Hamptons, Mill Valley, Telluride, New York, the L.A. Independent Film Festival, Slamdance, and a few others. In Canada, the pre-eminent film festival is Toronto, although Vancouver and Montreal are also important. In Europe, the big three film festivals are Cannes, Berlin, and Venice."

"We felt Sundance was going to have the highest media coverage to date, so we brought the film there with the director," says Bernard. "We hired two publicity firms, Block-Korenbrot in Los Angeles and Clein + White, to get interviews for the director and introduce him to critics from all over the country so that he could form relationships with them. That way the critics could get to know the director and hear his personal vision of the film, which ultimately helps the critics understand the film and have a feel for it."

One of the benefits of festival exposure is that films get reviewed by the media. Most publications have a policy of only reviewing films that will receive a theatrical release, and the review appears at about the time of the release. For films seeking a distributor, it can be difficult to demonstrate how the film will be critically received. The principal way for a film that does not have a release date to be reviewed is for the film to be screened at a festival. Thus, festivals help independent filmmakers in two ways: they expose the film to distributors who can observe how audiences receive it, and the festival screening often results in the film being reviewed by critics and the trade press.

"One advantage that these low-budget, independent films have is that critics don't judge them on the same criteria as they judge the major films," says Litwak. "Critics tend to be very forgiving of technical shortcomings of low-budget independent films, because they recognize that the filmmakers have minuscule budgets. In fact, in many instances, the filmmakers of low-budget independent films have less money to make their film than the meal and drink budget for a major studio production. But a lot of reviewers love to discover unknown films and become their champion, and of course this helps some filmmakers break through the clutter, attract the attention of distributors, and ultimately get distribution. Reviews matter to filmgoers who patronize specialty films, because they read reviews and can be influenced by them, unlike the people who patronize major studio films, who are less affected by reviews. Some would say that the people who see *Rambo* don't read reviews, with some cynics going so far as to claim that those who want to see a film like *Rambo* don't read. But clearly, reviews have much more influence among specialty moviegoers. An action-adventure film can be critically panned and still succeed at the box office. Moviegoers are not expecting great art. But I can't think of one specialty or foreign film that became a hit in the face of uniformly bad reviews."

Welcome to the Dollhouse won the award for the Best Dramatic Film at the 1996 Sundance Film Festival. (The year before, another Sony Classics film, *Crumb*, had won the Best Documentary Award at Sundance, which catapulted *Crumb* into the mainstream.) *Dollhouse* director Todd Solondz was in attendance and did numerous interviews, which put the film on the map. "People were now aware of the film," says Bernard. "It was a film that had to be dealt with in the marketplace." Solondz took the film to the Berlin Film Festival, adding to the publicity momentum. The Sony partners felt that the film still needed a higher profile in New York City, which it attained when it was invited to be the opening night film in Lincoln Center's New Director series. Another round of press followed, including a glowing review in the *New York Times,* which the distributor could reprint for further publicity when the film eventually opened. "The film opened to great publicity and fanfare at the New Director Series because it was a very unique and different film," says Bernhard. "There haven't been many American independent films about junior high school."

"We had originally planned to open the film right after the New Director's Series in March, but as we got closer to Sundance, it became obvious to us that this picture was going to have such great word-of-mouth that we shouldn't rush it," says Barker. "The more people buzz about this picture before it opens, the better off it is. So we decided, 'We'll be in Sundance, we'll be in the Lincoln Center New Director's Series, then we'll open on Memorial Day.' The reason we chose Memorial Day was because everyone else was running away from Memorial Day because that was the day *Mission: Impossible* was going to open. We purposely wanted to open opposite *Mission: Impossible* because three years earlier we opened *Orlando* opposite *Jurassic Park*. We were really criticized, but we put in our ads for *Orlando*, 'If you don't want to see a dinosaur this weekend, there is always *Orlando*.' And the fact of the matter is, there is a sizable audience out there that are in the movegoing habit from Memorial Day on, whose first choice is not *Jurassic Park* or *Mission: Impossible*. We also knew there would be very few, if any, openings other than *Mission: Impossible*. That meant a lot of space would be spent talking about our film, because we felt confident that our film would get good reviews. And sure enough, all of that happened. But even better than that, *Mission: Impossible* moved their date up two days so they opened on Wednesday instead of Friday. So in New York, L.A., San Francisco, and Seattle, *Welcome to the Dollhouse* virtually owned the editorial space on the front page of the arts sections on the Friday of Memorial Day weekend, because *Mission: Impossible* publicity had all appeared on Wednesday. Hence, house records!"

Welcome to the Dollhouse opened to box-office records in Los Angeles and near-records in New York, and in Bernard's estimation, "It was a tremendous hit." Sony then positioned the film to open in numerous regional film festivals shortly before its opening in each market. By doing so, Sony saved money on the director's travel expenses, which were usually paid by the film festivals, and had the director on hand to do interviews in person when the film opened. Flying the director to the festival in coach and housing him in a modest hotel was part of positioning the film as a movie that was *not* a high-profile, lavish, big-budget film. "This was positioned as an

American independent movie made on a shoestring by a director, financed with his credit cards and by his parents and private investors," says Bernard. "We also felt there was a large youth market eighteen-to-twenty-five for the film, even though it was rated 'R.'" The Sony partners had kept the young girl who starred in the film, Heather Matarazzo, out of the limelight until the film opened, with the intention of saving her story for a second round of publicity. Sony worked with their two public relations firms, Block-Korenbrot and Clein + White, to place interviews with Matarazzo and Solondz in youth-oriented magazines such as *Spin*, *Details*, *Rolling Stone*, and *The Village Voice*. "We arranged for Solondz to be interviewed by MTV when he was at Sundance, because we felt MTV was going to be important in creating a hipness to the film," says Bernard. "MTV took to the film and thought it was just perfect for their audience, so we set up a promotion where you could actually win a ticket to the opening of the Sundance Film Festival next year." Matarazzo's appearances on *Letterman*, *Good Morning America*, MTV, and *Conan O'Brien*, along with interviews in the *Los Angeles Times* and the *New York Times*, contributed to national awareness of the film.

Bernard says their biggest obstacle in marketing *Welcome to the Dollhouse* was that "it was an American independent, low-budget film about junior high school that no one had ever heard of. The goal was to make it a very cool, hip, entertaining thing to go see." Along with the publicity blitz, Sony purposely put the film in theaters so small that there would be long lines outside, making it difficult to see. Barker compares the growing awareness of *Welcome to the Dollhouse* to their experience marketing a film called *Slacker* when they were at Orion Classics: "Our goal with *Slacker* was somehow to get the word 'slacker' into the vernacular. It had already started being used in the culture as a generic term for a certain generation ['slacker' describes a highly educated, thirty-something underachiever]. To key into the popular culture and get recognized as part of the culture is the key to making the movie successful. With *Welcome to the Dollhouse*, I'm seeing more and more references in stories and different magazines to the 'Wienerdog' (the name given to the main character, Dawn Wiener, by the rest of the junior high school) and her clothing and fashion." Indeed, "Wienerdog" gave new meaning to that staple of fashion "journalism" in articles such as "*Welcome to the Dollhouse* Makeover: What To Do When Geek Isn't Chic."[1]

"One of the keys to the success of *Dollhouse* is that we really worked in partnership with the filmmaker on all the materials," says Barker. "A lot of filmmakers don't want to fool with the poster or the trailer and don't have a knack for it at all. Todd is someone who really did have strong feelings about it. His instincts were totally compatible with ours. The partnership resulted in a very unified campaign that was totally in keeping with the spirit of the film." While some production stills had been shot during the making of the film, the stills were not great, an affliction common to many low-budget films. So Barker arranged a post-production photo shoot that involved posing the young star, Heather Matarazzo, in a "Lolita-like" pose, which was then used for the poster and one-sheet.

From the beginning, Sony Pictures Classics has been known for its original, previously unheard-of approach to releasing films. "Our biggest success was *Howards End*, which brought in $26 million at the box office," says Bernard. "*Howards End* opened in one theater the first week. It ended up on 450 screens, but it was done in a very systematic way. David Putnam once said, 'The picture will tell you where to go.' With *Welcome to the Dollhouse*, we opened exclusively

in New York and Los Angeles on opening day. We positioned ourselves to be the only picture outside of *Mission: Impossible* on the
screen, which afforded us a lot of space in the newspaper. One of
our main pushes is that we don't want to buy your recognition of
our film. We want to get it through publicity. We'd much rather have
a full-page interview with Todd Solondz than a full-page ad. We feel
an interview adds more credibility to the film, gives you more information, and people pay more attention to it. One of the keys to our
marketing strategy is publicity—free space in the newspaper."

When Sony Pictures Classics is about to open a film, they study
each market across the country individually. If they're opening in Seattle, for example, they make sure they're not going up against several
other specialized films that might compete with them for newspaper
space and split the media coverage. They study the marketplace to
make certain that their opening is going to be the biggest event for
that weekend. "You have to monitor the release patterns of your
competition's picture throughout the country—you've got to be on
top of it," says Bernard. "We're in touch with the marketplace."

Both Barker and Bernhard are still involved in the day-to-day
operations of booking the theaters, setting the ad campaigns and
doing the marketing for Sony Pictures Classics. That's not the case
for many distribution companies, with a top-down command structure that involves communicating orders through several layers of
management, until the message often gets garbled in the translation.
Barker and Bernard are sensitive to the nuances of the entertainment marketplace. If the critic in Cincinnati who loves specialized
film suddenly gets fired or the filmmaker can't make it to Albuquerque for the opening, they arrange a wire-service interview to make
sure that the local paper still gets the story about their film. They're

tuned in to special events in a town, so that if there's a major event like Gay Pride Week that closes down the street right next to the theater where they're opening, they don't open that weekend. They appreciate the regional idiosyncrasies of marketplaces such as rainy Seattle, where it's better to open a movie early in the summer rather than later, because as the weather gets better, people don't go to the movies. Some cities are better than others for Memorial Day weekend openings, because of variations in summer vacation patterns. "Getting a feel for how the movies perform at different times of the year, in different places—these are things you learn after years of experience," says Bernard.

With *Welcome to the Dollhouse*, they went wide in New York and Los Angeles after three weeks, then expanded to eighty-five screens throughout the country. Bernard tried to expand the film as widely as possible in June and July, otherwise they would run into competition from the Olympics, which took place the last two weeks of July. Distributors generally try to avoid opening during events like the Olympics, the World Series, and NBA basketball championships, which have a negative impact on box office. *Welcome to the Dollhouse* eventually expanded to 700 theaters, grossing $6 million with an expenditure of $1.3 million on prints and advertising.

Bernard, Barker and Bloom perfected their marketing and distribution strategies with the release of *Howards End*, a Merchant Ivory Production, which was the first film they purchased at Sony Pictures Classics. "We chased the script," says Bernard. "We said, 'This is a movie that has got Oscars written all over it. [The film did receive Oscars for Best Actress, Screenplay, Art Direction, and Editing.] We felt, especially five years ago, that we could grow the picture. The picture was so good we felt it would have such legs that

we could set this picture up so that it would play for over a year."
They opened *Howards End* at the Paris Theater in Manhattan in
70mm. "The industry criticized us tremendously," says Bernard. "A
lot of the people that you talked to in this book went in print saying we were doing an insane thing. But it would have just been
wrong for us to be on 500 screens in two weeks."

Part of Sony's strategy on *Howards End* was to bring a couple of
the film's many characters to the United States on a publicity tour
every two months, rather like a rotating, continuous press conference. They sent Sam West and Helena Bonham Carter, two of the
film's stars, on a tour of the country beginning in Ohio and Or-
egon, timing their visits to coincide with the regional opening of
the film. When *Howards End* opened in Cincinnati in August, 1991,
it did $20,000 the first week, which among specialized films is sig-
nificant. The partners constantly added screens, and according to
Bernard, "Every time we added a screen, the movie just stuck in
there. It didn't come off." Sony picked theaters that were in upscale
neighborhoods, because they knew that they would have open playing time and would be able to play through the summer into the
fall. Box office drooped slightly in October, but as the year-end
awards rolled around, there was a resurgence in attendance. Momentum built as the film was honored on "Ten Best" lists and won numerous other awards, including the National Board of Review Best
Actress award for Emma Thompson, and the New York and Los Angeles Film Critics Awards. "In December, with Emma Thompson
winning the Golden Globe Awards for Best Actress, we felt we were
at maximum awareness of this picture, and we felt that was when we
should go out wide," says Bernhard. "We ended up on 450 screens
during the Oscar period, and ended up with $26 million at the box

office with an unheard-of expense of $4 million in P&A [prints and advertising]. Our critics ceased. Now you see a lot of the same people who criticized us using this distribution pattern, with the words, 'We're going to do it like *Howards End.*'" Bernard views with amusement the many movies he sees that have to open in an exclusive engagement at the Paris Theater in 70mm, followed by a slow rollout that peaks during the awards period, with the widest release going into the Oscars. Bernard points to films such as *Leaving Las Vegas, Dead Man Walking, Sense and Sensibility, Braveheart,* and *Remains of the Day* that followed this pattern. "*Howards End* was a landmark in this new crossover of specialized film distribution," says Bernard.

Crumb proved to be another profitable venture for Sony Pictures Classics. This was a documentary about the underground artist Robert Crumb, best known for his "Keep On Truckin'" poster, his Janis Joplin album covers, and his work in Zap Comix. Bernard characterizes it as a "pretty disturbing and racy" film, which they picked up "for a song," that is, for less than $200,000, at the Toronto Film Festival. The partners saw Crumb as a "mysterious underground character from the sixties" whose work was recognized by millions of people. Bernard felt "this was the movie that would finally introduce them to this guy's inner secrets, to who he really was."

Terry Zwigoff, the director of *Crumb,* worked closely with Sony on the marketing and distribution of the film. "He was a great interview, a real entertainer," says Bernard, "and he traveled to more cities and more regional film festivals than he ever intended to visit in America." Sony didn't have to spend a lot of money on marketing *Crumb* because they played it at virtually locked engagements, at calendar houses, which are considered the last of the real independent theaters. Calendar houses are art theaters that book films for a limited period of time. The advantage of playing at a calendar house is that the film distributor doesn't have to spend large amounts of money on newspaper advertising because the theater's calendar is circulated throughout the city.

Crumb played a four-week engagement at the Music Box in Chicago (grossing $63,000 the first week) and at the Castro Theater in San Francisco (grossing $78,000 the first week). The film took in $700,000 during its New York Film Forum run alone. Sony Pictures Classics eventually grossed more than $3 million with *Crumb*, with an expenditure of $600,000 on P&A. Bernard looks at the profitability of film distribution very critically, pointing out that profitability is determined not just by how much a film grosses, but by the percentage of advertising to box office. There are distributors who do what is called "grossing the film up," which means spending more in order to raise film grosses. In Bernard's estimation, a film is not really profitable if so much money has been spent on marketing that there are little or no profits, in the form of residuals or overages, left for the people involved in the film.

"A lot more pride used to be taken in making sure the filmmaker received some revenues at the end of the day," says Barker. "I find more and more, we are the sole oasis in the desert, or one of the few in the desert. I think today there is overspending in the marketing area, replacing creative ideas with spending more money. I think that's an irresponsible way of releasing pictures if you want to be responsible towards the bottom line, not only for yourself, but for the filmmaker."

Bernard finds marketing becomes more challenging each year, because there are more films competing for a certain audience, for space in the newspaper, for screen space, and for staying on the screen altogether. "It's become a business of survival of the fittest," says Bernard. "Even the theaters which used to hold the movies on for weeks at a time now say, 'Okay, the lowest box-office gross this week is off.' So you have to market better to keep your picture performing. You're also in a business to make money, so you've got to do it in a cost-effective way so that you can remain in business." Bernard points out that in the past fifteen years, more than 300 companies that distribute independent films have come and gone, companies like New World, Cinecom, Embassy Releasing, Filmways, the old Orion, Cinema Five.

Barker doesn't expect the job of marketing to get any easier, especially when it comes to foreign-language films, because the media no longer give foreign films the attention they used to give. "Whether it's the critics for the major magazines or the major newspapers, there's a real rush for the big Hollywood stuff and a lack of support for the foreign films," says Barker. "In years past, the people who were the head critics at a number of the major newspapers were huge fans of international cinema," says Bernard. "You could look at Charles Champlin of the *L.A. Times*, a legend in the world of criticism, Judy Stone, another legendary critic who was at the *San Francisco Chronicle* for years, Vincent Canby at the *New York Times*, Gary Arnold at the *Washington Post*—these are all the lead newspapers for film criticism in the country. The fact is, every one of those critics is gone. And the people who have taken their place are simply not as educated about foreign film. They seem to embrace the American independent movement now, and have put their emphasis in that arena, and just haven't given the coverage, in terms of reviews, as well as urging their editors to do interviews on these types of films. So the public has been focused, through the media, to look towards the American independent arena now, instead of the foreign film arena, which was the genre in specialized film in the seventies and eighties."

To some extent, the current orientation of film critics affects specialized distributors like Sony Pictures Classics. "We buy films that we think are good," says Bernard. "We may not take as many chances on smaller films as we used to, knowing that the critics aren't going to review them or that we're going to get the third-string critic, because there's no one really interested in discovering new directors in that arena. But we still are very much in the game of foreign film, have several out right now, and hope to find a bunch more for next year."

It was film festivals such as the Dallas International Film Festival as well as foreign films that first piqued Bernard's interest in film. Later, when he was a college student at the University of Maryland, he started a film series, which financed the rest of his college career. After college he went to work for Bob Shaye at New Line Cinema, who started out with movies like *Reefer Madness* and *Pink Flamingoes*. In Bernard's eyes, Shaye was "the original maverick, the guy who started out in his garage and is now one of the major forces in the industry, paying $3 to 4 million for scripts and making movies that make $100 million—the guy everyone wants to be like." One of Bernard's fondest memories of New Line was watching Bobby Seale (the black militant who was represented by New Line's speaker's bureau) sitting in the boss's office demanding his money or he was going to "punch his lights out." The boss gave him the money. Bernard worked in New Line's theatrical division, selling to theaters and colleges, until the nepotism of the old-boy network in the movie distribution business got to him. He left when he was hired to run a new theatrical distribution company for Films, Incorporated. After his first film there, *Shout*, directed by Jerzy Skolimowski and produced by Jeremy Thomas, went on to win Oscars, Bernard decided that he could distribute films out of New York with just a telephone, eliminating numerous field agents.

At Films, Incorporated, Bernard first crossed paths with Michael Barker, who was working for them selling 16mm films to prisons. Nathaniel Kwit at United Artists soon asked Bernard to start up a division at United Artists to distribute smaller films, and United Artists Classics was born. Barker teamed up with Bernard, and together they ran UA Classics for three years. At United Artists Classics, their first film was *The Last Metro*, which was very successful. "All of a sudden, there was a marketplace for these type of films, unlike ever before," says Bernard. He points to the films that came out of that era: John Sayles' *Secaucus Seven*, Paul Bartel's *Eating Raoul*, Louis Malle's *Atlantic City*. During their tenure at UA, the management changed seven times until, finally, Bernard and Barker were wooed to Orion by Arthur Krim. They formed Orion Classics, which they ran for eight years until Orion went bankrupt. While they were at Orion they became partners with Marcie Bloom, who had worked as a publicist on their major films. After Orion collapsed, they moved to form Sony Pictures Classics, which has been in business more than five years. After the genesis of Sony Pictures Classics, Disney bought Miramax, Fox Searchlight Films was formed under the Twentieth Century Fox banner, and Gramercy became part of Polygram, continuing the tradition of distributing small films.

For Barker, marketing films is not a business, it is more of a calling: "I've always loved movies in a substantial way, and they've always been a major part of my life. I've always felt, even when I was a young child, that there had to be a way that I could contribute. As I became older, I realized that I was not a filmmaker, I was not an artist. I was more someone in awe of the arts and the creative, the creators. So when I started to embark on my career, my goal was how to serve those filmmakers who were not being served well in the marketplace—how to serve them well. That's Marcie's and Tom's goal as well, and hopefully we've succeeded with the filmmakers we've been involved with."

Mark Litwak on Strategy and Tactics in Orchestrating the Distribution Deal

When a distributor negotiates with a filmmaker to acquire film rights, the distributor often has a lot of clout and the filmmaker may be desperate to make a deal. This is a perilous situation for the filmmaker. A filmmaker who makes a bad distribution deal will not be able to repay investors, and this often means that the filmmaker will find it very difficult, if not impossible, to raise financing for another film. Filmmakers must know how to orchestrate the selling of their film to achieve maximum clout when negotiating their deal.

Making a film is only half the battle. In order to secure favorable terms for distribution, a filmmaker needs to have a strategy designed to attract distributors. This often entails generating good word of mouth within the industry. This "buzz" or "heat" can be fanned by filmmakers who are willing to work the festival circuit and mount an aggressive campaign on behalf of the film.

Festivals are a cost-effective way to get films in front of potential distributors in a setting where they can view the film with a public audience. Acquisition executives attend a limited number of festivals. They prefer to attend those that show premieres of films that have not secured distribution yet. Consequently, festivals compete with each other to premiere such films. They each want to be first to discover a great film. Filmmakers need to understand that you only get one premiere per territory or region, and participation in one festival may make the film ineligible for acceptance to other festivals. For instance, the Sundance Festival prefers to premiere films and has a policy of only accepting into competition those films that have been in no more than one festival. Note that Sundance does not count a market, such as IFFM, as a festival, and Sundance has established a non-competitive section to exhibit films that have been shown elsewhere.

The festivals most important for filmmakers seeking distribution are those that are well attended by acquisition executives. There are many festivals and they each have their own selection criteria and point of view. Some are very specialized; others exhibit a broad range of motion pictures including animation, shorts, and documentaries. The nature of a film will determine which festivals are best to enter. Generally speaking, for independent filmmakers with feature-length films, the best festivals are Sundance, Hamptons, New York, Mill Valley, Seattle, and Telluride. Up-and-coming festivals are Slamdance, the Los Angeles Independent Film Festival (LAIFF), Ft. Lauderdale, and Palm Springs. The most important European festivals are Berlin, Cannes, and Venice. The top Canadian festival is Toronto, although Vancouver and Montreal are important as well. The Independent Feature Film Market (IFFM), while not a festival, provides a good opportunity for an independent filmmaker to have his film screened for foreign and domestic distributors.

When you attend a festival, come early, bring lots of marketing materials, and actively promote your film. Filmmakers who show up the day of their screening without preparation will be disappointed to find that only a handful of acquisition executives are attending their screening and distribution offers may never materialize. Savvy filmmakers will spend a considerable amount of time laying the groundwork for a successful festival. They often prepare professional one-sheets (8.5-by-11-inch leaflets with poster artwork), posters, T-shirts, and giveaway items. Sometimes they arrange publicity stunts to call attention to their films. It can be helpful to have the film's stars attend the festival.

In 1994, I attended the IFFM representing the film *Unconditional Love*. I met with the filmmaker and his collaborators beforehand and we plotted a strategy. The film is an autobiographical account of a young painter searching for his artistic vision amid various romantic entanglements. It is a classy, art-house film. We devised a professional, full-color, glossy one-sheet with still photos; a beautiful poster; and a press kit with photos, a synopsis, bios, and background information about the film. As a promotional item, we gave away a small artist's sketch pad with the film's title, key art, and screening times printed on the cover. This giveaway was very successful because it was thematically related to the film, it was unique (not the usual button, hat, or T-shirt) and it was a useful and desirable item. Indeed, acquisition executives used the pad throughout the market to take notes as they went from one screening to another, and every time they picked it up, they were reminded about our film.

The filmmaker was on excellent terms with his cast and crew. Unlike some productions, everyone was still talking to one another. Ten of the filmmaker's collaborators attended the market at their own expense. The editor, composer, co-producers, and several of the stars of the film arrived in New York prepared to work the festival. They passed out leaflets, asked local retailers to display the poster in store windows, and invited buyers to attend a screening. In many respects the effort resembled working on a political campaign. As a result of this work, fifty-seven buyers attended our first screening, and we generated strong positive word of mouth. The film was subsequently invited to exhibit at the Hamptons International Film Festival, where it won the top prize—an award of $110,000 in goods and services for the filmmaker's next film.

Once you are able to interest distributors in your film, you must be careful not to compromise your bargaining position. It is important not to brag about how little money you spent to make your film before you conclude all your distribution deals. You may feel justly proud of making a great-looking picture for a mere $200,000. But, if the distributor knows that is all the cash you have invested, you will find it difficult to get an advance beyond that. It would be wiser not to reveal your investment, recognizing that production costs are not readily discernible from viewing a film. Remember, the distributor has no right to examine your books. What you have spent is between you, your investors, and the IRS.

From the filmmaker's point of view, one will obtain the best deal if one has several distributors competing to acquire the movie. But, what if one distributor makes a pre-emptive bid for the film, offering a $500,000 advance, and giving the filmmaker twenty-four hours to decide? If the filmmaker passes, he may not be able to get a better deal later. It is possible that he may fail to obtain any distribution deal at all. On the other hand, if the filmmaker accepts the offer, he may be foreclosing the possibility of a more lucrative deal that might be offered later. That is why it is a good idea to screen your film to all potential distributors at the same time.

To maximize a filmmaker's leverage, it is important to orchestrate the release of the film to potential distributors. Here are some guidelines:

Orchestrating the Release

1. *Keep the film under wraps*: Don't show your film until it is finished. Executives may ask to see a rough cut. They will say, "Don't worry. We're professionals, we can extrapolate and envision what the film will look like with sound and titles." Don't believe them. Most people can't extrapolate. They will view your unfinished film and think it amateurish. First impressions last.

The only reason to show your film before completion is if you are desperate to raise funds to finish it. The terms you can obtain under these circumstances will be less than what you can get on completion. If you must show a work in progress, exhibit it on a Moviola or flatbed editing table. People have lower expectations viewing a film on an editing console than when it is projected in a theater.

2. *Arrange a screening*: Invite executives to a screening; don't send them a videocassette. If you send a tape to a busy executive, he will pop it in his VCR. Ten minutes later the phone rings and he hits the pause button. Then he watches another ten minutes until he is interrupted by his secretary. After being distracted ten times, he passes on your film because it is "too choppy." Well, of course it's choppy with all those interruptions.

You want to get acquisition executives in a dark room, away from diversions, surrounded with a live audience—hopefully one that will respond positively. The best venue is often a film festival. The next-best alternative is arranging your own screening. You can rent a screening room at a number of major studios, laboratories, and other sites. Invite all the acquisition executives you can, and pack the rest of the audience with your cast, friends, and relatives, especially Uncle Herb with his infectious laugh.

3. *Make the buyers compete against each other*: Screen the film for all distributors simultaneously. Some executives will attempt to get

an early look—that is their job. Your job is to keep them intrigued until it is completed. You can promise to let them see it "as soon as it is finished." They may be annoyed to arrive at the screening and see their competitors. But this will get their competitive juices flowing. They will know that they better make a decent offer fast if they hope to acquire the film.

4. *Obtain an experienced advisor*: Retain an experienced producer's rep or entertainment attorney to negotiate your deal. Filmmakers know about film, distributors know about distribution. Don't kid yourself and believe you can play in their arena and win. There are many pitfalls to avoid. Get yourself an experienced guide to protect your interests. Any decent negotiator can improve a distributor's offer enough to outweigh the cost of their services.

5. *Investigate the distributor.* Always check the track record and experience of potential distributors. As an entertainment attorney who represents many independent filmmakers, I often find myself in the position of trying to get unscrupulous distributors to live up to their contracts. I am amazed at how many distributors refuse to abide by the clear terms of their own agreements. The savvy filmmaker will carefully investigate potential distributors by calling filmmakers who have worked with them. One can also check court records to see if a company has been repeatedly sued. Check out my web site, which houses the Filmmaker's Clearing-house, a registry for filmmakers to evaluate and complain about distributors. The site is at: **http://www.laig.com/law/entlaw/** If you have had a bad experience, send in a report.

Selecting a Distributor: Checklist

1. Amount of advance.

2. Extent of rights conveyed. Domestic and/or foreign? Ancillary rights? Are any markets cross-collateralized?

3. Is there a guaranteed marketing commitment?

4. Does the producer have any input or veto power over artwork and theater selection in the top markets?

5. Track record and financial health of distributor.

6. Are monthly or quarterly accounting statements required?

7. To what extent does the distributor plan to involve the film-makers in promotion?

8. Marketing strategy: demographics of intended market, grassroots promotion efforts, film festivals, etc.

9. Split of revenues and accounting of profits: Is there a distribution fee? Overhead fees?

10. Distributor leverage with exhibitors: Can the distributor collect monies owed?

11. Any competing films handled by distributor? Conflicts of interest?

12. Does the producer have the right to regain distribution rights if the distributor pulls the plug early on distribution?

13. Personal chemistry between producer and distribution executives.

[Mark Litwak is an attorney with the entertainment law firm of Berton & Donaldson in Beverly Hills. He has acted as a producer's rep for numerous independent features. He is the author of *Reel Power, The Struggle for Influence and Success in the New Hollywood, Dealmaking in the Film and Television Industry*, and *Contracts for the Film and Television Industry*.]

Film Festivals and Markets

January

Nortel Palm Springs International Film Festival, P.O. Box 2230, Palm Springs, CA 92263-2230. Tel. (619) 322-2930. FAX. (619) 322-4087. (Contact: Craig Prater) Deadline: December 1.

National Association of TV Program Executives Conference, Tel. (213) 965-1990. FAX. (213) 965-1990. (Contact: Kate Chester).

Slamdance Film Festival, 2419 Oak St. - A, Santa Monica, CA 90405. Tel. (603) 643-5938. (Contact: Jon Fitzgerald).

Sundance Film Festival, 225 Santa Monica Blvd., 8th Floor, Santa Monica, CA 90401. Tel. (310) 394-4662. FAX. (801) 575-5175. (Contact: Geoffey Gilmore & Nicole Guillemet).

Rotterdam Intl. Film Festival, P. O. Box 21696, 3001 AR Rotterdam, The Netherlands. Tel. (011) (31) 10 4118080. FAX. (011) (31) 10 4135132. (Contact: Simon Field) Deadline: November.

February

CineMart, P. O. Box 21696, 3001 AR Rotterdam, The Netherlands, Tel. (011) (31) 10 4118080. FAX. (011) (31) 10 4135132. (Contact: Sandra Den Hamer) Deadline: September 1, 1996.

Berlin International Film Festival, Budapester Strasse 50, 10787 Berlin, Germany. Tel. (212) 877-8656. (U.S. Contact: Gordon Hitchens).

American Film Market, 10850 Wilshire Blvd., 9th Floor, Los Angeles, CA 90024. Tel. (310) 446-1000 FAX. (310) 446-1600. (Contact: Brady Craine).

March

SXSW Film Festival & Conference, P. O. Box 4999, Austin, TX 78765. Tel. (512) 467-7979 FAX. (512) 451-0754. (Contact: Nancy Schafer) Deadline: December 15.

Santa Barbara International Film Festival, 1216 State St., Suite 710, Santa Barbara, CA 93101. Tel. (805) 963-0023. FAX. (805) 962-2524. (Contact: Diane Durst) Deadline: December 1.

New Directors/New Films. Tel. (212) 875-5610. FAX. (212) 875-5636. (Contact: Richard Pena).

April

Los Angeles Independent Film Festival, 8306 Wilshire Blvd., Suite 28, Beverly Hills, CA 90211. Tel. (310) 358-6400. FAX. (213) 850-1713. (Contact: Thomas Ethan Harris).

San Francisco Intl. Film Festival. Tel. (415) 929-5000 Ext. 110. FAX. (415) 921-5032. (Contact: Peter Scarlet).

May

Cannes International Film Festival, 99, Boulevard Malherbes, 75008 Paris, France. Tel. (011) 33 1 45 61 66 00. FAX. (011) 33 1 45 61 97 60.

Seattle International Film Festival, 801 E. Pine St., Seattle, WA 98122. Tel. (206) 324-9996. FAX. (206) 324-9998. (Conntact: Carl Spence) Deadline: March 1.

June

Sydney Film Festival, P.O. Box 950, Glebe N.S.W., 2037, Australia. Tel. (011) 61 2 660 3844. FAX. (011) 2 692 8793. (Contact: Paul Byrnes) Deadline: March 7.

Banff Television Festival, P. O. Box 219, #9000, Banff, Alberta, T0L 0M0, Canada. Tel. (403) 678-9260. FAX. (403) 678-9269. (Contact: Jerry Ezekiel).

Florida Film Festival, 1300 S. Orlando Ave., Maitland, FL 32751. Tel. (407) 629-1088. FAX. (407) 929-6870. (Contact: Sigrid Tiedtke) Deadline: April 1.

July

Karlovy Vary Intl. Film Festival, Panska 1, Prague 1, ZIP 110 00, Czech Republic. Tel. (011) (42) (2) 2423 5412. FAX. (011) (42) (2) 2423 3408. (Contact: Eva Zaoralova).

Melbourne Intl. Film Festival, P. O. Box 2206, Fitzroy Mail Centre, Melbourne, 3065 Australia. Tel. (011) (61) (3) 9417 2011. FAX. (011) (61) (3) 9417 3804. Deadline: March 30.

August

Locarno Intl. Film Festival.,Via della Posta 6, P. O. Box 1621, 6600 Locarno, Switzerland. Tel. (011) (41) (91) 751- 0232. FAX. (011) (41) (91) 751-7465. (Contact: Marco Mueller) Deadline: May 31.

Montreal World Film Festival, 1432 De Bleury St., Montreal, Canada, H3A 2J1. Tel. (514) 848-3883. FAX. (514) 848-3886. (Contact: Serge Losique & Daniele Cauchard) Deadline: July 5.

Telluride Film Festival, 53 South Main St., Suite 212, Hanover, NH 03755. Tel. (603) 643-1255. FAX. (603) 643-5938. (Contact: Bill Pence).

Venice Film Festival, August/Ely. September, La Biennale di Venezia, S. Marco, Ca' Giustinian, 30124 Venice, Italy. Tel. (011) (39) (41) 521-8711. FAX. (011) (39) (41) 520-0569. (Contact: Gillo Ponteccorvo).

September

Deauville Festival of American Films, c/o Promo-2000, 36 rue Pierret, 92200, Neuilly-sur-Seine, France. Tel. (011) (1) 46-40-55-00. FAX. (011) (1) 46-40-55-39. (Contact: Corinne de Bury).

Toronto International Film Festival, 2 Carlton St., Suite 1600, Toronto, Ontario, Canada M5B 1J3. Tel. (416) 967-7371. FAX. (416) 967-9477. (Contact: Piers Handling) Deadline: June 28.

San Sebastian International Film Festival, Plaza de Oquendo, s/n 20004 San Sebastian, Spain. Tel. (011) 34 43 481 212. FAX. (011) 34 43 481 218. (Contact: Diego Galan).

Independant Feature Film Market, 104 W. 29th St., 12th Floor, New York, NY 10001. Tel. (212) 465-8200. FAX. (212) 465-8525. (Contact: Valerie Sheppard) Deadline: June 21.

New York Film Festival, 70 Lincoln Center Plaza, New York, NY 10023. Tel. (212) 875-5610. FAX. (212) 875-5636. (Contact: Richard Pena) Deadline: July.

October

Mill Valley Film Festival, 38 Miller Ave., Suite #6, Mill Valley, CA 94941. Tel. (415) 383-5256. FAX. (415) 383-8606. (Contact: Mark Fishkin) Deadline: June 30.

Hamptons International Film Festival, 3 Newton Mews, East Hampton, NY 11937. Tel. (516) 324-4600. FAX. (516) 324-5116. (Contact: Ken Tabachnick) Deadline: September 1.

Vancouver International Film Festival, 1008 Homer St., Suite 410, Vancouver, B.C. V6B 2X1 Canada. Tel. (604) 685-0260. FAX. (604) 688-8221. (Contact: Alan Franey) Deadline: July 20.

Mipcom, Reed Midem Organisation, P. O. Box 572, 11 rue du Colonel Pierre, 75726 Paris Cedex 15, France. Tel. (011) (33) (1) 4190 4580. FAX. (011) (33) (1) 4190 4570. (Contact: Andre Vaillant).

Mifed, E. A. Fiera Milano, Largo Domodossoea, 1, 20145 Milano, Italy. Tel. (39) (2) 480 12912. FAX. (39) (2) 499 77020. (Contact: Tullio Galleno) Deadline: October 18.

November

Northwest Film & Video Festival, 1219 SW Park Ave., Portland, OR, 97205. Tel. (503) 221-1156. FAX. (503) 226-4842. (Contact: Bill Foster).

A complete list of film festival web sites is available at Entertainment Law Resources: http://www.laig.com/law/entlaw/

---

1. "*Welcome to the Dollhouse* Makeover: What To Do When Geek Isn't Chic," Victoria Thomas, *The Outlook*, June 29, 1996, p. B1.

6
LOW-BUDGET
AND B-MOVIES:
Carnosaur

For many people, the term "B-movie" conjures up images of exploitative, low-quality entertainment, replete with ax murderers, erotic thrill killers, and assorted monsters running amok. One filmmaker, Roger Corman, has been universally acknowledged as the "King of the B's" for his prolific output of more than 250 films in every genre from Westerns and gangster films to sci-fi and teenage hot-rod and rock-'n'-roll movies. Corman is equally well-known for running what has become known as "The Roger Corman School of Filmmaking," a production company that spots young talent and gives it a chance to grow. Among the many producers, actors, writers, and directors he has nurtured are Francis Ford Coppola, Peter Bogdanovich, Robert DeNiro, Martin Scorsese, Ron Howard, Jack Nicholson, Charles Bronson, Joe Dante, Jonathan Demme, Gale Ann Hurd, John Sayles, James Cameron, Carl Franklin, Katt Shea, and Luis Llosa.

Those who have benefited from Corman's tutelage are not limited to the above-the-line "creative" people, because Corman is not just a talented filmmaker, he's a savvy, successful businessman. In fact, he is one of the few people in Hollywood who would dare claim that every film he's produced has turned a profit. Some young film lovers like Alex Kostich go to work for Corman with the intention of learning everything they can about the *marketing* of films as well as the making of them.

A communications graduate of Stanford University, Kostich was treading water as a newspaper advertising-space salesman when one of his Stanford professors suggested Kostich contact Corman in his search for a coveted entry-level job in the film business. Corman, a Stanford grad himself, supposedly has a predilection for hiring Stanford and Harvard grads. Kostich was willing to take any job just to get his foot in the door, and his timing was great. His résumé landed on Corman's desk the same day that Corman lost his executive assistant. Corman interviewed him, and hired him on the spot.

The education of Alex Kostich, executive assistant on-the-way-up, began with answering phones and expanded to reading scripts, writing coverage (script assessments), and creating titles and tag lines for the marketing campaigns for Corman's latest releases. "He had me do everything," recalls Kostich. "It's a great learning experience to be in that seat because you're basically his right-hand man and do everything that he does, but perhaps on a smaller scale . . . he'd have me think up titles to movies, come up with tag lines, and have me sketch out ideas for campaigns. He liked what I did . . . and in typical Roger Corman fashion, he just put me in the director's seat."

So at the ripe age of twenty-three, after six months of experience, Alex Kostich became Director of Marketing and Public Relations for Concorde/New Horizons Corporation, a company with twenty-four films on its yearly slate. He had worked himself up from writing tag lines to being in charge of two or three video campaigns a month. "These are all shot on film, but they're transferred to video and released on video, primarily. We're starting to do more theatrical releases, with the goal of doing what Trimark and New Line Cinema have done," says Kostich. One of Kostich's responsibilities was orchestrating the entire marketing campaign for two of Corman's most successful recent films, the dinosaur epic, *Carnosaur*, and its sequel, *Carnosaur II. Carnosaur* was released theatrically first, then to video; *Carnosaur II* was released directly to video.

Kostich eschews the "B-movie" label, insisting that Corman flicks should be placed in the more respectable *low-budget* film category. "We like to think of ourselves as a low-budget film company," says Kostich. "*B-movie* carries a sort of connotation of exploitative, low-quality entertainment, which was usually tacked onto an '*A*' title at the end of a double bill in the fifties. We specialize in films done on a low budget, but we really try to make them in the best possible way we can, given our limitations. I think they end up a little more creative and more quality-oriented."

Technically, a B-movie is indeed the second half of a double feature. Adam Simon, who directed *Carnosaur* for Corman, also defines it in marketing terms: "A B-movie is a film whose main selling points to the audience are not going to be the scale of the production, the stars who are in it, or the reputation of the people who made it. The main selling points are going to be the *exploitable* elements of the film, ergo the term *exploitation film*. The term does not refer to the exploitation of women, children, or animals, but refers to the exploitation of story and visual elements that are so appealing to an audience that the audience will want to go see the movie, regardless of whether they've heard of the movie or not. In the sense that 'Oh, this is a movie about drag strip racers and I like movies about drag strips,' or 'this is a movie about serial killers,' or 'this is an erotic thriller or a sci-fi movie, so cool, I want to see that.' As opposed to 'I want to see that because Clint Eastwood or Harrison Ford's in it,' or 'I want to see it because Ridley Scott directed it,' or 'I want to see it because it's based on a Stephen King novel.'"

Carnosaur, one of Corman's contributions to the horror genre, is a low-budget film about a mad scientist who creates dinosaurs from genetically altered chicken eggs and sets them loose in an effort to wipe out the human race. Kostich unabashedly admits that *Carnosaur*'s April 1993 release, just two months before the release of the much bigger-budget dinosaur pic, *Jurassic Park*, was designed to ride on the publicity wave generated by the Spielberg movie. Which filmmaker came up with the idea for a dinosaur movie first is a matter of debate: Corman had the foresight to buy the rights to *Carnosaur*, the English novel written by Harry Knight, which was published six years before Michael Crichton's *Jurassic Park*, and time the release of his movie to maximum advantage with minimum investment. At the time, Corman said, "These things work in cycles . . . there's always been a fascination with dinosaurs—they were the greatest, strongest creatures to ever walk the earth—but interest has been building for the past few years. The public has seen enough of outer-space pictures and now the horror and mystery of dinosaurs is coming back."[1]

No one understands the "cycles" of marketing better than Roger Corman, whose films are marketing driven, rather than driven by an artistic vision. Adam Simon, who has directed three films for Corman (*Brain Dead*, one of the *Body Chemistry* series, and *Carnosaur*), knows from experience how this focus on marketing affects the director of a Corman film. "With a film like *Carnosaur*, the whole meaning of marketing is different than it would be for studio films," says Simon. "In a big studio movie they're thinking about the movie and *then* they market it. With a lot of Roger's stuff, the marketing concept of it probably comes first. The very desire to make it doesn't come from the fact that 'here's a book or an idea that would make a good movie,' but 'here's something that a big studio is doing that they're going to be spending a fortune on marketing, and that we can do quicker and cheaper and get out in some proximity, preferably before theirs.' Actually, it's a real sign of Roger's brilliance.

"Probably around the time they announced the *Jurassic Park* movie, Roger began to develop the script of *Carnosaur*," recalls Simon, who also wrote the script for *Carnosaur* after Corman rejected various earlier drafts by other writers. "He didn't want me to read the novel and wanted me to start from scratch . . . *Carnosaur* was a very pulpy, almost parody novel written by a pretty good British science-fiction writer who was slumming. The book *Carnosaur* had been written before *Jurassic Park* and dimly contains the idea of genetically engineered dinosaurs—not in a particularly coherent, brilliant way, and certainly not with the degree of intensity or of scientific ideas that Crichton had."

Corman had just a few requirements for the script: the dinosaurs had to be genetically engineered, and one of the dinosaurs *had* to be a tyrannosaurus rex. From Simon's point of view, the requirements are a good example of how marketing can affect a movie: "I think in his mind's eye he had always seen the image of the tyrannosaurus rex, because that's the dinosaur people have in their heads. He had the image of this tyrannosaurus rex walking through the main street of a small town. Now that shot turned out to be one of the crappiest shots in the movie. We only shot it because we realized, 'Roger really demands this shot.' And of course it's in the movie and in the trailer, so it was not optional. On the other hand, because the dinosaurs were going to be the selling point, the film didn't require the things that a Corman film might normally require. Normally you might go, 'Okay, it's got to have two sex scenes, one car crash.' Here, the dinosaurs were all that was important."

"*Jurassic Park* has a huge awareness in people's minds as a book and as a movie in production from the teasers onward," says Simon. "You've got a studio spending tens and tens and tens of millions of dollars marketing that. With *Carnosaur*, you have to figure out how to use *their* marketing budget to help sell *your* film, so that you spend very little marketing. When he created the poster for *Carnosaur*, Roger went so far as to use the line 'based on the chilling bestselling novel.' Of course he has such good humor about it, which is one of the reasons I think he gets away with that. He's really a brilliant man, he's of the highest intelligence."

This description of Corman may surprise some who read reviews of his films. Tony Scott's review of *Roger Corman Presents: Suspect Device*, published in *Variety*, isn't atypical: "Showtime's new weekly film series under the aegis of Roger Corman lifts off with a frenetic tale loaded with mindless shootings, pinging bullets, brutal (if dull) fights, cars on fire, and countless bodies. Topped off with a nuclear detonation, *Suspect Device* works the gem of an idea through violence, foul lingo, and monotony to a bomb: it's just what the bam–wham–slam lovers will adore."[2]

Simon maintains that Corman's oeuvre reflects a man who is both a supreme marketer and a fine artist. "He's very much an intellectual," says Simon. "People need to understand that even if they sometimes think these movies are stupid, they're not done by stupid people. That's particularly true in Roger's case. These are really acts of a man who completely knows what he's doing."

If moviegoers were making comparisons of the two films, they couldn't help but notice that *Carnosaur*'s dinosaur models and special effects were not quite as slick as the computer-generated special effects of the megabuck-budget *Jurassic Park*. While *Jurassic Park* relied on state-of-the-art computer animation to depict its world of dinosaurs run amok, the makers of *Carnosaur* relied on the type of miniature mechanical models of dinosaurs that were originally created by Ray Harryhausen and have served as the staple of dinosaur and monster flicks since they first hit the screen.

"Roger said he could have expended more money on computer-generated effects, but he really didn't trust them since they were relatively new and never really done before," recalls marketer Kostich. "He was more comfortable using the tried-and-true techniques of the past thirty or forty years. A lot can also be hidden and done in editing. Where Steven Spielberg might have spent millions of dollars to create five seconds of film, with clever editing you can mask things that would look obvious. For example, if you use puppets, you shoot them in the dark. If you're using stop motion, and you have a miniature, you cut it very quickly so you just see little bits and pieces of something happening. You move the objects really quickly—there are tricks to make it more real. In *Jurassic Park* you might get more dinosaurs for your buck, but in *Carnosaur*, frankly, there's more action and more excitement and more blood, which is

what we're known for. *Jurassic Park* was the big-studio, family-ori-
ented dinosaur movie, or at least they tried to position it that way.
Carnosaur was an R-rated, blood-and-guts horror film which didn't
shy away from what would really happen if dinosaurs were to come
back from extinction. That was another of our marketing tools. We
said, 'This is what you won't see in *Jurassic Park*—flying limbs and
blood and guts.'"

Director Simon wasn't nearly as sanguine about the special effects in *Carnosaur*. "I'm pleased with some of the effects. I think
most of them look exceedingly cheesy. The whole point of the script
was to play on the new idea that dinosaurs actually are the direct
ancestors of birds, not reptiles, and that they were fast moving and
agile. The story's based on the fact that these dinosaurs get bred in a
chicken plant from chicken DNA and have bird-like qualities. But
the dinosaurs they built for *Carnosaur* didn't move like birds, that's
for sure. The only bird they moved like was Jim Henson's 'Big Bird.'

"When you're making this kind of a film, something small like
a B horror movie, usually there's two routes to trying to make it
effective," explains Simon. "One is to make it really explicit, in a
way that a studio couldn't or wouldn't, à la *Night of the Living Dead*
or *Texas Chainsaw Massacre*. Another route is to make it very subtle
and use lots of suggestion, rather than explicitness. The master of
that was Val Lewton, a producer at RKO in the forties. Lewton
would be given a title like *The Cat People* or *I Walked with a Zombie*
or *The Body Snatchers* and be told to make a movie to fit that title.
That's how marketing affects B-movies: the title often precedes the
story. The Lewton films are famous for their subtlety, the fact that
everything's in shadows. There's always two routes to go when you
don't really have the money to do it right: one is to go over the top

and the other is to keep it in the shadows. In *Carnosaur*, as anybody who sees it will testify, we went over the top. It could have been a better movie by showing less. But to show the dinosaurs less would be to violate the whole marketing-driven desire to make a film that showed lots and lots of dinosaurs acting in gory ways."

Even the casting for *Carnosaur* was designed to encourage comparisons with *Jurassic Park*. "One great idea that Roger had was to cast Diane Ladd in the lead for *Carnosaur*, because he knew that her daughter, Laura Dern, was the lead in *Jurassic Park*," says Kostich. "He thought, 'Wouldn't this make a great story: two people from the same family battling dinosaurs in separate films. Which one is going to be the top-grossing film of the year?' You make the call on that one."

Although *Carnosaur* had a theatrical release, standard operating procedure for Corman productions is to shoot on 35mm film, transfer to video, and release on video. "It's really *like* a theatrical release," says Kostich, of the Corman direct-to-video modus operandi. "We do a poster, trailers, and a lot of promotional work. The goal is to make the video release look like a theatrical release—like a big-budget film that people might have missed in theaters, because there is a lot of video product now."

While the demise of drive-in movie theaters in the seventies fueled the market for home videos, the market also became increasingly competitive, observes Kostich. "Not only did the big studios have their A products—their *Diehard*s and *Nightmare on Elm Streets*—but you had all the little video companies doing their products as well, and the market became really saturated. It became really hard to position a title in the video market when you have thirty or forty titles debuting on video each month."

Corman released *Carnosaur* in April, during the period immediately preceding the summer blockbuster season, which begins on
Memorial Day. *Jurassic Park* was released in June. "Our strategy was
to obviously ride on the coattails of this huge blockbuster monster
which was about to take America by storm," says Kostich. "For a
small company like Concorde/New Horizons, that's really our only
hope of breaking out of the straight-to-video molds and doing something that people will stand up and take notice."

Carnosaur's Los Angeles opening at the Cinerama Dome in Hollywood was done in style. "In my opinion, the Cinerama Dome is
the nicest theater in L.A.," says Kostich, "We got it for a one-week
engagement and we just promoted—excuse my French—the hell
out of it. On the opening day, we had Diane Ladd and the cast down
in front of the theater signing autographs. We had the life-size, foam-
core dinosaur brought in and assembled in front of the theater. A lot
of TV stations, E! Entertainment, and *Entertainment Weekly* covered
it. We had a lot of publicity, because we weren't ashamed to ride on
the coattails of *Jurassic Park* six weeks before that movie opened. There
was so much hysteria for that movie that people were willing to go
for another dinosaur film to whet their appetites."

Carnosaur's theatrical run consisted of the Cinerama Dome and
Laemmle Sunset 5 theaters in Los Angeles, as well as in theaters in
Fort Lauderdale, Miami, Tucson, and Boston. "We released it in these
territories to see how it would do," says Kostich. "It outperformed
against all the films, including some big-budget studio films. For us,
the theatrical opening was just a way to get a few good reviews, a
few quotes, a little publicity here and there, a few spots on the local
TV channels that reviewed the film. The theatrical release was really just a part of our marketing plan for the video premiere.

Carnosaur was in the theaters for a couple of weeks. There were a couple of big hits that opened on Memorial Day that summer, and there was just no way we could compete. So *Carnosaur* was relegated to the midnight-movie circuit and a couple of art houses in Los Angeles and Boston and it found a little audience there."

From director Simon's perspective, *Carnosaur* wasn't trying to compete with *Jurassic Park*. Instead, says Simon, "*Carnosaur* plays on the anticipation people have for that movie. They are definitely going to go see *Jurassic Park*. In the meantime, here's this movie playing that's released two months before *Jurassic Park*. So great, they'll go see that, too. Then, during the long theatrical release of *Jurassic* and long before the video for *Jurassic* is out, the video of *Carnosaur* is on the video store shelves. Meanwhile, MCA is paying for a media blitz for *Jurassic Park*. Finally, when the *Jurassic* video comes out, you walk into your neighborhood Blockbuster and all the copies of *Jurassic Park* are taken. But on the shelf right next to it a sign says, 'Looking for *Jurassic Park*? Try these.' A lot of video stores will put up movies that are related in theme. And that never failed to happen with *Carnosaur* in relation to *Jurassic Park*.

"Even the big studios are happy when they break even on a theatrical release," observes Simon. "The theatrical release is active marketing for the video in the sense that the real money is coming from the video. It's not unlike publishers—with the exception of some real best-sellers, they don't expect to make the big money off their hardcover, the money is made on the paperback. That's how it is with the video. Roger, I'm sure, did okay on the theatrical. He certainly didn't lose money on that. Then he made lots selling the cable rights. I believe he sold the foreign rights, both theatrical and video, to this film for more than he'd ever sold anything. It wouldn't surprise me given how smart he is and how well he knows what he is doing with a film like this, if he might have turned his million-dollar investment into considerably more than $10 million."

Although Corman originally hyped *Carnosaur* as a movie budgeted at $5 million, Simon says he believes that the budget was actually closer to the $900,000 to $1 million range. The discrepancy between hype and reality demonstrates one of the ways Simon feels Concorde/New Horizons' marketing orientation had an adverse effect on the film and the director. "Initially I had written it as a $3 million movie," says Simon. "Very shortly before we started shooting, he [Corman] told me that we would have something closer to the usual Corman budget which is a little less than $1 million. That meant tossing out huge gobs of the script that couldn't be done and doing effects that I didn't think were very good. I was actually quite pleased with the script, as was everybody, including Roger and Diane Ladd. One of the main reasons she agreed to do it, in addition to her old associations with Roger, was that she liked this character I'd written for her, this crazy, mad scientist. But the script was massively compromised in the process, in terms of the actual shooting schedule, the amount of time you have to do it, the quality of the effects." Budgetary limitations also forced Simon to cast amateurs in some of the roles, which resulted in the "great performances" of the finest actors juxtaposed with "some really stiff piece of amateur work from someone else."

"Where the marketing hurt me was that, to a certain extent, I was proud of what I had accomplished in making this film within the budgetary constraints that had been set," says Simon. The director recalls the creation of the dinosaur-attack sequences using a minuscule crew, a couple of actors, and miniatures on a tabletop, which turned out pretty well, given the limitations. Still, this was no megabuck production:"Roger doesn't like people to know how small those movies really are. So he is running around telling people and having it printed in the press that it's a $5 million movie. There I am, working my ass off to feel proud that maybe I made a $1 million production look like a $3 million production. Instead people are going to go see the movie expecting a $5 million production, and saying, 'Oh my god, it looks like a $1 million production.'"

Unlike many Hollywood production houses, Corman's film factory creates most of its advertising materials and trailers in-house. "Some of these pictures really need to be marketed in order to find an audience, because they aren't necessarily the big-budget, $40 million extravaganza that you pay $7.50 for at the box office," says Kostich. "Sometimes all you have going for the movie is the one-sheet or the video box cover, so you have to make it really impressive, and I don't want to say misleading, but you have to make it sell the best elements of the movie that's possible." With Corman producing twenty-four films per year, Kostich has only two to three weeks per film to get the marketing campaign together. Under Corman's tutelage, Kostich sketches ideas for video box covers, supervises photo shoots, hires vendors to produce the poster and one-sheet, and comes up with tag lines (for *Carnosaur*, "Driven to Extinction but Back for Revenge").

"People are becoming more sophisticated and discriminating," says Kostich, reflecting on the changing approach to marketing Corman films. "I think people are a little skeptical when they see a fuzzy, out-of-focus picture of a woman with a gun. They say, "Ugh, another low-budget, straight-to-video product that's not going to make any sense and it's going to be a waste of money.' And they don't rent it. They know to look for packages that seem to aim for something higher, not something that will hit you over the head. An example of that is one of those horror films, *Friday the 13th*, which had a video box which showed a person getting an ax cut in their forehead."

Corman didn't produce *Friday the 13th*, but he did produce a series called *Slumber Party Massacre*, which Kostich says "pushed the limits on the front of the box as much as you could—show as much blood, cleavage, and gore as possible and the titles sold. But now if kids want to rent a horror movie, they don't look for that. They think, 'Oh, it's showing everything on the front of the box, there's nothing left to see.' A lot of times, the scenes on the box never appeared in the movie. So now what they try to do on horror movies, for instance, is to have a very subtle box—something dark, with maybe a pair of eyes peeking out from behind a tree, and it's that subtle sale. It makes it look more big budget because that's what the studios do. You can call it classier, more sophisticated, or whatever, but that's essentially the direction it's going and I think people are looking for higher-quality entertainment. We're not talking Merchant Ivory productions here, but it's still a step up from the guns and cleavage approach."

During his tenure at Concorde/New Horizons, Kostich has developed a sense of the audience for Corman films, and they aren't the people lining up in front of art houses for the latest John Sayles film: "You'd be surprised at how many people go to a video store and look for straight-to-video products. There are people out there who don't grasp major theatrical releases. I don't want to sound elitist or snobby, but sometimes even major studio films are a little too highbrow for middle America. We're talking about the people who think *Married . . . With Children* is *Gone With the Wind*. They will go into a video store and look for something very simple on the cover of the box that says it all about the movie. They can watch the movie and not have to think about whodunit and not think about where the plot is going to go next. It's an easy story: A, B, C. They just want to be entertained and they want their requisite guns, action, and perhaps a topless woman in there. So really, the trick is in the packaging—what's inside isn't nearly as important as the packaging." Kostich cites the example of films that are written and shot in three days, literally, with leftover sets from other Corman productions. These often prove to be more profitable than much bigger-budget Corman films, and Kostich attributes their success in the marketplace to the creativity of the video box cover alone.

While Corman does make use of some market research, he doesn't pay for it. "We don't pay an outside agency to do market research," says Kostich. "I hire interns from various schools around the area—UCLA, USC—who are in marketing programs. They're willing to work for free, and especially for an entertainment-industry company. I say, 'Look, make this a project you can turn in to your professor. Give me a survey on the following titles.' For instance, the title I'm working on now is tentatively titled *Strip Teaser*. I have four titles which I'd like to work from and my intern designs a survey around those four titles and we test them. She goes to a theater, a video or record store, or a high school and asks people what they prefer for a title for a movie."

For the sequel to *Carnosaur*, called *Carnosaur II*, Kostich did research to see how to position the sequel after the success of the original *Carnosaur*, and in the absence of a *Jurassic Park* sequel to hitch a ride on. "We decided that we couldn't position it as a low-budget

B-movie," says Kostich. We had to make it look like a legitimate theatrical sequel to a film that people may or may not have remembered." Research indicated that the audience for *Carnosaur II* wasn't young adults in their twenties, but teens from thirteen to sixteen. "This was unusual, because it's an R-rated film, which technically people under seventeen shouldn't see without a parent," says Kostich. "Who knows what they're doing these days, but I guess at the video store they can go away with anything. We ended up targeting a lot of younger publications like *Fangoria* and *Film Threat*, which is kind of a *Premiere* magazine about the low-budget exploitation industry. We also had a couple of spots in *Entertainment Weekly*." (Ironically, Kostich attributes his lifelong love of movies to the fact that television viewing wasn't allowed in his home when he was growing up, and he had cachet among his friends because on weekends he would go to the movies to see the latest R-rated films.)

Corman's marketing strategy paid off big-time when it came to *Carnosaur*'s video sales. Says Kostich, "*Carnosaur* did very well for us. I don't know the exact figures because Roger keeps those pretty close to his heart, but I know theatrically we grossed over $2 million and on video we made a killing. We sold 80,000 video cassettes direct to the retailer for $60 to $90. Our average title sells from 25,000 to 30,000 units. If the retailer rents it from thirty to fifty times, they turn a profit. Then it goes directly to the customer and then it's $19.99 or $24.99. So we made a killing on that on video, which was our intention all along."

Kostich promotes Corman's straight-to-video product through a number of channels. For *The Spy Within*, starring Teresa Russell and Scott Glenn, Kostich designed a sweepstakes for video retailers. Kostich placed clues on ads in video trade magazines; the magazine readers had to piece together the clues from four different ads, then mail in the answer on a postcard to win a night-vision scope, which was featured in the film. "I did a little research on this, and the bigger studios will pay a promotional company $40,000 and $60,000 to set up this type of thing for them and sort the postcards," says Kostich. "I did the whole thing on my own, just kind of cutting and pasting ideas from cereal boxes and other sweepstakes I saw around. I came up with the program and it's been a real success. We're going to do it again, with an 800 number for an upcoming film we have called *Dillinger and Capone*, where there's going to be clues on the recording—we're trying audio this time as opposed to visual. I also designed a frequent-flier-style program for our retailers. If they keep coming back to our company and buying product from us they get points, and after a certain time they can cash in those points and get prizes. We try to do incentives like that on the big titles. Being in a company like this and being able to do what I want, I tend to be inspired by the big studios. I'll look at what the big guys are doing and try to funnel it down to something small enough in scope for me to do."

Corman's marketing formulae continue to be successfully applied to a variety of film genres, including erotic thrillers and action-adventure films, which Kostich puts into the "kickboxing-adventure" category. "Don 'The Dragon' Wilson is a famous kickboxer who has made a career out of doing Roger Corman movies," says Kostich. "These are movies basically where the hero goes out, avenges the death of his brother or sister in some foreign country. He has to enter a kickboxing contest to get out alive. It's just an excuse to have grunting men in a big ring kicking each other's heads in, so it's been a successful genre for us." In another genre altogether,

Corman's family division, run by producer Julie Corman (Roger Corman is her husband), has been very successful with films like *Cry in the Wild*, the *White Wolves* series, *Little Ms. Millions*, *The Crazy Sitter*, *The Skateboard Kid*, and *Munchie*.

Roger Corman's continuing profitability relies as much on his legendary "frugality" as on his undisputed understanding of the marketplace. While those who work for him may chafe under his financial strictures, neither Simon nor Kostich feel Corman has taken advantage of them.

"He's absolutely not mean-spirited in any sense," says Simon. "He has never been anything but gracious and respectful to me. Is he cheap? I have no idea how he lives personally. In terms of making the movies, yes, absolutely he is. That's the method. But one thing I will say for him—having worked a couple years post-Corman in bigger Hollywood—he stands out in my mind for his honesty and his directness. I always tell people who are thinking about going to work or write for Roger that in fact I trust him completely, in certain ways. He doesn't rob people, he doesn't rip them off. I don't think he cheats them or exploits them. He absolutely will spend the minimum possible to get the result he wants, and he will purposely pick people either because they're just starting in their career or because they're just finishing in their career or because they have no career, for whom that's a good wage or for whom that's a good budget. Look at the quality of people who have worked for him. Look at the number of his films which, regardless of their budget, continue to be watched today. We used to try to do this as a game: you cannot pick up any week's *TV Guide* without finding a half a dozen films that he made being shown. Lots of people still like to watch those movies. Not to mention the fact that this is a guy whose relationships with the banks and the ultimate financiers is golden, because they utterly trust him. It's because he is totally above board in those ways and because he always delivers."

Kostich feels that "Roger Corman is a great person to work for," and for him, a modest salary is a fair price to pay for experience. Kostich's salary as Director of Marketing is $28,000, which Kostich considers decent. "Roger's known in the industry for not paying his employees very much, but that's okay because he gives them titles and gives them experience, which I think is more important when you're starting out. That is why a lot of young people flock to his door. He's very hands-off once he learns to trust you. When I first had this job, he was in here every ten minutes checking out whether I had done a survey or checking out what a campaign was going to look like, but the last eight campaigns I have done, he has really let me run with it where he would have never done that before."

This is not to say that Corman and Kostich haven't differed on the best way to market his films. "The most difficult part of my job is probably convincing Roger to try something new in terms of a marketing approach because he's been in the industry for forty-some-odd years, and I'm coming in off the street with very little experience," says Kostich. "We're constantly sort of not arguing but struggling, because he thinks he's been in it so long that he knows what he's doing, and I feel I'm closer in tune with my generation. I'm not that removed from the thirteen-to-sixteen demographic that might flock to these films, whereas he might want to market a film today like he did in the sixties—the drive-in pictures where you had a big bad mama standing on the hood of a car in high-heeled shoes and a machine gun. That doesn't work today. That's the tough part of my job—convincing him to let me do what I want to do, then proving myself. There have been times where I have fought him to the end and I've ended up coming back with my tail between my legs and saying, 'Roger, you were right. I should have listened to you.' That's part of the learning curve. Lately, the last six to eight campaigns he let me do what I want, and we've been very successful. So I'm assuming he's going to let me do what I want until one of these bombs, then we're going to go back to doing the old stuff again. But he's really easy to get along with. It's tough for me to go in to somebody with so much more experience than myself and tell him I think he should listen to me, but he's extremely receptive and open-minded to that."

For its young recruits, The Roger Corman School of Filmmaking provides a milieu for learning and the camaraderie of kindred spirits. "It's very much like a family," says Kostich. "There're probably twenty to twenty-five employees roaming these halls, and everyone has a say in everybody else's business. I can walk down the hall to creative development and say, 'Hey, I've read this script and I think this part of the script doesn't work. Why don't you consider changing it?' Sometimes they'll listen to me and sometimes they won't, but the fact that I can walk down the hall and do that I think is pretty special. I have everyone walking into my office and saying, 'Oh, is that the poster for so and so movie? Gosh, why didn't you do this' or 'Wow, that looks really great.' It's kind of like brothers and sisters. There's a lot of teasing and constructive criticism going on, but people pat you on the back, too."

For Simon, the most important thing Corman has done is give people like him a chance to practice their art and craft during a time, from the fifties to the present, when few producers were willing to do that. When asked about his own education in film, Simon will tell you that he received his undergraduate education at Harvard, then went to the USC Film School, and did his "post-doc work" at The Roger Corman School of Filmmaking. "Number one, the most important thing you get from Roger is that he's simply giving you the opportunity to play with the real stuff," says Simon. "Number two, you get an inner strength that comes from surviving the process, from doing it and pulling it off—the sense that, 'well shit, if you can do that, you can do anything.' A lot of the lessons I learned there involved ways to make very little go much further. You could watch a James Cameron movie now where he has the $100 million budget and still see individual shots that he's doing in a manner that he would have done when he was running the special effects at Corman. Because one of the things you do learn from Roger is if there's ways to do it well in the cheaper way, then do that. Save the money for where you need it, and put that money on the screen."

Simon sees Corman's role in Hollywood changing with the advent of low-low-cost, independent filmmaking, which has opened doors to many more young filmmakers: "Now people are making no-budget independent films like *Slacker* or *El Mariachi*, and getting festival play. That was not true even ten years ago. Times have changed. It's the end of an era. I don't think that filmmakers, for example like me or like the people who came out of Roger's studio in the last ten, twenty years, would make Roger Corman B-movies if we were just coming out of film school today. We would be more likely to go out and make *Slacker* or *El Mariachi* now. But at the time, who else but Roger would give people their first shots?"

Corman took his own shots at producing more highbrow films when he first started directing and producing, long before he became the man who caters to some of the lower common denominators of the film audience. Corman's cycle of Vincent Price/Edgar Allen Poe horror classics brought him international recognition in the 1960s. The French Film Institute honored him with a retrospective of his work in 1964. "A lot of Roger's films, especially the films he directed himself, actually are very good films, and to this day have a real following," says Simon. "A handful of the ones he produced even as an exploitation filmmaker, including films like *Brain Dead*, are still shown every year at festivals all around the world. At the same time Roger was producing those kinds of *B*-movies, he was the sole person in this country distributing films by people like Ingmar Bergman, François Truffaut, Jean-Luc Godard. In that period, I think he got a lot of his cultural satisfaction from the fact that he was distributing art films here, and from the fact that the Europeans always viewed him as being quite an artist himself. I asked that question of myself, that you asked, in the sense that 'If it was me, I would want to make a different kind of movie.' I think at a certain point, that wasn't what he wanted to do. He was making a company to make a certain type of movie and to make money, and he succeeded in doing that beyond anybody, beyond any of the studios. His company has been consistently enormously successful and he's made enormous amounts of money. I think the other area where he got a lot of satisfaction was in effect being in a place where other directors could get their start."

Clearly, Corman created a place where marketing people could get a start as well. When we interviewed Alex Kostich, he was already sending his résumé out, looking to move up the next rung on the ladder of success, having put in nearly two years at The Roger Corman School of Filmmaking. "You can pretty much walk out having learned what you wanted to learn in the first place and then some," says Kostich of his stint at Corman. "For instance, I have always wanted to work in creative advertising at a film studio. Fortunately and unfortunately, this experience is a double-edged sword. On the one hand, at twenty-five, I have run a marketing division of a major company and I understand the whole process from A to Z. At twenty-five years of age, with only two years of experience under my belt, I may have overseen forty campaigns, but at companies like Warner Bros., the only people that do that are the president and vice-president who have been there ten or fifteen years and are forty or fifty years old. People are impressed by what you do, but they don't want to give you the chance because they don't think you put in the time. But it's been a great experience. I have gained confidence in this job, knowing I can pull off a campaign even if it's a small picture and bring in money." A few weeks after this interview, Kostich successfully marketed himself, moving on to a position at Warner Bros. in creative advertising.

Marketing Expenditures: *Carnosaur*
January '93 – December '93
$(000)

Magazines	28.0
Newspapers	43.5
Spot Television	2.5
Grand Total	74.0

© Copyright 1966 Competitive Media Reporting and Publishers Information Bureau.

1. *Entertainment Weekly*, June 18, 1993, p. 23.

2. Review of *Roger Corman Presents: Suspect Device*, Tony Scott, *Variety*, July 12, 1995, p. 9.

7
SUSPENSE THRILLER:
Malice

One of the most important elements in a movie marketing campaign is the trailer. The trailer gives marketers their best shot at intriguing and enticing moviegoers to make their movie the moviegoers' first choice above all others. Producing a provocative trailer that stimulates "wannasee" is not a simple matter. It requires the combined talents of a storyteller, advertiser, and tease, because the best trailers whet your appetite without giving away the story.

When Jim Fredrick, President of Marketing at Castle Rock Entertainment, set out to create a trailer for *Malice*, a contemporary thriller, he faced a thorny marketing problem: how to give prospective moviegoers enough information to get them interested in the story, but not give away so much of the plot that by the time they see the film, the thrill is gone.

"*Malice* was a movie with a lot of secrets in it," recalls Fredrick, "secrets that the filmmakers refused to give up in the advertising.

And we agreed with that. We felt the movie would be more enjoyable if people would come in cold, thinking they were going to get one thing, and when the surprise happens, several surprises in the case of *Malice*, they would enjoy the film a lot more. That particular problem also arose with *The Shawshank Redemption* and a few other films that we've done here. It's been a real challenge to coerce people, to get them to see a film and yet not tell them everything about that film. That's advertising's job—to do everything you can to get people in the seats opening weekend. When your hands are tied, so to speak, when you can't show every single intriguing element of the movie, it makes our job very difficult. That was the case with *Malice*."

Malice was touted as a "suspense thriller" about a young New England couple (Bill Pullman and Nicole Kidman) whose lives intersect with a brilliant surgeon (Alec Baldwin). As the story unfolds, according to the PR production notes, "the three of them embark on a relationship that leads them into a world of intrigue, betrayal, and deception . . . where nothing is what it appears to be."

Castle Rock's philosophy in creating its marketing campaign with *Malice*, as with all their films, is to involve the filmmaker every step of the way. "A studio has every right to say, 'Mr. Director, I don't care what you think. We're gonna market it, we've got $40 million tied up in this movie, we're going to do what we want.' But like most studios, we don't do that here. We're very deferential to the filmmakers," says Fredrick. "They're very much partners in the marketing strategies, in the creation of the trailers and the TV spots, and certainly the poster, which is very important to them because it usually becomes the trademark for their film in its everlasting life after the theatrical release, the image that is on laser discs, home videos, etc."

At Castle Rock, including the filmmakers in the creation of marketing materials makes sense and gives Fredrick the assurance that responsibility for successes—and failures—will be shared. "Having a supportive management helps. This company is incredible at shouldering responsibility," says Fredrick. "My bosses are involved every step of the way. They've never said, 'Well, Jim if you had marketed it differently . . .' They're real pros. We also involve the film's talent as much as we can. We never ship a poster without seeking the approval of the people who are on it, even though most have no legal right to approve the final concept. Usually, they have the right of approval of their photographic image, and that approval is obtained long before we begin working on the one-sheet. We want them to be aware of everything that we're doing to promote the movie and consequently we hope to gain their trust and their loyalty. Having your talent promote your film is obviously crucial to its success. Tim Robbins apparently had been known not to push certain films he'd been in. That was not the case with *Shawshank*. He was out there publicizing the daylights out of it."

"In the case of *Malice*, Harold Becker was the producer and the director of the film. He felt very strongly that 'Jim, you're not giving up my secrets, I want people to enjoy the film in discovering those secrets.' That was the hook of the film—whodunit? Who's good, who's bad? So with that limitation, away we went in making the trailer."

Most marketing heads farm out trailer production. At Castle Rock, Fredrick cuts all the trailers and most of the TV spots himself. The company's modus operandi is for Fredrick and the filmmaker to sit down with Castle Rock management and come up with a marketing approach that all can agree on. "Filmmakers very often come and sit with me at my little editing system and we create a trailer," says Fredrick. In the case of *Malice*, Fredrick worked with an early cut of the feature that ran two and a half hours, and his objective was to "create a piece that would intrigue people but not tell them everything about the film—to be mysterious, and it was a chore." He was limited to using scenes from only the first half of the film, "because after a certain point in the film, things start changing, people who you thought were good turn out to be bad, and vice versa."

At their strategy sessions, everyone agreed the trailer should focus on the sexy stars, Alec Baldwin and Nicole Kidman, and on director Harold Becker, who was known for directing *Sea of Love*. The strategists also agreed on what to exclude from the trailer. Says Fredrick, "What you don't want to address is the fact that—and forgive me for giving away the secrets of *Malice* here—that the Nicole Kidman and Alec Baldwin characters are actually in cahoots. That's something no one wanted to give away. In the movie, Bill Pullman is married to Nicole Kidman, they have this life together in this bucolic town near Boston. Alec Baldwin is this mysterious surgeon who you think is a bad guy, and it turns out that he and Nicole are out to scam Bill Pullman. So I had to find ways around that secret. I tried a zillion different tacks at it. The first cut of the trailer was the one that actually went forward. We set up this mysterious stranger in Alec Baldwin and the sparks that fly with Nicole Kidman. Although we never show them embracing, we hint at seduction. We show this doctor who is power-crazy and you know he's up to something. There's wrongdoing going on. We show a little bit of a murder that has taken place. It wasn't a trailer that started at A and went to B, C, and D and told a very linear story. That was risky, because people, before they leave their house and their VCR machine, want to know what they're getting for their $8.00. What we've been told is 'give us information, tell us, the audience, what the movie's about.' We didn't do that with *Malice*. We took a chance. So the trailer basically was more of what we call a teaser than anything. It was more of a mood piece, really, that titillated rather than informed. We gave them lots of intriguing, mysterious images, eerie music, a little star power, a little sex, a little violence, and the pedigree of 'A New Film from the Director of *Sea of Love*'—which also was a thriller. Then we prayed that this 'teaser of a trailer' would be enough to get audiences interested."

Once the trailer is finished, there is no guarantee that movie theaters will show it. Distributors can cajole exhibitors to show their trailers, but ultimately, exhibitors will show the trailers they deem are in their best interest to show. "If you have a trailer with big stars, like Tom Cruise, those trailers never have trouble getting played," says Fredrick. "Whether it's a 'good' trailer or a 'bad' trailer isn't the point. If a film looks like it will do business, that's the trailer exhibitors will play with greater frequency. Our trailer for *Malice* created a buzz, thank goodness. It may not have pleased every audience member in giving them all the information they required, but there was an audible buzz after it finished. That's something, particularly in a dramatic trailer, that you listen for. I often finish a trailer, go into a theater, and run it before we actually ship ten thousand or so prints. You can tell if a trailer isn't working. A comedy trailer is easier to judge—people laugh, it's an easier response to gauge, but a dramatic trailer is more difficult. For me, the tell-tale sign is that buzz when it's over. You could see people's heads turning, you hear the murmur, and you know you have something."

Most teaser trailers are shown in theaters six months before the film is released. They're usually followed by a regular trailer that hits theaters ten to eight weeks before the film opens. "In this case, since we had a trailer that was more like a teaser in its concept, we went out a little earlier," says Fredrick. "We went out three months before we opened, so it got a lot of play because theater owners saw the buzz and they saw something that was potentially commercial."

From Fredrick's perspective, the trailer prepares audiences for the final pitch, which is delivered in TV spots. "The TV campaign, I think, really closed the deal on *Malice*," says Fredrick. "It's the TV campaign where most of your media dollars go. It's the thing that makes people want to go see the film, not the print, not the poster. In the TV campaign, rather than being so mysterious and titillating, we hit them harder, which I think television spots have to do— anything to keep folks from running to their refrigerators. Two things happened that I think really helped us: one, we got a really strong review early on that called the film 'the sexiest thriller of the year.'" Fredrick took that kudo and used it to create a TV spot that juxtaposed the line from the review with a shot from the movie of Nicole Kidman taking off her shirt. "All of a sudden, you've got young males across the country turning off their Game Boys," says Fredrick of the response to the spot.

"Those two elements—and I hate to narrow it down to that one shot and that one line—seemed to make a big difference. We saw our tracking go up significantly once that spot started running. We hinted more definitely at sparks between Alec and Nicole. So rather than just a thriller, it also played as a hot, sexy romance and now you've got a date movie," says Fredrick. In contrast to the soft, eerie music used in the trailer, the *Malice* TV spots had access to the more hard-hitting, provocative music Jerry Goldsmith had scored for the movie. "It's rare to have a film's score early in the trailer-making process," says Fredrick.

"One month before we opened, we began our cable buy; our network spots ran about ten days prior to our sneak," recalls Fredrick. Part of Castle Rock's release strategy, which has been successful for them in the past, was having a sneak preview of the film on the Saturday before the wide release. "That's a more expensive way to release a film because you have to throw a lot of advertising money prior to the sneak and then also continue to advertise in the week leading up to your release," says Fredrick. Their rationale for this strategy was simple: "We had a film that did not have Tom Cruise. I mean, there are very few actors who can open a film. Up to that point in their careers, Alec and Nicole hadn't opened any films. Based on our testing of the film, we felt the word-of-mouth would be very good. People liked the movie, and we felt that by sneaking the film we would generate word-of-mouth prior to our opening weekend a week later." The objective of sneak previews, which usually take place the Saturday night before the film's opening, is to generate good word-of-mouth for a movie that has a complicated storyline or unusual character development. Studios normally don't sneak comedies, no-brainer action films, or films with A-list stars. They do sneak films that aren't easily marketed in a thirty-second TV spot. TV ads for a sneak can cost $2 million or more, and newspapers ads can cost an additional $1 million.[1]

In conjunction with the National Research Group (NRG), Castle Rock tested *Malice* three times, making changes after each test. "We test all our films through NRG, as many times as we and the filmmakers feel it necessary," says Fredrick. "The scores were very good on *Malice*. They continued to get better every time we screened it, and every time changes were made, the movie continued to improve. The movie got shorter, we clarified points that confused people, eliminated offensive moments, and it consequently became a better film."

Fredrick has faith in market research—up to a point: "I'm a believer in researching movies. I'm *not* a huge believer in testing advertising materials. We've never tested a print image as long as I've been here. . . . Why? We've had materials test spectacularly well and then the movie doesn't do any business. I don't think testing ad materials translates very well to how your film is going to do. We'd rather go with our gut, particularly in a trailer, because it's not a science, obviously. I don't think we need to be told by numbers if our trailer is working or not. We have such a plethora of talent in this company. We have Rob Reiner, we have Martin Schafer, who's the president of our motion picture division and my boss; Andy Scheinman, who's produced a lot of great movies, Alan Horn [Chairman and CEO]—all these guys are the partners of Castle Rock. They bring a lot of years of experience to the process. We feel that after testing our trailers, we didn't learn anything. TV spots are a little different. Testing them can be helpful in isolating one spot to a particular demographic. For instance, if you tested four different spots and found out that a spot tests better for older females, we'd more than likely run that spot on *Good Morning America*, the soaps, or *Ellen*—TV shows geared to that audience."

Castle Rock movies are distributed by Columbia Pictures. Sony Pictures Releasing's President, Jeff Blake, works with Castle Rock President Martin Schafer to come up with a distribution plan for each film. In the case of *Malice*, they decided to sneak it in approximately 800 theaters the Saturday before the film went into release. A week later *Malice* opened on 1,500 screens. "We were set to go at 1,200, but the sneaks went so well, we kicked it up another 300," says Fredrick. "All our sneaks were very well-attended. It was interesting because, as you know, films track—there's a tracking report that NRG does which systematically gauges how a movie is being perceived by the public. It's a barometer of how people are responding to the marketing campaign and the movie itself. What's the awareness of the movie, is there a definite interest, would it be your first choice, those three categories. And those numbers change daily based on us throwing millions of dollars of advertising into the marketplace. It's a real litmus test of our TV campaign, our publicity campaign, our marketing campaign. I'm terrified by tracking because my day is made or broken by these daily numbers."

The National Research Group dominates the movie tracking business in Hollywood, for the time being. They interview 1,200 randomly selected people in seventeen U.S. markets every week, asking them three questions similar to these: "What films are you aware of currently in theaters or about to be released? Based on everything you know about film X, would you say you are definitely interested or definitely not interested in seeing it? What is your first choice among films playing this weekend?"[2]

Fredrick isn't the only Hollywood marketing exec traumatized by tracking. Leonard Klady, who writes about marketing for *Variety*, reports that "more than any other detail, industry honchos want to know the percentage of respondents that select a picture as their first choice for each weekend. . . . But a straw poll of marketing execs and researchers indicates widespread frustration that, despite a formidable database, the ability to accurately predict a film's appeal isn't improving."[3]

"Those tracking numbers come in every morning on the week that you open, and it's a very nerve-racking process!" says Fredrick. "Because there have been times when the tracking has been huge on a film and it doesn't open. Raised expectations are crushed. You just have to wait and see how the public reacts. That's the great mystery of movies. 'Nobody knows anything,' as Bill Goldman [screenwriter and author of *Adventures in the Screen Trade*] says. People want to predict how their film is going to do ahead of time. It helps secure screens and it affects your media buy—there's a lot of money at stake. The other day Martin said, 'You know, I don't want to open, I just want to track well.' He was kidding of course, but it becomes a score card. It's like watching stock prices or the box scores everyday and your team, that is, your movie, is in a pennant race.

"The tracking on this movie started very slowly because it did not have a story that was easily digested," recalls Fredrick. "It was a very complex, sophisticated piece of business. It didn't have huge stars in it that drew people, but as the TV spots began to run, we saw the tracking numbers go up. You never know what you've got until you walk into the theater and there they are or there they aren't. I'll never forget that sneak preview Saturday, not knowing whether it was going to be a hit or not. The tracking was really on the border, it could have gone either way. I remember swinging the doors open at my local theater, and there they were—it was sold out, and it was the best feeling in the world. The sneaks were well-attended across the country. Sometimes you have a film like *The Shawshank Redemption*, which does a huge business in New York and Los Angeles, but does not gain the interest of those in middle America or the South. *Malice* sold out across the country. Ninety percent of the theaters were sold out. So given that information, we kicked up our screens for opening day. And we opened to nine and a half million dollars and eventually grossed over $50 million. We were very happy. We made money. If a film has success in the domestic market place, you'll most likely have ancillary success in the area of international, home video, television, etc. It's a chain reaction. If your movie doesn't open well, doesn't perform well, it's not going to do well in those ancillary markets."

Ultimately, *Malice* cost around $30 million to make. Castle Rock spent approximately $8 to 9 million to open the film. By the end of the run, Castle Rock had spent $13 million in advertising, which Frederick considers a "very reasonable amount with regard to its payoff."

Fredrick's efforts at Castle Rock are complemented by the work of John DeSimio, Vice President of Publicity for Castle Rock. "In the case of *Malice*," says Fredrick, "John's job was to arrange talent photo shoots with magazines, to get Nicole, Alec, and Bill on *The Tonight Show*, the *Letterman* show, and the morning shows. The junket's very important. John always does a terrific job at that. It also helped to have someone like Alec who's very smart and personable on talk shows and interviews. The talent was also careful not to give away the film's twists and turns. Of course, when the reviews came out, all bets were off. It's a reviewer's prerogative to give up any secrets—I think they did in most cases. It wasn't like the *Crying Game*, which came out around that time, too. Their 'secret' was a little different than ours! Miramax consequently made it a cause célèbre. They made that secret the focal point of their campaign: 'Don't Give Up The Secret' was their ad line. We had thought about doing something like that, but the *Crying Game* had just come out, so . . ."

Fredrick is an L.A. native who learned the business of marketing from the ground up. Looking for a more intimate atmosphere than the UCLA film school, he migrated to the University of California at Santa Cruz ("home of the Banana Slugs"), where he majored in film. After college he returned to Los Angeles and found his first job in the biz as a driver for Cinema Research, a special effects company. "I was a driver, a shipping clerk—I was at the bottom," recalls Fredrick, with good humor. "I drove around a lot and got to know where all the studios were. I think it's a great job to have when you start in this business. You get to know the town, you get to know where things are and who does what." After a year and a half, Fredrick moved on to a job as an assistant editor at a computer effects company called Digital, which has since gone out of business. "They were at the absolute ground-breaking edge of computer generation images, and consequently, they had too many bugs in their system. They helped push what is now happening with *Forrest Gump* and *Twister*—they created a lot of the hardware and technology that's allowed those effects to happen. They created all the effects in a movie called *The Last Starfighter*, which was a real ground-breaking film. It wasn't a great movie, but it had forty minutes of total computer animation. Unfortunately, they were mismanaged and went under."

During his two years at Digital, Fredrick learned the trade of assistant editing as well as the more technical aspects of postproduction. His next job was with Intralink, a company that produced posters, trailers and other advertising materials for studios. Anthony Goldschmidt, the proprietor of Intralink, gave Fredrick a chance to start working on trailers. "I started out on a technical level there, finishing the stuff, doing the mixes, and slowly got more interested in the creative side of it," says Fredrick. "I was there for six years and worked on some great projects, *The Color Purple*, *The Last Temptation of Christ*, *Fabulous Baker Boys*, and consequently started editing trailers for a company called Castle Rock. I cut a trailer for *Misery* and got to know the guys over here, and after working on *City Slickers* and a couple other films, Martin hired me as their head of advertising. So I came here three and a half years ago with the understanding that I would continue to do what I enjoyed most, and that was creating trailers and TV spots. I also handle the print work, hiring vendors to create posters for our films. Of course the job consists of many things—budgets, media placement, dealing with filmmakers, corporate image, etc. We created our own in-house operation to handle the bulk of the audio-visual campaigns. We often hire companies to do TV spots. But since I've been here we've done all the trailers in-house and so far, everyone seems happy with the results."

Fredrick says that the most difficult thing about his job is "maintaining optimism—because it's a position where everybody can have differing opinions. Everybody on the street has an opinion, my bosses have an opinion, the filmmakers have their opinion. It's a very subjective thing—how to create an image for a film. It can be a real roller coaster for me. One day, people are loving a trailer, the next day somebody happens to see it and responds badly and the next thing you know it's dead and you have to start from scratch. Maintaining that sense of being a Teflon man and not taking it personally is very important. My job is to open films and to create the best advertising possible to get people to want to see our movies. When a film doesn't open, I take it personally. Very personally! When a film opens and does well like *Malice*, it's the greatest feeling in the world, and it's just the opposite feeling when a movie fails."

When a film like *The Shawshank Redemption* stumbles, Fredrick finds it perplexing and disappointing: "Frankly, it's been a frustration for us because we felt it was a wonderful film. It was a very difficult film to market, it had a tough title. It's a prison film and a lot of people had trouble getting beyond that. The movie has been rereleased in 800 theaters since it has been nominated for several awards, including Best Picture, and it has done very well. The international box office has been great because of the Oscar nominations, and the home video release should really benefit. It's rare these days for a film to slowly roll out, find its audience, and have a successful life outside of that important opening weekend. I think *Shawshank* is one of those films that will continually be 'discovered.'"

As President of Marketing, Fredrick isn't consulted on the films Castle Rock greenlights. "Martin Schafer's policy is to make the best movies we can from the best scripts we can develop," says Fredrick. "We spend an enormous amount of time on our scripts. Our track record is pretty good with regard to the amount of movies that we make that are hits. Castle Rock's philosophy is pretty simple: we make the best films we can, we do the best we can in marketing them, and we support them financially. After that, it's up to the public. Our company (sometimes to a fault) takes the high road in marketing our films. But that's the way we choose to do it and it has worked in the past for us and I think it will work in the future.

"We used to test our materials a lot," says Fredrick. "We just felt that it wasn't making our materials better, it really wasn't helping us, and that's why you test, to get help. I think test results are a way of pointing a finger. Because if a film doesn't open, you can always point to the testing and say, 'Well, as you can see by these terrific test results, the film's failure can't be blamed on the trailer!'

It's a real scapegoat. I'm fortunate in that my guys don't point fingers. We look in the mirror and point."

Two ways Castle Rock promotes its films is by having premieres and promotional screenings in conjunction with radio stations and magazines. "We do that a lot because most of our films are word-of-mouth pictures," says Fredrick. "With *City Slickers*, we felt we had a film that was working, so we created a ton of radio-promoted screenings: 'Be the first to see a free screening of *City Slickers.*' Why? To create word-of-mouth. Get the buzz going. With *Malice*, we did the same thing. We screened the daylights out of it." The radio-promoted screenings took place in the top sixty markets throughout the country, in conjunction with stations featuring classic rock, talk shows, and news radio and targeted to older demographics.

With the type of adult movie fare that dominates Castle Rock's agenda, favorable movie reviews are very important. Fredrick recognizes that some movies rely more on reviews than others. "You look at a film like *Billy Madison*—Universal chose not to screen it for the press prior to its release, feeling that it might get lambasted. But for young males eager to see Adam Sandler be funny—who cares what critics think?" says Fredrick. "So far we haven't made a *Billy Madison*-type of movie aimed at that young male audience. Those films obviously don't count on reviews. *Dumb and Dumber* didn't count on reviews. As a rule, our films tend to be upscale. We count on reviews for our movies. *Malice* was finished in plenty of time where we had lots of long-lead press on it. The critical response was very good. It definitely benefited from the good reviews. We have a movie opening next weekend called *Dolores Claiborne*, which is getting sensational reviews. With that type of movie, we're going to do review spots, we're going to paper our newspaper ads with all those wonderful reviews. Reviews are strange. Everybody puts these glowing remarks in their ads; does it make people want to go see the movie? Maybe. But I believe you can't afford *not* to use reviews in your ads. If you have just an ad without wonderful adjectives splattered across it, you can't compete with *Outbreak*, which has all these glowing phrases plastered all over it. That's one way you compete with the other studios."

Stars are important for promoting films, and Castle Rock's collaborative approach to marketing often gains them the cooperation of their star talent. "We opened *Before Sunrise* this year, and it had Ethan Hawke in it. Now Ethan Hawke is not Tom Cruise or Brad Pitt, yet, but he is an up-and-comer. He's good looking and I think he's a great actor. Young girls love him. He's a heart throb. Without Ethan Hawke pushing *Before Sunrise*, it would have been a very difficult film to market. Because it was a very chancy film. Richard Linklater did a great job directing it. It's about two people walking around Vienna, a love story, but a very dialogue-heavy, sophisticated piece of work—something that you would never in a million years call commercial. But Ethan Hawke on the cover of *Rolling Stone*, Ethan Hawke on talk shows, Ethan Hawke in magazines features made our job a lot easier. He really did a wonderful job promoting the film."

Like many other marketing mavens, Fredrick will never be heard whispering, "But what I really want to do is direct." "I love making two-minute movies; I mean, trailers are little movies," says Fredrick gleefully. "I don't have to sit around on a set for hours to get one shot. I don't miss that. I think production is very tedious and I don't have the patience for it. Rob [Reiner] is amazing to watch direct. He's patient, passionate, and so detail-oriented. I really admire that.

But I wouldn't trade places with him. I get handed this piece of clay—this movie. And from that, I whittle it down to its essence. You write narration, you create graphics, you score music, just like a feature film. It has a beginning, middle, and end—just like a movie. And if that two-minute trailer isn't as good as the film it's trying to sell, you're screwed!"

Marketing Expenditures: *Malice*
January '93 – December '94
$(000)

Magazines	349.0
Newspapers	2,340.8
Outdoor	231.3
Network Television	3,784.1
Spot Television	1,658.1
Syndicated Television	361.3
Cable TV Networks	666.9
National Spot Radio	161.4
Grand Total	19,552.9

© Copyright 1996 Competitive Media Reporting and Publishers Information Bureau.

1. "Art of the Sneak: Creating a Buzz: How Studios Use Advance Showings to Sell 'Tough' Films," Patrick Goldstein, *Los Angeles Times*, October 8, 1996, pp. F1, F6.

2. "Human Nature Stumps Tracking Science," Leonard Klady, *Variety*, August 19-25, pp. 1, 10, 14.

3. Ibid.

8

SELF-DISTRIBUTION/
DO-IT-YOURSELF MARKETING:
Brother's Keeper

Brother's Keeper is a film that is known not only for the imagination of its filmmakers, Joe Berlinger and Bruce Sinofsky, but also for their ingenuity in distributing and marketing the film themselves. *Brother's Keeper* is the story of four illiterate bachelor brothers who live a quiet—albeit squalid—existence in a two-room shack without running water until one of the brothers, Delbert, is accused of suffocating his brother Bill in the bed they shared. Berlinger and Sinofsky refer to their film as a "non-fiction feature film," intentionally avoiding the "d-word" ("documentary"), which often closes people's minds to the possibilities of a film before they ever see it. Their savvy, gutsy approach to distribution resulted in a thirteen-month/250-city theatrical release for *Brother's Keeper*, grossing nearly $1.5 million. After the theatrical release, *Brother's Keeper* had a successful home video release through Fox Lorber, was broadcast on PBS's *American Playhouse* (the filmmakers' primary source of postproduction financing), and was televised in seventeen countries worldwide. During this process, they learned the distribution business inside-out, gained first-hand knowledge of their target audience, and earned a "respectable profit," says Berlinger.

These two mavericks exhibited an independent streak long before they made the decision to self-distribute *Brother's Keeper*. For some time, Berlinger and Sinofsky both had felt there weren't enough non-fiction films made in the present tense, following a real story as it unfolds. "It's difficult to do," says Berlinger, "because you're not guaranteed of the outcome." They set out to find a story "that unfolds in the present tense, and which can be filmed and edited in such a way that it has all the narrative drive and dramatic structure of any good fiction film, in the sense of a story with a beginning, middle, and end. Right from the get-go, we had theatricality in mind. We feel that's our niche in the marketplace."

The filmmakers were inspired by the success of *The Thin Blue Line* and *Roger & Me*, which demonstrated that "the door has opened in the past ten years for allowing good-quality, entertaining, non-fiction films to play in movie theaters."

"So every day we just combed the newspapers, looking for the right story to come along," recalls Berlinger. "The story had to have the right combination of ingredients: obviously, something had to have happened so there would be a story about it, otherwise we wouldn't have known about some event out there. It had to have the promise of a lot of stuff in the future that could be captured on film. So when we read about this case, it seemed like a whole bunch of stuff was about to happen, and that it was quirky and interesting, and it seemed like it was going to capture a certain level of Americana, which we felt was necessary to bring an audience in to see it.

When we saw the story, we said this is it, this is going to be the film we're going to make.'"

The article they saw in the *New York Times* said that Delbert Ward, one of four brothers in the upstate New York town of Munnsville, had just been arrested for allegedly killing his brother, and the town thought he was innocent. "When you have two opposing sides that believe the exact opposite, you have the classic definition of drama, which is that all drama is conflict," says Berlinger. "We said, 'Hmm, there's going to be some drama here.' Of course it's a risky thing, because when you're following a story as it unfolds, there's no script—the story could peter out at any moment. That's why a lot of these films aren't made. In fact, when we started our second non-fiction film, we realized, after one shoot, that it was not going the way we hoped it would go and abandoned ship. There's no guarantee that you're going to have a story that has a dramatic arc in real life. So there's a certain amount of faith involved."

Berlinger and Sinofsky took their faith and drove five hours to upstate New York, where they met with Delbert's defense attorney, who had already been besieged with offers from feature film companies for the rights to Delbert's story. "There were Hollywood companies waving blank checks at him, wanting to do recreations, casting Andy Griffith as Delbert, for example," recalls Berlinger. "They wanted to quickly crank out an MOW [Movie of the Week]. We had no money to offer—just our promise that we were going to make a film that had integrity and that the film would not come out until after the trial was over." Apparently, that was more attractive to the defendant's attorney than the offers from Hollywood film companies, so in June of 1990, the no-budget, weekend filmmakers began their opus.

When they first sought the Ward brothers' cooperation, the film-makers were both employed at Maysles Brothers, Inc. a film production company where Berlinger worked as an executive producer of TV commercials and Sinofsky worked as an editor. Every week they would put in a fifty- to sixty-hour work week at the Maysles Brothers, and on weekends they would drive five hours to upstate Munnsville, New York, to film. "This was truly a leap of faith," recalls Berlinger. "We had no production funding, we had no support from our employer: they weren't loaning us any equipment, moral support, or financing. In fact, we were concerned about losing our jobs. We got the film in the can ourselves—buying short-ends and recans and renting other people's equipment—for about $100,000 of debt. [Short-ends are short pieces of leftover, unexposed film stock from a finished production that is recanned for resale; recans are 400- to 1,000-foot rolls of film that were loaded into film magazines in preparation for use during another production, but not used. They were subsequently recanned for resale. Both are usually sold at a discount to struggling filmmakers.] Both Bruce and I took second mortgages on our homes. At that point, we had sixty hours of dailies, and the one thing that hadn't been shot yet was the murder trial. We knew we couldn't continue, so we approached *American Playhouse*."

In looking for finishing funds, Berlinger and Sinofsky ran into the obstacle that all documentary filmmakers face. Most distributors don't want to pay for the theatrical release of an unknown documentary film. This was particularly true at the time *Brother's Keeper* was produced, before several documentary breakthroughs. "The only place a documentary is picked up is after it's already finished and it's won some award at Sundance and people are going crazy over it," says Berlinger. "No movie company ever gets involved with a documentary, which means that you have to go to a TV entity. The problem with that is that when the TV window gets exploited first, it's very hard to release it theatrically. The one exception in the business—the only place we could have gone to—was *American Playhouse*, which was a PBS program that no longer exists. *American Playhouse* was executive-produced by Lindsay Law, and even though it was a television show, their mandate was to help the film to develop a theatrical pedigree, unlike other television outlets. For example, if you do a show on *POV* [a PBS show] or HBO, it has to go on TV first, so it's very hard to do a theatrical release. With *Brother's Keeper*, we knew that if we went to a television funder, we would not be able to do a theatrical release, which was the whole goal. If *American Playhouse* picks up your film, they give you the funding, they buy the TV rights, but they want you to go out and release it theatrically first, and then after it's out theatrically for two years, and has its own video release, then it comes back for television. The problem with *American Playhouse* was that they were a dramatic series, they weren't a documentary series. The one exception, of course, was that they had funded *The Thin Blue Line*. Our challenge, as unknown filmmakers, was to convince them that *Brother's Keeper* was the next *Thin Blue Line*, that they should give us some money so that it could be released theatrically first and then go back to them eventually, which thankfully is what happened. If they had said no, the film would never have had the life that it did, because it would have just gone on television."

Berlinger and Sinofsky eventually received $400,000 from *American Playhouse* and $100,000 from Channel Four in England. They invested $50,000 of their own money, bringing the total production budget to $550,000. Berlinger jokes that their budget was equivalent to "the cost of a honeywagon [the trailer with portable toilets] on a feature film."

In March 1991, after Sinofsky and Berlinger made the deal with *American Playhouse*, they finally had enough money to film the murder trial and edit the film, and were able to leave their jobs at Maysles Films. They formed their own production company, Creative Thinking International, to facilitate the production of *Brother's Keeper*.

Berlinger pooh-poohs those who refer to the nineties as "the golden age of documentaries in theaters." "I think that's sort of ridiculous," chides Berlinger. "According to *Variety*, only one-tenth of one percent of the domestic box-office gross in 1995 was earned by documentaries at a time when there were three major documentaries—*Crumb*, *Hoop Dreams*, and *Unzipped* (the documentary about fashion designer Isaac Mizrahi)—released by major distributors (Sony Pictures Classics, Fine Line, and Miramax). It's always a struggle to get your documentary out there."

One of the things that attracted Berlinger to the story about the Ward Brothers was the area detail map in the *New York Times* that pinpointed the site of the alleged murder as Munnsville, New York, a town just eight miles from Colgate University in Hamilton, which just happened to be Berlinger's alma mater.

Ironically, during his years at Colgate, Berlinger's perception of Munnsville was colored by campus jokes that ridiculed the citizens of the small town. "One of the interesting things for me, in the whole experience of making the film, was breaking down my own stereotypes, as we hoped to break down the stereotypes of the viewers who were watching the movie. I think the first twenty minutes of the film, people are laughing *at* the brothers. Eventually, you start caring about them as people, you see them in three-dimensions, you care about the outcome, which is why the trial becomes so moving.

"The first time you drive down that dead-end country road that says 'No Outlet,' the dirt road at the end of Munnsville, you see strewn tractor parts, a rusted-out refrigerator in the high grass, you knock on their door, you see how they live," says Berlinger. "They're dirty, they're smelly. The first time we met them we couldn't help but have images of *Deliverance North* and wonder, 'Gee, what kind of people are these?' You heard all sorts of stories from people in town about how they have sex with cows and little boys—stuff that we later realized was just false. It's the type of stuff that when there's a ghost house at the end of the road, everyone likes to throw stones at it and tell stories about it. As we got to know the brothers as human beings, all that stuff—their home and their hygiene—didn't matter. To this day, we stay in touch with them, we really care about these guys, we saw them as human beings. It was a very important personal experience, getting to know these guys. The life experience of making that film was actually more important to me than what's on the screen. At some point in the film, you start really caring about them, so that when you see Lyman breaking down on the stand, or Delbert testifying, you really feel for them, and you want them to get off.

"Not that we did it on purpose, but I think the film has a really positive structure. Ironically, for a non-fiction film, it has a classic dramatic structure. Even though it's an odd film and an odd story, it's like a fairy tale. I think it's like the perfect theatrical offering, in the sense that it's intellectually provocative, it's real, so it's very interesting, but it's ultimately a feel-good movie, like a fairy tale. By the end of the film, everything is neatly wrapped up, the boys have been acquitted. When they drive off waving in that tractor shot, and the end credits roll, it really feels like any good story that you've seen, but yet it's real. It's a satisfying movie experience."

Berlinger won't say whether he thinks Delbert Ward was guilty or innocent of killing his brother. "One of the great things about *Brother's Keeper* that sets us apart from traditional documentarians, and what makes this film theatrical, is that we embrace ambiguity," says Berlinger. "There is a whole school of traditional documentary filmmaking which says you have to dot every *i* and cross every *t*, and if you raise an issue you have to resolve it, and you have to present the filmmaker's point of view, which is usually delivered through narration, which we hate. In the traditional approach, the filmmaker's point of view has to be explicit in the film, you have to walk away knowing exactly what the filmmaker thinks. We don't like to tell people whether or not we think Delbert is guilty. Of the people who watch the film, there are as many moviegoers who think Delbert is guilty as there are those who think he is innocent. Some people who think he's guilty think he's still *an innocent*. We certainly had a feeling, but we keep vacillating throughout the entire making of the film, and that is the experience we want to give the audience. Really, the guilt or innocence is almost not relevant. It's the excuse for making the film, the skeleton we hang everything on in terms of dramatic structure, but the film is about something else. It's a film that is really a portrait of a time and a place. It's a portrait of these brothers, it's a portrait of a community. We're not there on a mission to prove guilt or innocence, we're there on a mission to tell a story in the present tense, which is the aesthetic goal, to capture what's happening as it unfolds. We're there to tell a story about small-town camaraderie, about the justice system. The ambiguity—

people go out and talk about the film, from a practical standpoint, in terms of theatrical success. If you watch *Dumb and Dumber*, that stays with you for about an hour. If you watched this film at the time it was playing in movie theaters, people are still thinking about the film and talking about it days later. After watching the film they go off and have coffee and debate the guilt or innocence question, and from a practical standpoint, that can only enhance the word-of-mouth value of a film. In terms of the theatrical success of this movie, that was one of our major, grassroots, word-of-mouth marketing tools."

When the film was completed, Berlinger and Sinofsky approached "everybody" for distribution. They were optimistic. After all, they had the *American Playhouse* imprimatur, which was the equivalent of the *Good Housekeeping* Seal of Approval for independent films, and their film won the Audience Award at the Sundance Film Festival in 1992. "We fully expected to walk away with a distribution deal from Sundance," says Berlinger. "We were surprised, because there was a lot of critical and popular heat on our film, but the phone was not ringing at our condo." After Sundance, Berlinger took what he characterizes as a "very humiliating trip" to Hollywood. Warner Bros. provided him with a plane ticket, but the Warner distribution executive who was supposed to meet with him wasn't available and passed Berlinger on to a low-level home video executive.

"It was obvious they really weren't interested in the film, and how I got the ticket out of them is beyond me," says Berlinger. "Here I am flying out to Hollywood on a Warner Bros. ticket, to see the people who had picked up *Roger & Me* the year before for a $3 million advance to the filmmaker. I thought our film was as good, certainly the reviews and the reaction at Sundance testified to it being as high quality as *Roger & Me*. We thought for sure we would get—not $3 million—but certainly a deal. In hindsight, now that I know more about the business, that Warner Bros. deal was just a strange anomaly in the history of Hollywood. It was an anti-Reagan film, championing the little man, and I think they thought it was going to hit a much bigger audience than it ultimately did. Ironically, *Roger & Me* grossed $7 million at the box office. Warner Bros. spent $6 million in prints and advertising to get that $7 million, plus they gave an advance to the filmmaker of $3 million, so they were in the hole $9 million. The $7 million at the box office really means only about $3.5 million to Warner Brothers, so they took a bath on that film, which hurt future generations of people like myself. Instead of really analyzing and saying, 'Maybe if we had given *Roger & Me* a $500,000 advance and only spent a million dollars, we would have had a success.' And then the door would have been opened by Hollywood to more documentaries. One legacy of the *Roger & Me* deal was that it was great for Michael Moore, it established his career. A $7 million box-office gross still means that a lot of people saw the film. He pocketed a lot of cash. But I think it was bad in the long run for non-fiction filmmakers. Myths arise. All that's talked about on the *Roger & Me* deal is that the film lost a lot of money. Here we're going at it a year later, not knowing all this stuff, just knowing that they got $3 million, and knowing that *Roger & Me* is playing at theaters all over the place, and here we have the hot new documentary, fully expecting to get a deal, and the Warner Bros.' executive who bought the ticket didn't even show up at the meeting."

During Berlinger's week-long sojourn in Los Angeles, he carried his only 16mm print of *Brother's Keeper* from distributor to distributor. He dropped the print off at Goldwyn on Wednesday and Thursday for screenings that never took place. By Friday, Berlinger was running out of time. He was due back in New York for a Monday morning screening with Miramax, so he spent the entire day at the mall across from the Goldwyn Company offices, making calls and waiting to pick up the print after Friday's promised 5:00 P.M. screening. Finally, at 6:30 P.M., in pouring rain, he rang the buzzer at the Goldwyn building, which was locked up for the weekend. No answer. Finally someone answered the phone, removed Berlinger's print from the projection room, and slid it through to him through the iron grille that fortified the back door. For Berlinger, it was an "incredibly humiliating and eye-opening experience. I was returning to New York with my tail between my legs, having been treated with such indifference by Hollywood that I couldn't believe it." Other distributors, including Fine Line, Miramax, October Films, and Sony Classics passed on the film, although they treated the filmmakers with more respect. "They said, 'It's a really high-quality film, we just don't know what we can do with it,'" recalls Berlinger. "I don't necessarily argue with that, because what Bruce and I really did, in the marketing of the film, is something that I don't think a distributor could afford to do: spend a lot of time doing grassroots, tender-loving-care type of marketing for just one title."

When Berlinger and Sinofsky decided to distribute *Brother's Keeper* themselves, they knew the effort would take all their energies, but they had no choice. They launched their distribution effort with a loan of $85,000 from *American Playhouse* and started making television sales. The filmmakers invested a lot of sweat equity, taking a year off from filmmaking, and paying $40,000 for the blowup themselves. The original *American Playhouse* production monies had paid back the filmmakers' initial $100,000 investment. Now they plowed that sum and more back into the distribution effort, once again going into debt. Once the film started generating box-office receipts, they were able to pay themselves a salary, but until then, says Berlinger, "times were tight. We spent a total of $250,000 on prints and advertising, but that was not all at once. Once the film starting generating a profit and buzz and the theaters starting paying us, we would roll the profits from one market into the next market. Both for practical reasons, in terms of allowing the film to find its audience, and for financial reasons, we platformed the release from city to city. We slowly rolled the film to New York, then to San Francisco, then to Boston. It was not like we opened in ten cities at once, because we couldn't afford to do that. Sometimes when we went into college towns we would also do speaking engagements and get a small fee. There were different ways we made money. Believe it or not, at one point we were living off of the merchandising of the T-shirts, buttons, hats, and posters."

"Our strategy for the release involved three very simple things," says Berlinger. "One was to not use the word *documentary*. We positioned the film as a non-fiction feature film, with the emphasis on *feature*. We wanted to lose the word documentary, because the d-word carries tremendous baggage. We felt that if people thought it was a documentary, they would feel it was an educational film. It's like a spoonful of castor oil to get them to go to the theater to see a documentary. Our second strategy was to go into mainstream theaters when appropriate. Certain markets cry out for a traditional alternative screen—for example, the Film Forum in New York is the obvious place for a film like this. The conservative approach to releasing a documentary is that you do it in 16mm, which limits you to seventy theatrical venues around the country. They are generally calendar houses [theaters with prearranged, limited-run engagements] where you have a closed-end run. In the closed-end-run calendar houses, no matter how well you're doing, you can't move over to another screen and that's it. We did the open-end-run calendar houses where we felt we *could* move over, but in certain markets we really wanted to play at mainstream theaters, which involved the commitment to blowing up your film to 35mm, which is a huge expense. At that time, a 35mm print was $1,600 a pop, a 16mm print was $450 a pop. Ultimately we had thirty prints, which was expensive. So we wanted to blow-up the film to 35mm, treat it like a movie, go to real theaters. Of course the upside of an open-ended run is, if you ignite, you can last for weeks—in theory. Sometimes we got pulled off the screen prematurely, which we didn't anticipate. We just assumed that if the business was there, the theater would leave us on screen—that's not always the case, and that was something we learned the hard way.

"The downside to an open-ended run is that it costs a lot more to support," says Berlinger. "You have to do a lot more advertising. The nice thing about a calendar house is that they have a built-in audience. The Film Forum's calendar goes out to 55,000 people. When you go in with an open-ended run, you're paying for the first week's advertising *and* you're competing with everything out in Hollywood. When a Hollywood movie comes out, they take out a two-page, double-truck ad [double-truck refers to an ad spanning two full adjacent newspaper pages] and you've got your little one-inch ad at the bottom corner of the *Boston Globe*, it's tough competition. We wanted to take that risk. We wanted the film to be perceived as a regular film, so we blew it up to 35mm and went for regular theaters—that was the second part of our strategy."

For their New York opening at the Film Forum, the filmmakers launched an aggressive public-relations effort, calling the press directly. "We appealed to the press, saying we made this film on credit cards and now we are distributing it ourselves," says Berlinger. "The distributors have passed it over, but we think it is an interesting film that people will want to see. Will you look at it?' Once they looked at it, they liked it and they would tell us. Then we would ask for their support. Because it was our debut market, the film was not really well-known. When the press feels like they are discovering something, they seem to champion it more. We had a tremendous amount of press for our opening."

The filmmakers chose to debut their film at the Film Forum because they knew they couldn't afford to spend a lot of money on advertising. "New York is a very tough market to make money in," says Berlinger. "You have to do some advertising when you go with the Film Forum, but it was minimal compared to what we would have had to spend if we had opened at the Angelika or the City Cinema."

Their advertising expenditures for the first week came to $12,000. That paid for a pre-opening ad in the *New York Times* (two-inch by one column) on Wednesday, an opening-day ad (three-inch by one column) on Friday, and a cooperative ad with the Film Forum (paying for one-third of a one-third-page ad, plus a one-inch listing ad), which ran in *The Village Voice*. By far, their biggest advertising device was mailings. They began their direct-mail effort before they took their film to the Sundance Film Festival, mailing 5,000 postcards of the three Ward brothers standing in their home with the message, "The Ward brothers are taking their first trip out of New York City . . . to Park City, Utah." For Sundance, Berlinger built his own database of every agent and movie executive in Hollywood, using the *Hollywood Bluebook* and other sources. Berlinger and Sinofsky mailed out 15,000 cards in New York alone, just for the opening, with the message, "The Ward Boys Are Coming to a Theater Near You." "We knew we were successful because people showed up at the screenings with the postcards in their hands," says Berlinger. "It was incredibly successful—I'm a real believer in postcards. If you have a good image sent to the right people, you capture people's attention quickly. We were nobodies and *Brother's Keeper* did not have much pre-Sundance buzz, other than this postcard, and yet all of our screenings were sold out within a day of the festival opening, which wasn't a common occurrence in '92. Even now, when I visit people's offices, I still see the postcard up on bulletin boards, yellowing with age—it's something people kept."

Berlinger and Sinofsky used the same direct-mail strategy for all their openings, coming up with some hook and mailing to everyone they could think of. Berlinger tapped old school ties, mailing postcards to fellow alumni from Horace Greeley High School in Chappaqua, New York ("Joe Berlinger, Class of '79, Horace Greeley H.S."), and to Colgate University alumni. Sinofsky contacted his alma maters, the University of Massachusetts and New York University School of Film. Berlinger went to his home town, Chappaqua, New York, and handed out flyers at the train station. The filmmakers obtained mailing lists of lawyer's groups and the American Civil Liberties Union, among others. "Some people look at *Brother's Keeper* and see it as a film about the plight of the elderly and the plight of people who live in poverty," says Berlinger. "I don't necessarily see the film that way, but as long as people were telling us they were seeing that in the film, we found groups like that," says Berlinger. "We put up ads at NYU and Columbia and successfully recruited interns to help us hand out flyers. A few weeks before our film was about to open, we went to uptown art screens like Lincoln Plaza Cinemas where other films, like Errol Morris's *A Brief History of Time*, were opening, and handed out flyers. We did things as silly as standing in line at other people's movies, talking up our film as though we were viewers: 'Hey, did you see that film *Brother's Keeper?*' We did everything, it was all word-of-mouth grassroots." The filmmakers efforts also resulted in a lot of radio coverage for *Brother's Keeper* on various local New York City stations and National Public Radio. Vin Scelsa, a local radio personality, championed the film on his show *Idiot's Delight*, and promoted a special screening for KROQ listeners.

The pièce de résistance of their marketing effort, however, was the provocative trailer for the film, which consisted of a "testimonial" by the idiosyncratic monologist Spalding Gray (known for his film *Swimming to Cambodia*). "We woke up one day and said, 'Oh my God, we need a trailer,' but our negatives were tied up in making the blow-up and not available. Plus, we were afraid because of the whole d-word thing. We were afraid that if we showed footage from the film, it might not do the film justice and people would see that as a little grainy and documentary-like and might stay away. We remembered that Spalding Gray, who presented the audience award to us at Sundance, really loved the film and offered to do anything to help promote the film. During the award presentation, he said, 'This film is terrific. It's the first film I've ever seen where I couldn't get up and tear myself away to go take a leak, even though I really had to take a leak throughout the entire film.' He told this really funny story about how he just could not move to go pee, because he didn't want to miss a frame. So we said let's get Spalding and shoot a 35mm trailer, give it a really rich look and have Spalding just tell the story about how great the film is. We went out to the Hamptons, and in a day we just shot him in his writer's studio talking about the film in a very deadpan, funny sort of way, telling the story about how he had to take a leak and we intercut it with some of the press quotes that we had. We didn't show a frame of the film, which is a highly unusual approach to a trailer—just to have it described in very evocative terms. In some markets, this trailer was very effective, in other markets, it wasn't. If you don't like or don't know about Spalding Gray, the trailer was a disaster—in twenty-five percent of the markets that we sent the trailer, they sent it back, saying, 'This is useless.' In places where Spalding does well, which generally are in the same places where art films do well, this trailer worked like magic. In fact in New York, the trailer itself was talked about and itself achieved semi-cult status. You know how people talk during the trailers and don't really pay attention because they're busy munching on popcorn—when our trailer came on, you could hear a pin drop and people laughing and really paying attention to it. Intercut with regular trailers it was even more effective. People always talk about the trailer as having brought them into the theater, so that was something we invested a lot of time in. We convinced the Film Forum to play it earlier than usual, for four weeks, before every show prior to the opening of *Brother's Keeper.*

"Since one of our strategies with this release was to play at mainstream art houses, or crossover places," says Berlinger, "we did not want to release the film in 16mm, we wanted to do it in 35mm. We wanted to have open-ended runs at regular theaters, instead of the typical documentary approach, with one day here at some dumpy art screen, or two days there. That was the risk we took, and we spent accordingly. That was a major strategic decision: to play at the Nickelodeon in Boston, which was at the time a Loew's theater, instead of the Coolidge Corner for two days. To play at The Ritz in Philadelphia, which is the theater you would go to see Hollywood product as well as art product, instead of The Roxy. That's a major thing that most documentaries don't do, especially self-distributed ones. In New York, playing at the Film Forum was the right thing to do, playing at The Roxie in San Francisco was the right thing to do. Now part of the problem with *Brother's Keeper* is we were unknowns and some markets were reluctant to commit to booking us. Philadelphia was one of them. In Philadelphia, there's one really great place, called The Ritz, to play art films. It's a beautiful theater and it's got a great audience. We really wanted The Ritz, we wanted an upscale release, we wanted to be at the same theater that *The Crying Game* was at. So every month we would send the theater manager our grosses and our reviews, and eventually he agreed to book us. So then we did our job: we did our grassroots mailings, we got groups to come, we got Stephen Ray of the *Philadelphia Inquirer* to do a big feature piece. The reviews were glowing, and indeed, the first week we were on screen we did incredible numbers. If we were a Miramax film or a Fine Line film, we would have stayed for weeks, but we were pulled off the screen the second week. First, they split the screen with another film, then by the third week we were completely taken off the screen, because the other distributors were muscling us out of the theater. That hurt our grosses. We were not allowed to fully exploit our market. And I think that happened in a lot of places around the country. Had we had a distributor's clout, where we could say, 'Don't take us off the screen because we've got ten more films coming down the pike, and if you want them, you've got to play this film.' Because we did not have that ability, it probably cost us at least a half-a-million dollars to our gross. That's the big problem with self-distribution. You're the first to be pulled off the screen and you're the last to be paid by a lot of people. A lot of theaters were terrific and paid right on time. Collecting money was a big pain. I would say we collected eighty-five percent of what we should have been paid on paper, and ninety-five percent when you take a settled amount as the full amount.

"The third part of our strategy was just doing tender loving, grassroots marketing," says Berlinger. "We knew that we couldn't afford real advertising. We knew that our marketing effort would be press-driven and word-of-mouth driven. So we just got on the phone and courted the press. Now this sounds like an obvious thing to do, but I think there's a big difference between a studio publicist calling some press contact with his weekly call, 'Well, this is what's coming out.' There's a big difference between that and filmmakers calling almost naively and saying we've got this film, we got it in the can with credit cards, we're releasing it ourselves, we hope you like it, if you like it we could use your support.' Somehow the press responded to that approach, because the press support of our film was incredible. Our press book is three inches thick, and we got incredible press everywhere. A lot of people ignore the press in the smaller markets. For example, Joanna Conners at the *Cleveland Plain Dealer* is an intelligent, excellent reviewer. We would call these markets and offer to come in to do an interview. These are people who don't normally get that kind of attention. Usually they're overlooked by studios, by the general publicity machine. Because we were willing to go to those markets, and talk personally with the press, we were put on the front page of a lot of local papers. The net result was that we had great press in small markets, and consequently, in a place like Albany, at the Spectrum Theater, we had a bigger gross and a bigger profit than we had in Los Angeles. The success in Albany is attributable to the fact that Munnsville is a hundred miles away, and it's sort of a local story, and we took advantage of that. In the hinterlands of upstate New York, in places like Utica, Syracuse, Rochester, usually not big-ticket places for art films, this film was the biggest film up there. In the two theaters opposite of Munnsville, in Hamilton, New York, and Oneida, New York, this film outgrossed every film you can name from *Star Wars* to *Batman* to *Jurassic Park*. We made about $30,000 gross in Oneida and about $35,000 in Hamilton. Obviously, not huge numbers—but those are theaters no one would pay any attention to. Multiply that by fifty to sixty markets where we did the same thing. I think the real reason we were successful is that we treated every market like New York City or Los Angeles, we did it slowly, and it was all grass roots. Not just press-oriented. We identified target groups such as advocacy groups for rural people, the elderly, and civil rights. We tried to find as many people who might respond to this film, aside from just people interested in good filmmaking."

Although both Berlinger and Sinofsky had to delay their next film for a year while they distributed *Brother's Keeper*, they are convinced that their strategy paid off for both *Brother's Keeper* and their careers. "A lot of the independent distributors grab up a number of titles at once and throw them against the wall in exactly the same way, like spaghetti, and whichever piece of spaghetti sticks to the wall, that's the one they then follow up and nurture. The rest fall into box-office oblivion. No-one ever hears of these films, not because the films necessarily are unmarketable, because there is such pressure for a film to produce results immediately, that if an independent film does not automatically hit a home run, then it's abandoned within weeks. We didn't start off with a home run, we nurtured and found our audience. We did not get discouraged and we allowed the film to build, which is how they used to distribute films, especially foreign art product. A film was allowed to find its audience, people didn't freak-out after the first weekend. Obviously, the same thing is happening in feature films now. If a film doesn't do $20 million its first weekend, it means it won't do the $150 million it has to do, which is sort of absurd, but that's where the business has moved. Those ripples have gone into the independent world as well. A decade ago, it used to be that if a film cost $1 million and did $2 million at the box office, then made some video sales, that was a big hit. Now, a lot of these companies are owned by bigger distributors—Fine Line is owned by Turner, Miramax is owned by Disney. Independent film has become like a brand name, a genre almost, like there's 'romantic comedies,' there's 'film noir,' there's 'independent films' in quotation marks. They want to make films that cost $5 to $8 million and the film has to do $10 million at the box office to be a success. It's a mirror of what's happening in the Hollywood traditional world. So, there's no time to allow a film to find its audience. As a result of our release we won numerous awards. We had the Sundance award already, that wouldn't have changed, but I don't know if we would have gotten the Directors Guild Award, the National Board of Review, and the D.W. Griffith Award of the New York Film Critics Circle. All those things have made us much higher-profile filmmakers. It has enhanced our reputation in the independent film world because, frankly, we are sort of folk heroes for having done what we did."

Berlinger warns that not everyone is capable of self-distribution. "I think one thing that gave us the confidence to proceed with self-distribution was the fact that in my former life, I had a lot of practical skills," says Berlinger. After he graduated from Colgate University with majors in English and German, he went to work as an assistant account executive on the Nescafé coffee and Gillette pens accounts at McCann-Erickson, an ad agency in New York City. He parlayed his fluency in German and his agency experience into a job with Ogilvy & Mather in Frankfurt, working as an international account executive, coordinating numerous international film shoots, which is where Berlinger caught "the production bug." While he was living in Germany, Jim Jarmusch's *Stranger Than Paradise* came out. "That really affected me, and made me want to become a filmmaker," recalls Berlinger. "I thought it was a great film and it was accessible. I said I want to go back to New York and become a filmmaker.'" He returned to New York, still working for Ogilvy & Mather on the American Express account. American Express decided they wanted to shoot documentary-style commercials for the Green Card, and by coincidence, Ogilvy & Mather hired the Maysles Brothers to shoot those documentary commercials. "The Maysles Brothers were looking for somebody who had ad agency and marketing experience to formalize their presence and market their services on Madison Avenue. I was looking to get into film, and David Maysles and I hit it off," says Berlinger. "David hired me to be their marketing director and later, their executive producer. Within seven months, David died, unfortunately. He was really the guy I had responded to; I felt a real distance with his brother Albert. I was still a marketing person, but now I was at a film production company, so I spent the next five years using my experience there as my film school and learned the nuts and bolts of production. I didn't really have an interest in documentaries per se, it was just where I ended up and where I've learned my filmmaking. I consider myself a filmmaker more than a documentarian. Right now I'm working in nonfiction, but I plan to work in fiction films as well. That's why we emphasize stories. We are much more about storytelling than about journalism per se."

Berlinger's marketing experience at the Maysles Brothers proved invaluable. "When I launched the Maysles home video line, I designed all the video box covers. I had the practical marketing skills that I think a lot of filmmakers do not have because I came to filmmaking late. I was a marketer who decided he wanted to be a filmmaker. I have an advertising background, so I know how to make a poster. I knew enough about putting ads together that I could go to somebody and say, 'How do you put together an ad slick for a newspaper?' I had the writing skills along with really good PR skills. I know how to write a pitch letter, how to promote, and how to talk to the press. I did all of our press release writing. It was interesting to see what happened when the film was properly positioned and properly written about. I'm a good prose writer and I noticed that some of the stuff I wrote for the press kit was just reprinted with somebody else's name put on it. I wasn't upset, I was actually very proud of that, that people were plagiarizing me wholesale.

"In 1989, prior to *Brother's Keeper*, I decided I would try my own film, so I made this short film called *Outrageous Taxi Stories*, which was shot in a day for $7,000. The film is twenty-five minutes' worth of New York city cabbies telling the most outrageous thing that's ever happened in their life. It was a funny documentary, not a boring lecture about something. Even back then, I was looking for ways, in my own way, to push the boundaries of what a documentary could be. At the time, I called it a 'Funumentary.' It was important for two reasons: one, it did extraordinarily well at film festivals, I sold it to several countries for broadcast, and it won an IDA [International Documentary Association] nomination for distinguished documentary achievement. Because of all that success with relatively little effort, it encouraged me to believe that I was on the right path. It is possible to be a filmmaker, you just have to figure out how to do it. The other benefit was that I asked my friend Bruce Sinofsky, who also worked at Maysles, to edit it for me. In the editing room we got along really well, and realized we could collaborate and that we had the same vision for wanting to expand the boundaries of non-fiction filmmaking by making feature-length films that could play in the theaters. While Bruce was editing my film *Outrageous Taxi Stories*, we started talking about doing a film like *Brother's Keeper*. Within a year, in June of 1990, *Brother's Keeper* came along. *Brother's Keeper* was really the first real big film for both of us. Since then, we've formed a company and made twenty-five TV commercials together. We've done a *Frontline* called *The Begging Game* in between *Brother's Keeper* and *Paradise Lost*."

The Begging Game was an hour-long portrait of New York City panhandlers. The film was produced in the midst of an ongoing public debate about the quality of life in cities. The city of San Francisco had just cracked down on homeless panhandlers, forbidding them to sleep on the streets, and many people were questioning what society should do with the armies of homeless beggars populating city streets. Berlinger and Sinofsky spent a year following these panhandlers as they plied their trade. "This film is really a portrait of five panhandlers to see how they live their lives and why they need the money. No one was getting to know these people as people. Our approach was not to deal with the public policy, but to have this very ambiguous portrait of the lower depths without any value judgments or conclusions about what to do with them. It was shot on video for television, and it was successful. We have a pretty successful little production company I would say, based on the success of *Brother's Keeper*. We support ourselves. But the real money is in TV commercials, sadly." Berlinger and Sinofsky spend twenty-five percent of their time producing TV commercials under the banner of Gray Matter Productions but receive seventy-five percent of their incomes from that source. Their feature film division, called Hand to Mouth Productions, acquired its moniker from the fact that Berlinger and Sinofsky were making their film hand-to-mouth on the weekends, and also because Delbert was accused of placing his hand over the mouth of brother Bill, asphyxiating him in the process.

Since they began their adventures in self-distribution, Berlinger and Sinofsky have been besieged by other filmmakers asking them to distribute their work. Berlinger says they're not interested, because "it's a lot of work and you don't make a huge amount of money. I don't think I could muster the same enthusiasm for someone else's work. The reason we get so enthusiastic is because it's *our* film."

Like anyone learning the business of distribution from scratch, the filmmakers made some serious mistakes. The biggest one was neglecting to make a poster until after the New York opening, a decision that was dictated by finances. "We just couldn't afford it," says Berlinger. "It's very expensive to make a poster and very expensive to put up 1,000 of them. There is a poster army or mafia that you pay to put up posters where you're not supposed to put posters. If there's a construction site, they will plaster the plywood wall that's hiding the construction site with posters. The city is divided into territories, and the mafia that works it out knows that after three days *Brother's Keeper* will get covered over for the next film. If you try to put up posters for yourself and don't go through this mafia, they immediately get covered over. We just made the decision to save money and do these half-size posters. That was a big mistake because people want to see posters. Instead of posters for the initial New York engagement, we had these displays with stills and items from our press kit. It looked really unprofessional. So we didn't have posters, but the trailers, the postcards, and the outreach to specialty groups worked really effectively. And of course this whole effort was press driven and we consciously nurtured that press."

The success of *Brother's Keeper* has been followed by the success of the filmmakers' second non-fiction feature film, *Paradise Lost: The Child Murders at Robin Hood Hills*. Produced for broadcast on the cable network Home Box Office, the film is another look at the American justice system, this time as revealed through the trial of three teenagers accused of ritualistically killing three young boys in the town of West Memphis, Arkansas. "Heavy-metal Monsters?" was the headline for the front-page coverage of the film in the "Calendar" (entertainment) section of the *Los Angeles Times*, with praises from none-too-easy-to-please TV critic Howard Rosenberg: "These guys really can tell a story, in this case a revealing X-ray of a small community that addresses the universality of human contradictions, all of it to a background of heavy metal by Metallica."

The distribution deal for *Paradise Lost* echoed that of *Brother's Keeper*. HBO paid for the film as part of a three-picture deal with Berlinger and Sinofsky. But unlike the PBS deal for *Brother's Keeper*,

Paradise Lost was first broadcast on HBO, with the theatrical release to follow. "Some people look at that as a problem," says Berlinger, "because they think we are cannibalizing our audience. We look on it as a potential problem, if it's not managed properly. Generally, I have the philosophy that the HBO showing is going to act as a word-of-mouth device. HBO is only in about eighteen million homes, but not everybody who gets HBO is going to watch the film. If it's on PBS, too many people see it because PBS is in ninety-nine percent of the country. We can't afford large-scale advertising. I think the TV press that we're going to get and the broadcast itself will help spread the word-of-mouth, because the type of people who go to the NuArt in Los Angeles, the Music Box in Chicago, or the Film Forum in New York, where this film will be shown, do not get HBO per se or would rather see a film like this in the movie theater. Obviously, we are going to lose some of our audience, but I think what we will lose, we will more than make up for in word-of-mouth that will be spread by those people who see it and talk to other people. So, I am hoping that it will work as a giant TV commercial or a giant preview for the film."

Having a television broadcast *before* the theatrical release also creates delicate public relations problems. Berlinger is aware that many publications that review the film's TV premiere won't review it again for its theatrical premiere. "We have to get enough TV broadcast press coverage to make the broadcast a hit. All that HBO cares about is its TV broadcast, but of course we have to be careful that we don't eat up all of our press opportunities, because this film, like *Brother's Keeper*, will be press-driven." Even before the TV broadcast, the filmmakers had pre-booked the film in 100 theaters, an accomplishment they attribute to their tenacity in maintaining contact with their exhibitor friends. "Since *Paradise Lost* went into production, we have done four mailings to our theaters that played *Brother's Keeper*, letting them know about the film and making it sound exciting to them. The other thing we did, which no one else does, is we went to Show East, the exhibitors' convention, in October. Most people go there to look at the latest urinal, newest seat, or popcorn device, but of course the major studios unveil their products there as well. No independent filmmakers go down, so we piggy-backed on one of the theaters that we had a good relationship with and we went in under their umbrella. Once we were in the convention, we had our press kits and our postcards. When we looked at name tags, we recognized the name of our friend from the Spectrum Theater, who we may never have actually met, but have spoken to on the phone. We made a lot of personal appearances for *Brother's Keeper*, so a lot of people were familiar to us. We went down and shook everyone's hand and said, 'Look, this film is going to Sundance and it will be out in the theaters.' It was a really smart way to network with theater owners. Of course, if the film stunk, did terribly at Sundance, and got terrible reviews, no amount of networking and handshaking is going to get them to book the film. Luckily, the film was getting the kind of attention that *Brother's Keeper* got. What is harder with this film is that we have a higher profile and we are busier. We don't want to abandon filmmaking the way we did on *Brother's Keeper*, so we are hiring more people to oversee the distribution of *Paradise Lost*. We have a three-picture deal with HBO and other opportunities, so the real challenge is going to be not doing everything ourselves. Also, that genuinely naive approach that we used with the press isn't going to fly anymore. We are much more sophisticated and we're established filmmakers. We've hired a publicist and we're doing things a little more traditionally." The filmmakers hired Sharon Kahn, a publicist known for her expertise in independent films, to handle traditional entertainment press publicity for *Paradise Lost*. They also hired Dan Klores Associates, a non-entertainment publicity firm in an effort to bring press attention to the issues of politics and justice raised by the film. "Our strategy with this film," says Berlinger, "is to move the press off the entertainment page."

Like many "D" filmmakers, Berlinger and Sinofsky would like to exercise their storytelling talents in the arena of fiction films. Berlinger hopes to be in production on a "traditional" fiction film by mid-1997, although he promises that while the film is scripted, it will not be done in a traditional way. Given their track records, few doubt that whatever Berlinger and Sinofsky create, it will not follow the rules, and it will provide filmgoers with a fresh experience—a rarity in today's world of recycled ideas and predictable plot lines.

9
COMING ATTRACTIONS: CREATING THE TRAILER

Coming Attractions were what they used to call movie trailers—those short advertising previews of soon-to-be-released movies that are shown before the feature. Trailers are one of the filmmakers' best chances to seduce a captive, demographically desirable audience into seeing their film when it comes out. In order to accomplish this, according to New Line marketing and distribution chief Mitchell Goldman, "trailers have to be better than the movies they promote. . . . If that's not the case, you haven't done your job."[1]

"Doing the job" with trailers is the life's work of Chris Arnold, one of the managing partners of Cimarron, Bacon, O'Brien, behind-the-scenes producers of primo trailers for numerous Hollywood clients. His is a niche business that Madison Avenue never really mastered, in Arnold's estimation: "People ask me, 'What's the difference between what you do and what Madison Avenue does when it comes to advertising?' I answer, 'In the trailer business we get to do something that Madison Avenue doesn't very often get to do with their products—we get to give away free samples.' That means if you have a horror movie that you're advertising, you make a scary trailer, something that will make people in the theater jump. If you have a comedy, you make the funniest trailer you can. Many people say that by the time you've told three or four jokes from a movie, that's all there is. They've gone to the movie and waited for two and a half hours and haven't seen anything more than they saw in the trailer. That's true—sometimes the product we're advertising is not quite as good as we make it look. But it's not our job to do anything more than get people in for the first weekend."

According to John Jacobs, President of Worldwide Media for Mandalay Entertainment, distilling a movie down to its essential sound bites has a long history in Hollywood. "All a movie needs is three big scenes," says Jacobs. "When people walk out of a movie theater and ultimately talk about movies, they really only distill it into a couple of moments. In *The Fugitive*, you had the train crash and the jump off the bridge and that was it. People thought it was worth the price of admission. In *Indiana Jones*, you had the ball running down the thing and that's it. That was worth my seven bucks. In *Sister Act*, Whoopi Goldberg has two singing numbers. Done deal. I'm there. We used to joke about *Driving Miss Daisy*—in the last scene, when Morgan Freeman brings the pumpkin pie to her in the wheelchair and she says, 'You're my best friend,' that's it. Three or four great sound bites from *Casablanca* have lived on forever. All you need is one or two sound bites for *Gone With the Wind*, and it emotes for everybody."

Those collections of sound bites and action sequences known as trailers are apparently quite successful at pulling in moviegoers, according to a 1995 Gallup/*Variety* telephone poll of 1,200 Americans questioning the effectiveness of motion picture trailers. The survey showed that the majority of people wanted to see a specific movie after seeing the trailer for it.[2] An earlier Gallup/*Variety* poll showed that movie trailers are the most memorable and influential forms of motion picture marketing next to television advertising. Marketers consider trailers a very cost-efficient avenue for creating word-of-mouth for a film because they reach a very specific target audience. Compared to other methods of film marketing, trailers require relatively modest budgets—the average trailer costs between $40,000 and $100,000 to produce.

There are two types of trailers: teaser trailers and standard trailers. Teaser trailers run about ninety seconds, and are designed to tease the audience and pique their interest in an upcoming movie. They can start running in theaters three to six months before a film is released. Standard theatrical trailers run about two and a half minutes and are shown six to eight weeks before the movie opens in order to properly position the film for its target audience.

The most recent Gallup/*Variety* poll revealed that most moviegoers vividly remembered "an incident, gag, or memorable line" from a trailer, and that "it was rare for someone who had seen a trailer to be able to discuss a film on a plot basis."[3]

Successful trailers are built around an idea and have a point of view. Conveying the essence of a two-hour movie is considerably more complicated than advertising a bar of soap, for example, which is why Madison Avenue never "got it" when it came to creating trailers. "Advertising of trailers or motion pictures eventually fell to people who had a good deal more motion picture background than most Madison Avenue advertising executives had," says Arnold.

Gradually, trailer production was farmed out to "people who understood how motion pictures and drama work, because these little pieces are microcosmic films," according to Arnold. "I think the closest thing you can compare a trailer to is a song. A trailer is to a movie what a song is to a symphony. It's three minutes, it's much shorter, but it has a beginning, a middle, and an end. It has a theme. It needs to go somewhere and leave you on some kind of a high, if it's going to work at all. It needs to be made by somebody who understands the principles of constructing it. That's how someone like me, who became an editor and wanted to cut films, ended up in this business and is still happy. This is a wonderful way to move from movie to movie to movie without being stuck on the same picture for twelve months. Projects come in and out of here in a matter of weeks and we're in a very privileged position."

When his firm receives an assignment to produce a trailer, the first thing they see is the script for the movie. "You read the script for a movie like *Mask* and think, 'That's crazy—nobody can produce that. I don't see how the sky is going to turn inside out and do all those things,'" says Arnold. "Then you see the movie itself, and suddenly it has a life of its own. A director writes a script and has something in mind, but almost any director will tell you that once he's finished shooting it, it doesn't have too much resemblance to the original script he started out with—and here I'm not talking about *Mask*, I'm talking about many movies. It's a project on its own and bears the marks of everyone who has worked on it, because this business is extremely collaborative. So as trailer-makers, we are standing at this sort of crossroads, where the idea meets the reality of what the project became and we have two choices. We can either take the idea that the movie had originally, whether or not it was well-executed, and sell that, or we can take the product, what finally happened, and sell that—I mean the stars, the package, the production. When I first started in the business, in the days of what they called 'high-concept movies,' I tended to think in terms of the first of these things. I'd say to myself as a trailer-maker, 'Here's this director who just spent two and a half years of his life trying to get this movie off the ground: trying to get paid for it, trying to get it cast, trying to get it shot, trying to get it cut, trying to get it sold, trying to get it out. By the time he's through with that process, he had put pretty much of his life on the line. He'd certainly put his career on the line, because if it's a flop, he may never get another job again. What would it take for someone to sacrifice that much of their life, that much of their time, that much of their personal cred-ibility in the business? What would it take to make them do that? What kind of an idea would drive them to want to sacrifice that much for it?' If you can come up with that idea, if you can isolate that, I say, you have at least a head start in figuring out how to talk somebody into spending five dollars to see it. Whether or not the movie was successful, there ought to be an idea or concept in it somewhere that is magic and that is powerful enough to cause all these people to expend all that energy to make it come to the screen. It ought to be powerful enough to get somebody out of their couch and into a movie theater. So that's one premise I start with."

Trailers over the years have been subject to the vicissitudes of style, just like other popular art forms. Arnold recalls some of the variations that appeared even before MTV: "There was a time when Simpson & Bruckheimer were throwing major rock-'n'-roll soundtracks at motion pictures like *Top Gun* and trailers tended to look like what later became rock videos. People in those days would look at our trailers and say, 'Well, it certainly is exciting, and that certainly is good music, but I don't know whether there's a story to this movie or not.' Nowadays, people are very impressed with special effects, and special effects are getting better and better. That's a process that started way back in 1977 with *Star Wars*. But I think that the audience gets wise very quickly. Nowadays, you need more than special effects because everybody has seen a few special effects and can also see them on TV. Of course, there are stars who bring people in, stars that people want to see, but stars rise in the heavens and fall over the horizon faster than many people would expect. You don't always catch them quite where you want them. Right now, Jim Carrey, who's in *The Mask*, is having a meteoric rise, but what happened to the guy who did *Ford Fairlane* who was so hot three and a half years ago for about three and a half minutes?"

From Arnold's perspective, too many movie trailers suffer from a lack of subtlety; in fact, they often give away the whole story. "The audience out there is very smart and savvy," says Arnold. "When they look at certain trailers, for example for comedies, they'll say, 'Um, it looks like there may not be much more to this movie than is in the trailer.' The complaint I hear most often is that trailers tell too much of the story and sort of let it all hang out. The main reason for that is that for the last ten years, research is a big part of determining what we do. Market research has been used as a tool by marketing departments and studios because you can take out the advertising materials and trailers and show them to various audiences. They'll give you ratings and tell you how good this looks, what turns them on, what turns them off, how this works and how this doesn't work. Invariably, you discover the lowest common denominator, which is that the more story you tell somebody, the more they seem to understand what the movie is about. The more they think they grasp, about what the movie is, the better your test results will be. And since marketing executives are just like everyone else—they like to keep their jobs—research becomes a wonderful way for them to justify what happened when a movie doesn't do well. Let's face it: only one out of eight or ten movies in Hollywood breaks even. That means that more often than not, a marketing executive is not standing on top of the pinnacle of successes. But if he can turn to his bosses and say, 'Here was the trailer we showed, it tested ninety-eight percent in the top two boxes; we had a seventy-five percent want-to-see, and the fact that the movie didn't perform was certainly unexpected to those of us in the marketing department for whom our advertising materials were working quite well.' And frankly, it's important that we have some way to measure the effectiveness of advertising. If it weren't for that, every time a movie doesn't do as well as it was expected, somebody's ass, or at least their job, is going to be on the line."

Arnold is not fond of what he calls the "kitchen sink trailers," those that have everything in them, which he's called on occasionally to produce. He finds it much more interesting to make teaser trailers, those shown in theaters three to six months before the release of the movie. "Teaser trailers are there mainly to give an initial impression to an audience, to register the title and stars and the subject matter of the movie," says Arnold. "The object is to tickle whatever interest may be there, so that people will start talking about it, or at least recognize it when the regular trailer comes along and tells them a little bit more about the movie. It will be in their consciousness and they'll say, 'Oh, I've heard about that.' Well, maybe they haven't heard about it. Maybe they just saw a teaser trailer that they forgot about six months ago. Teaser trailers, therefore, are done at a time probably long before the movie is even cut, sometimes before the movie is even shot."

People often ask Arnold how much influence directors, writers, and producers have on the marketing of a movie. "Most of the time, very little impact," says Arnold. "However, stars and directors like Arnold Schwarzenegger, Clint Eastwood—we do all his trailers—and Larry Kasdan have some clout at the studios and can play a fairly significant role in the marketing of a movie. They get to say what they want and people will listen. So when we work on a Larry Kasdan picture, we very often find ourselves working with the man himself. In the case of *French Kiss*, he was looking for a trailer that did not have any copy, that is, narration. Larry comes from the school of thought that the movie should sell itself, nobody needs to be given a lot of sell-speak, nobody needs to be told what to think about a movie. If they don't like it, they don't come to see it. Often, some of the best trailers don't have narration, but I don't have hard and fast rules about that myself."

Arnold has observed that the demographics of the moviegoing public are changing. "Not long ago everybody said the major moviegoing public was young—under twenty-five—and that's really no longer true," says Arnold. "Now the baby-boom generation is entering its forties or is well into its forties, in my case. The younger audience is being matched by an older, more mature audience who is interested in a little more content, so nowadays you have a much wider demographic spectrum to choose from. Ten years ago, you had a movie like *Top Gun*, today you have a movie like *True Lies*. The differences between those two movies are suggestive of maybe the difference between the audiences out there. With *True*

Lies you have Arnold Schwarzenegger in an action picture, but it has a strong comedy element in it. The challenge in this trailer was how to balance the comedy and the domestic situation with Jamie Lee against the action and against the expected want-to-see of the young male audiences out there whom we are obviously trying to reach."

Bill Mechanic, who was President of 20th Century Fox at the time *True Lies* was released, says that the Fox marketing team faced a number of issues in coming up with a strategy to market *True Lies*. One of the issues was how to proceed given the track record of the previous Schwarzenegger picture, *Last Action Hero*, which was not successful at the box office. "We felt that the mixture of comedy and action was not something we really wanted to sell," says Mechanic. "We wanted to make sure that we had one audience in there for sure. Strategically, the first decision was to stay on the side of an action picture—not a down-and-dirty action picture, but an action picture, nevertheless. There were a lot of other issues: Does Arnold have a gun or not? Does Arnold dress to look like a spy or like James Bond?"

In creating the trailer, the Fox marketers had to determine which shots they had available early in the process, because a lot of the special effects shots were digitally enhanced and not yet available for use. Mechanic says that their objective with the trailer was "to show this is a big-league film with action, focusing on Arnold Schwarzenegger doing what you expect, with the director that Schwarzenegger made his reputation with." After *Last Action Hero*, Schwarzenegger was very concerned about not confusing an audience about whether *True Lies* was a comedy or an action adventure film. Mechanic characterizes Schwarzenegger as "a smart guy who participates actively in his movies." Apparently Schwarzenegger and Cameron didn't agree on his sartorial image, that is, whether he should be dressed in a raincoat or dressed in a tux. "I think he [Schwarzenegger] preferred the raincoat—the tougher look, and Jim preferred a more sophisticated look," says Mechanic. "We prepared it both ways and we ended up going with the tougher look, but softening it by using the hand grenade with the wedding ring on it, which said there's a sense of humor to the picture."

Learning from what didn't work with *Last Action Hero*, the Fox marketers were careful not to overhype the movie. They wanted the movie to speak for itself, not declare it "the most important picture of the summer" or an event movie, so they played it low-key during production and postproduction. Schwarzenegger did a few long-lead interviews about the making of the movie, but most of the publicity began shortly before the release. Mechanic says that Jamie Lee Curtis also played a key role in the publicity, because she gave them the opportunity to sell the comedic side of the movie and attract women.

Another factor in the marketing was the fact that *True Lies* was one of the most expensive movies ever made up to that point (estimated to cost $100 million). One of the objectives of the marketing team was to keep the movie out of the press as much as possible, and have it be judged not on its cost but on the movie itself. The film wasn't completed until a few weeks before the release date, which meant that critics didn't see it until shortly before it opened, which didn't seem to hurt it. "A movie like *True Lies* is helped by good reviews, but the good reviews weren't necessary to us opening it," says Mechanic. "I think we needed some [good reviews], just because we wanted credibility that it wasn't *The Last Action Hero*. Generally, big movies are review-proof. If you have a high-end movie like *Four Weddings and a Funeral* or *The Madness of King George*, then you are completely review-dependent."

Whatever the scale of the movie he's working on, Mechanic says the biggest danger in marketing is simply "not opening. It's always trying to decide what is the best way to sell a movie. If you want to attract an audience, you're fighting, not only in competitive situations with other movies, but the inertia of the public. A few people go a lot, a lot of people go a few times, and some people don't go at all. You have two jobs: one is motivating the regular filmgoer, and the second is to motivate the irregular filmgoer."

When Chris Arnold set out to create a trailer for *Star Trek Generations*, he had to motivate regular filmgoers who were also among a very specific group of *Star Trek* cognoscenti. In this case, as with many of his assignments, Arnold had to create a teaser trailer out of his imagination, because little or no footage of the film has been shot when it's time for him to create the trailer. "Much of the opening of the trailer for *Star Trek Generations* is a piece of computer graphics which we designed downstairs in our own computers and then took out to a place called Digital Magic, which did the rest," says Arnold. "There was no original photography, there were no models, the whole image was created totally inside of a computer." To create the trailer, Arnold combined the computer-generated imagery with shots of the spaceship from other *Star Trek* movies, shots from the *Star Trek Generations* TV show, and shots of Captain Kirk and other cast members that were culled from the fifteen minutes of dailies of *Star Trek Generations* that were available at the time.

Arnold thinks it's essential to "understand the ballpark you're playing in" when creating a trailer. *True Lies* and *Star Trek Generations* are good examples of two very different "ballparks." "On the one hand, you're playing in an Arnold Schwarzenegger ballpark, on the other hand, you're playing in a *Star Trek* ballpark," says Arnold. "Not only that, we discovered after getting into it a little bit, we were playing in a *Star Trek Generations* ballpark, which is even different than a *Star Trek* ballpark. What is the audience I'm targeting really looking for? The Arnold [Schwarzenegger] audience is looking for big-time action. In the case of *True Lies*, Jim Cameron is a major factor. Jim Cameron was the director and the creator of *T-2* [*Terminator II*], so there was a lot of anticipation for his next movie, which was *True Lies*. His audience would expect some major hardware and effects that looked more real than anything they had seen before. Why? Because of the way Jim Cameron shoots his movies. When Jim Cameron goes out and does a scene with a Harrier [a jet], he doesn't do it with a model in a studio; he goes and gets a Harrier. And he doesn't do it with a blue screen against a skyscraper model, he does it by hoisting the Harrier 500 feet in the air on a skyscraper, and waving it around over a city. And if Arnold is in the Harrier, and has to go pee—he's spoken about this on talk shows—and he calls on his two-way radio, 'I'm sorry, you can't start the take now, I have to go to the bathroom,' Jim says, 'Stay there, do it there.' People are used to a certain degree of reality in an Arnold Schwarzenegger movie—I'd say a greater degree of reality than, let's say, Jean-Claude Van Damme. Arnold is doing this stuff, Arnold is big, Arnold is strong, and there's a really big canvas and a big subject you're working with. So that's what you do—you try to work with the size of the thing and you try to project that and you try to excite people with that, because that's what they come for.

"Now, *Star Trek Generations* is in another ballpark," says Arnold. "The original *Star Trek* was a wonderful piece because of the characters in the ship and because of the wonderful imagination of some of the clever stories and the situations they got into. Now the *Star Trek Generations* audience is a bigger audience than the *Star Trek* audience and that audience is a smarter audience. It's the next generation, Generation-X audiences, the over-twenty audience. They are interested in a little more intellectual stuff. They've got characters in here who have quite complex character development. For instance, Dato, who is actually a robot, can have certain feelings, can't have certain other feelings. We have a shot of him laughing hysterically in here, which probably didn't mean anything to you, but a *Star Trek Generations* audience would go, 'My God! Dato's laughing! That's impossible! I've got to go to this movie and find out why he's laughing!' Because Dato never laughs. There are all kinds of hidden secrets in *Star Trek Generations*, there are stories that people know that go back over many other situations. We have a couple of people on our editorial staff, particularly the person who cut this, who are Trekkies and understand these things. So the significance of little images that you put into these things will push buttons and trigger things in parts of the audience that you wouldn't suspect. This *Star Trek Generations* audience wants to know why things happen. They want to know the ins and outs and the because of—what will happen if this planet blows up? Will the force field on the planets next to it suddenly go screwy and the seasons suddenly change? It's complicated and it's interesting."

"Now I'll go to another extreme," says Arnold. "We've done every one of the Steven Segal movies. Steven Segal's audience likes this attitude that Steven has. They like this really angry person who goes after the bad guys and makes them pay. That's what you sell them. So you have to steep yourself in the arena that you're in and try to understand what your target audience is really coming there for, then deliver it in spades in the trailer."

Creating a trailer for the touching romantic comedy *Sleepless in Seattle* required a simpler approach. "I've always thought that romance sells when you take a little thought or a pure idea and float it out there in a clear way," says Arnold. "For instance, *Sleepless in Seattle*, which we worked on, was a delightful romantic comedy. What was most delightful about it was the idea, What if there was a person out there that you heard on the radio, you were moved by his plight, and you fell in love with who he was? How far would you go to meet that person? To my way of thinking, romances sell best with beautiful little ideas like that. What you try to do when you do a trailer for a movie like that is simply platform that idea the way you would a jewel in a ring and make sure that people appreciate it. You don't load it up with the kitchen sink and you don't try to overwhelm people."

If romance is complicated, making trailers about complicated romances is tricky, as Arnold found when they produced the trailer for *Mrs. Doubtfire*. "There were problems associated with this movie that the studio was worried about, and that's what we're in business to try to avoid. The studio says, 'Here's what we need to overcome if this movie's going to make $100 million.' Now this movie eventually made $200 million, and more, but the problem with the movie was that it was about divorce. It was about Robin Williams, who is a guy everybody learned to love, who was no longer loved by Sally Field and who had to leave all his children. What grounds is this for comedy? We had been through this before, with a previous Chris Columbus movie, *Home Alone*, which we did. I remember Warner Bros., when they first had the movie, man they got rid of it and it went to Fox. Warner Bros. thought, 'What's funny about a family leaving a child alone in a house? Who's possibly going to go to that? What mother is going to take their children to see a movie that's going to make their children paranoid every night when they go to bed that they're going to wake up one morning and nobody's going to be around!' Well, history provides the answer, but at the time, this seemed like a major, major problem. Those are the kinds of issues that we have to face sometimes at an early stage and overcome. In the case of *Mrs. Doubtfire*, we tried to key in on Robin Williams and talk about his particular problem of a father trying to get back to his kids."

In the case of *Mrs. Doubtfire*, Arnold also cut the television spots, television being a medium that he says allows him "a little bit more freedom and a little bit less freedom. You have more freedom to choose targets, specific audiences, because you know that a television spot is going to air on a specific time slot or show. For instance, on *Mrs. Doubtfire*, we made spots for every conceivable audience. We made *Mrs. Doubtfire* Superbowl spots with a football concept in them, as we did with *Home Alone*. You can make spots for women, you can make spots for kids, you can make spots for men that air during sporting events, you can make spots that are upscale, that play during *L.A. Law*, you can make a specific spot for a specific audience. Although you have less time to do it in, you have a better idea of what it is you need to do. While you're doing a lot of advertising that is much better targeted, you're paying a lot more money for it. For example, it costs the studio the same amount of money to air one commercial as it costs for us to make an entire TV campaign. Studios pay millions of dollars in television time for showing spots. Our *Mrs. Doubtfire* Superbowl spot cost $3 million to air.

The spot itself cost $30,000. Television is a very, very expensive medium to buy time in. Trailers, on the other hand, play free. The theaters put them on at the request of the studios, and the truth is that very often, theaters don't put them on. Theaters are selective about what they show and what they don't show. Sometimes they'd rather sell popcorn."

More often than not, Chris Arnold's trailers make it onto the honor roll of "Coming Attractions." Even if they don't, well, he still feels privileged to inhabit his particular niche in the movie business. "I get to see where projects start, to see what was in people's minds to begin with, then I get to see the movie being put together and brought to fruition. I see how the final product compares to the original intent, and that's an education. Then I get to package that product into what I think is the most appealing way for an audience. Then I get to see it go out into the big, wide world and see what happens to it. Not everybody gets to have that kind of incredible experience. I've seen a thousand movies go through that process. Even John Huston, who was one of the greatest geniuses of our time, only got to see this process happen, what—twenty times?"

1. "Truth About Trailers: They Work," Leonard Klady, *International Variety*, Nov. 28 - Dec. 24, 1995, p. 13.

2. Ibid, p. 24.

3. Ibid, p. 24.

10

BLACK-THEMED FILMS BY BLACK FILMMAKERS

Young blacks attend movies more frequently than other segments of the U.S. population, and by virtue of that, they have a great deal of power at the box office. Their influence has been felt as far back as the "blaxploitation" films of the seventies, and more recently with the renaissance in black film that some say began in 1986, when Spike Lee wrote, edited, and directed his first film, *She's Gotta Have It*. Since then, moviegoers have flocked to black-themed films such as John Singleton's *Boyz N the Hood*, the single most profitable black-themed film in the industry's history,[1] which also elicited the first Best Director Oscar nomination for an African-American director. *Waiting to Exhale*, a film about the man troubles of four black women, directed by Forest Whitaker, surprised everyone in the industry by grossing nearly $67 million domestically in the biggest crossover box-office success of 1996.

Black filmmakers such as Spike Lee, John Singleton, the Hughes

Brothers (*Menace II Society, Dead Presidents*), Reginald and Warrington Hudlin (the *House Party* franchise), F. Gary Gray (*Set it Off, Friday*), and Tim Reid (*Once Upon a Time . . . When We Were Colored*) have succeeded in making films about the black experience that are marketable. "When John Singleton or Spike Lee directs a film, it's an additional selling point," says Mitchell Goldman, President/Chief Operating Officer New Line Cinema Marketing and Distribution. "Gary Gray is getting there, if not there already. In terms of the black community, a Hughes Brothers movie is an event, almost regardless of what it is. The Hudlin Brothers have been very active in the Black Filmmakers Association in New York. When they're involved in a movie, it also represents another star, or another imprimatur."

When New Line distributes a film by the Hughes Brothers, for example, the filmmakers are very involved in the publicity and marketing. "They go on the talk shows and do publicity along with the stars," says Goldman. "Their name is a little larger than life on the advertising materials, in light of what they deserve, which is their notoriety. We make sure people know—if they see the trailer, see the TV spots, listen to the radio spots, or read the newspaper—that it's a Hughes Brothers film, or a Hudlin Brothers film, or a Spike Lee film, or a John Singleton film. That's kind of important. They become, in essence, another star, besides the cast."

Although marketers may put black-themed films in a niche, black filmmakers don't necessarily like being categorized. "We don't like being lumped together, and we don't like our culture being taken into account with our filmmaking," says Allen Hughes. "Mario, John, Spike—we don't all think alike. We're not all the same people."[2]

Goldman feels black-themed films occupy a singular territory: "I would define a 'black film' as one that is about the black experience. I wouldn't say *Preacher's Wife* is a black film. I would go so far as to say that maybe *Waiting to Exhale* isn't a black film. I do think *Menace II Society* is certainly a black film, I do think *House Party* is a black film, I do think *Friday* is a black film. It is more specifically about the black experience. I do think a black film has to be directed by a black. That's my only nod to affirmative action. I think it's hard to call a film a black film if a white person has directed it. That's tough. I do think that a white person is capable of making a film that is noteworthy and important for the black community to see. I don't think it has to be a black director. I think when you're talking about a black film, that alone ghettoizes the film, I think almost correctly so, because what we call a black film is made specifically for a black audience, and not even made for a white audience to enjoy. So I think there's a definite determination on the part of the filmmaker and the producer and the writer at some point in time to say, 'Hey, we would love white people to see this movie, but we're not going to make it for them, we're going to make it for a black audience to appreciate the most, and hope that white people can also appreciate it.'"

Some argue that black-themed films have yet to meet their potential at the box office, for many reasons. "I feel badly for black films in the future, because I think there are some real problems ahead," says Goldman. "I think the economics of the business are not favorable for the kind of movies they're making because of the lack of foreign business. But I do think if they are properly produced, if the budget is properly controlled, and the film is properly marketed, a lot of films could be made about the black experience. Fortunately, for $5 to $10 million, you can still make a profit making a film about the black experience in America." Goldman doesn't think the prospects of making profitable black films are as good "anytime you go afield of that, if you start talking about periods, if you start going back in history, or if you start dealing with other subjects that aren't relevant to a contemporary black audience.

"I also believe there is a giant chasm between age groups in the black community, in the exact same manner there is in the white community," says Goldman. "They just want to see different movies. They have different tastes, different desires, different stars, different storylines. I think you can do well for an older black audience with a picture like *Corinna, Corinna*, which I essentially wouldn't call a black film, but it was a Whoopi Goldberg film. The older black audience can help you a lot with your box office. But the younger audience is not interested in seeing Whoopi Goldberg as a maid. On the other hand, a lot of the older black audience may not necessarily be interested in seeing a thing like a *Friday*, which is basically a young people's comedy about young black people. There is a difference in appeal. If I felt that the subject matter was appealing to mostly young blacks, I think it would be easier to make that movie, from a financial standpoint, than it would be to make a movie that's basically for older blacks, which is a smaller piece of the pie, in terms of frequent moviegoing."

Some black filmmakers like Warrington Hudlin, producer of the *House Party* movies and founder of the Black Filmmakers Foundation, say that assumptions about older black audiences become self-fulfilling prophecies. According to Hudlin, studios advertise with the assumption that *older* black audiences don't go to the movies very frequently: "If you are only advertising on hip-hop radio stations and in hip-hop magazines, then you are only reaching the under-twenty-five black moviegoer. Then the executives say, 'This is who comes.' Well, I say, 'That's who you invited.'"[3]

There is little agreement about whether black-themed films underperform at the box office because of the assumptions of movie executives, or because white audiences shy away from black-themed films. "In reality, the white audience looks at [a movie with an African-American theme] and says, 'It's not for me,'" according to Tom Sherak, who is now Chairman of the 20th Domestic Film Group, 20th Century Fox.[4]

In the opinion of Ivan Juzang, president of Philadelphia-based Motivational Educational Entertainment (MEE) Productions, the subgroup of adolescents that constitute the hip-hop generation define the youth film scene, because these black teens go to the movies three or four times a month.[5] MEE holds focus-group discussions for clients such as New Line Cinema, Disney and MGM to find out what appeals to urban youth and how best to reach them. Juzang attributes the success of *Menace II Society*, a New Line Cinema film about gangsters in L.A.'s Watts neighborhood, to its realistic portrayal of life in that milieu. "Kids tell us that they want to see movies that deal with the realities of their lives," says Juzang: "Is the movie logical? Does it make sense? It does not have to be hard-core about the urban scene, but if it is, it has to be real. To a lot of people, *Menace* was an extremely violent film. For the L.A. gang members in our focus group, it was a cautionary tale. Kids saw a lot of positive images in it."[6] According to Juzang, black teens want their humor "raw and R-rated,"[7] and he says that's why *Meteor Man*, a comedy starring Robert Townsend, didn't succeed in the marketplace.

Goldman says his research also indicates that young blacks are "very frequent moviegoers. They go to the movies more often than whites. They are easier to target in terms of media, because they are more specific about their wants or desires with regard to what shows to watch. They're less spread out." To reach young black audiences, Goldman places advertising for New Line films on shows like *New York Undercover*, popular sitcoms with predominantly black casts, shows on Fox and WB that are aimed at this core group, and in magazines like *Vibe*, which have a primarily black readership. Goldman defines blacks eighteen to thirty-four as one audience and blacks thirty-five and above as a totally different audience. He says there is a closer intersection between the fourteen-to-eighteen and the eighteen-to-twenty-five age group among blacks than among whites, perhaps because there are fewer pictures specifically targeted to black moviegoers.

According to a report by BJK&E Media Group, based on data from Nielsen Media Research, Fox is the most-watched network among black viewers, who represent about eleven percent of all TV households. The report also says that blacks are heavy viewers of the new WB and UPN networks, and that shows with black casts or main characters get higher ratings in black households. The shows that get the highest ratings from black viewers are Fox's *New York Undercover* and *Living Single*, NBC's *In the House*, Fox's *The Crew*, NBC's *The Fresh Prince of Bel-Air*, Fox's *Martin*, and ABC's *Family Matters*. According to the study, blacks watch more television than whites, with an average of 75.1 hours of television per week for black households and 50.2 hours per week for non-black households.[8]

"When it comes to distribution, reaching a black audience is a matter of knowing where they reside and what theaters they would like to go to, and being close to their homes, in the same way that any film would be distributed, no matter what their color is," says Goldman. "We have census information and historical theater information about cities, which tells us a little about moviegoing habits from an ethnic standpoint, so we pretty much know what we should be grossing in certain theaters in those cities if we're successful.

"You hit a home run domestically, theatrically, when you can make a picture for both black and white," says Goldman. "That doesn't mean you can't hit a home run without hitting black. It's almost impossible to hit a home run just hitting black. Certainly, when you can find a property or a casting or a subject matter that appeals to both black and white, you're really looking at much larger numbers when you have the support of both of those groups coming to the same movie. It doesn't happen as often as it used to.

"In terms of marketing, the idea is to reach as many people as possible. Just like any marketed movie, you have to buy the shows they're more likely to watch," says Goldman. "We know that there are certain ratings that delineate the black audience that we look at. But for certain pictures, we also know that there's an awful lot of ethnic viewing of shows that have nothing to do with ethnic programming, for example, sporting events, certain comedies, and drama shows. There may not necessarily be a black cast member, but they're still highly rated shows for an ethnic audience.

"You try to be in front of their eyeballs as much as possible with the right message, and the message changes based on the movie," says Goldman. "If a movie has action, there will probably be an action component in sales materials. If it's romantic, as in the movie *Love Jones*, you have a situation where you're showing no violence and no action. It has a different appeal, so you're showing moments of romanticism, human moments of relatable dialogue whenever possible. The idea is to convey that you're going to feel romantic when you see this movie.

"*Menace II Society* was a film that had a strong action component, but it also had a critical respectability and honor that went along with it," says Goldman. "It was a very unusual film in that regard. So we tried desperately to appeal to white audiences for, in essence, a very, very violent story about the black condition. Even with good reviews, we had great difficulties doing that—there was a great deal of resistance from the white audience to going to a movie theater to see *Menace II Society*. We don't exactly know why; we might have some guesses. The fact is, they just didn't respond theatrically, but we know that they've caught up with the film on video and cable. We do know that we've got the attention of the entire black community for that film. It had terrific legs. The word-of-mouth was terrific on it, and it became the movie you had to see in the black community. But unfortunately, it didn't become the movie you had to see in the white community at the time, despite our efforts. It was true and honest and real. I think people related to it, people knew that it was the truth, and not glossed over. Maybe for the first time, they knew it wasn't a Hollywood depiction of their life. They had a great deal of respect for the actors and they took to the story. *Menace II Society* grossed $30 million domestically. Video rentals were more successful than the $30 million would indicate, which tells us that the movie was rented very often in non-ethnic areas, which was very gratifying for us." (*Menace II Society* reportedly cost $3 million to produce and grossed $30 million; the *Menace* soundtrack sold 1.3 million units.[9] The Hughes Brothers' second film, *Dead Presidents*, cost between $13 and $15 million to produce and grossed $25 million.)

While *Menace II Society* may be considered a black-themed movie, its subject matter may well touch the lives of urban residents, black and white, according to a *Los Angeles Times* article reporting that the "Nationwide Spread of L.A. Gangs Is Alarming, FBI Says."[10] The FBI reports that criminal groups affiliated with the Los Angeles Bloods or Crips gangs have been reported in 180 cities in forty-two states. The Justice Department estimates that there are 652,000 gang members across the nation, wreaking the kind of havoc so graphically portrayed in *Menace II Society*. It is precisely the lives of those young gangsters the Hughes Brothers set out to chronicle in *Menace II Society*. Tyger Williams, who wrote the script from a story by him and the Hughes Brothers, says, "For every 'good' kid who makes it out of the ghetto, there are five more who don't. We asked the question, 'What's *their* story?'" *Menace* tells the story of a young black man who has hopes and dreams for a better life, but can't escape the violence of his surroundings, and ultimately gets killed. "This is a story about the guys who didn't have fathers for role models," says Allen Hughes. "They're hustling," says Albert Hughes. "One, the street. Two, make a buck. Good or bad. It's based on true, day-to-day life in Watts."[11]

While the lives of gangsters were the focus of *Menace II Society*, gang activity was largely in the background of another New Line film, *House Party*. "*House Party* was created initially from an independent short by the Hudlin Brothers, with a similar theme that was expanded upon," says Goldman of the film that has turned into a franchise for New Line. "For lack of a better description, it was sort of a black *Risky Business* in its day. It was about the kid who was trying to get away with having a party when his parents were out of town, without getting caught. It was also somewhat relatable, but also very strong in terms of music. Hip-hop was just blowing up at the time, and Kid 'N' Play [the young stars of the film] were hip-hop stars. It was the result of young filmmakers trying to depict what their life is like in a comic way."

House Party writer/director Reginald Hudlin says, "*House Party* is important because it portrays black teenagers as fully developed characters, not stereotypes. . . . It delivers a message without heavy-handed moralizing . . . sneaking out to a party is a great American tradition."[12] Hudlin's directorial debut—which mixed a comedic look at teenage dilemmas with moral questions of family values, teenage drinking, and sexual responsibility—received recognition from the directors in competition at the Sundance Film Festival, who awarded the film The Filmmakers Trophy and The Cinematography Award.

"*House Party* is almost the polar opposite of *Menace II Society*, but both have black filmmakers telling a story," says Goldman. "The pictures wound up appealing to the black audiences, probably in many cases the same people who had a taste for drama on one hand and comedy on the other."

The first *House Party* cost $2.5 million to produce, grossed nearly $27 million theatrically, and sold more than 150,000 videocassettes.[13] In addition to its theatrical release, it was also broadcast on Showtime. In 1991, the first installment was followed by *House Party 2*. It is the story of "The Mother of All House Parties—a Pajama Jammie Jam," held to raise tuition money for an African-American student (whose tuition money was stolen) at a predominantly white college. The film was so popular on college campuses that students throughout the country arrived at *House Party 2* screenings in their pajamas. The series did so well at the box office that New Line went on to produce *House Party 3*.

One of the biggest obstacles facing black-themed films is their lack of appeal in overseas markets. Even *Waiting to Exhale*, which brought in $67 million in domestic box-office, fell flat overseas. In Great Britain, for example, *Waiting to Exhale* grossed an anemic $2 million. This, in spite of the fact that *Waiting to Exhale* received the award for the Best Marketed Film of December 1995, from the Film Information Council (FIC). The FIC said they were "impressed by Fox's ability to surprise the industry by making a huge, crossover box-office success of a film starring four black women."[14] In giving the award, the FIC pointed to the marketing efforts they think contributed most to the film, including "the production and distribution of five separate music videos, three themed exposures on the *Oprah Winfrey Show*, star tours in twenty-five top markets, promotions in 10,000 beauty salons and 11,000 bookstores, satellite interviews on three days before opening, long-lead publicity approaches, and the teaming up, whenever possible, of Whitney Houston and Angela Bassett."[15]

"The response to *Exhale* shows that Hollywood has done an abysmal job of depicting African-Americans, serving up primarily crime-related portrayals and all but ignoring the middle class," said Fox chief Peter Chernin after the domestic box-office success of the movie.[16]

20th Century Fox produced *Waiting to Exhale* for about $17 million, estimating that it would gross $40 million from primarily black, female audiences. Fox opened the film on 1,300 screens, and aimed for a broad audience with their advertising. "We spent weeks and weeks trying to get middle white America to buy into this movie," says Tom Sherak. "We never succeeded. This would have been a $100 million movie if we had succeeded."[17] With its $67 million domestic gross, *Waiting to Exhale* was considered a solid hit, but not a blockbuster.

Goldman thinks foreign box-office is determined more by subject matter than by the skin color of the cast, in particular. "You can certainly agree, for example, that *Nutty Professor* is not a black film," says Goldman. "However, it's a predominantly black cast and there are no significant white stars whatsoever in the film. It happens to be a white director, it happens to be a white writer, and it's doing a lot of business overseas. So I think it's more about the subject matter of the film, as opposed to the color of the faces of the people. I would agree with you that Eddie Murphy is not exactly only a black star in the black community. But you would not expect an Eddie Murphy movie to do the kind of business *The Nutty Professor* did overseas either. The good news is, it's really about the film. But I think that when you talk about black films with black stars that are about the black experience, there's definitely a great distance between what is relatable in this country in certain neighborhoods, and what is relatable in foreign countries to the American black experience. That doesn't mean they can't appreciate a *Menace II Society* when they see it, as was the case at the Cannes Film Festival. But when you get out into the hinterlands of France, and England and Spain, it's less likely there's any interest at all in seeing a movie about the black American experience. *Waiting to Exhale* was unlike *Nutty Professor*, which had other things to sell—it was really about black men and women, their social situation and their problems with relationships, and their attempts to get out of relationships successfully, emotionally. I just don't think it was that relatable to white people who might even have the same problem. Without that component of comedy or action or special effects to go along with it, I think when you have to connect emotionally with a black character, it helps to be black."

When *Waiting to Exhale* opened in the United States, it brought in $14.1 million in box-office receipts, giving it the number one spot for the 1995 four-day Christmas holiday weekend. Exit polls showed that seventy percent of the audience was female and sixty-five percent were black. *Newsweek* film critic David Ansen says the film was filling a void, because "the black audience is fed up with inner-city, ghetto stories that speak to only a small section of their community. . . . There's a great hunger for projects about the middle-class experience, especially from a female point of view."[18]

"Studios have got to give audiences a broader view," says Tim Reid, director of *Once Upon a Time . . . When We Were Colored.* "Until they stop turning out this urban, dysfunctional stuff, I've no respect for them. Their stories leave me sad and sickened."[19] Based on Clifton L. Taulbert's best-selling novel, *Once Upon a Time . . . When We Were Colored* is a poignant story of a young boy's growing up in the midst of a loving family of sharecroppers in the segregated south, an unusual film that shows the strength and character of blacks in the face of the indignities of racism. Reid reports that after a screening in Chicago, he was approached by a black woman of about sixty-five who "came up and hugged me as hard as when I was a kid and my Aunt Dora grabbed me. She told me, 'In the last ten, fifteen years I've been watching the movies and this is the first time I've seen a black person die of natural causes.'"[20] Reid, an actor known for his roles in *WKRP in Cincinnati, Frank's Place,* and *Sister, Sister,* fought an uphill battle to get his film produced and distributed. Before the film was financed by Black Entertainment Television Pictures, Reid's film faced rejections from every studio in town, all the networks, *American Playhouse, Hallmark Hall of Fame,* and the Sundance Film Festival. Reid says that some studio executives told him the movie was "too soft," but they would make the movie if the conflict with the Ku Klux Klan was a more prominent part of the film. "They were telling me what black people want to see in a movie and what black people feel, and the closest they've come to a black person is a Lakers' game," says Reid. "What they're really saying is, 'I don't know if I'm ready to see this kind of dignity in black people on the screen. If we admit this, if we do this, does it mean we're living a lie if people like this really exist?'"[21] The film, shot for $2.5 million, was eventually distributed in five cities by Republic Pictures. "In some regards I think the film is subversive, in regard to the controlling of images of racially defined groups of people . . . along comes a movie about a time when character and courage, and all those wonderful values that many of us over thirty years old were brought up on, prevailed. It doesn't fit. And when it doesn't fit, distributors don't know how to sell it," says Reid.[22]

Reid may see black-themed films produced by Hollywood as the embodiment of dysfunctional urban black anger, but some distributors, like Goldman, say that such anger is color-blind. "I think you could say the same thing about Tarantino," says Goldman. "I don't think it has anything to do with being black. I think it has to do with movies being good and movies being commercial and movies being about something that other people are interested in. I'm not saying *Once Upon a Time . . . When We Were Colored* was a bad movie. I'm just saying that there's a lack of commerciality in the same way there's a lack of commerciality in Michael Apted's exploration of three generations of British children [*28 Up*, *35 Up*, etc.]. They weren't big box-office successes either, but Apted wanted to do them, and he was doing a subject that was interesting to some but mostly not to others. I don't think it's a black and white issue at all, it's about making small movies versus making big movies, making commercial movies versus non-commercial movies."

Allen Hughes, in an on-camera interview at the end of the *Menace II Society* video, gives his point of view on this controversy. "People nowadays, with black cinema especially, they want you to teach instead of entertain," says Allen Hughes. "It's all up to the individual coming in the theater, what they think. The weird thing is, we're not even being considered artists anymore, because you have to have this social responsibility. In art, you should be able to do what you want to do; if your vision is crooked, if your vision is racist, it's still your artistic—that's you, that's what you're doing, that's your personality. You shouldn't be imposed on by this outside—by people going 'don't do this' or 'do this,' or whatever." Adds Albert Hughes, "If it's glorifying violence, so be it, that's the way American history has been." Allen Hughes adds a qualification: "Not to say we're glorifying it [violence]. It's making money, it's exploitation and it's entertainment. People who aren't intelligent enough to realize that this is the underclass of a certain group of people, that's the way they operate, have no business even seeing a film. . . . It's not the whole race. A lot of people don't want to see that. . . . Our only message we were sending out was, understand how these kids can become these criminals, out of desperate conditions."[23]

Marketing Expenditures: *Menace II Society*
January '93 – September '94

$(000)

Sunday Magazines	0.1
Newspapers	1,976.8
National Newspapers	41.1
Outdoor	2.7
Network Television	1,434.9
Spot Television	109.3
Syndicated Television	42.6
National Spot Radio	567.9
Grand Total	4,175.4

© Copyright 1997 Competitive Media Reporting and Publishers Information Bureau.

Marketing Expenditures: *House Party*
January – December '90

$(000)

Newspapers	707.4
Network Television	153.0
Spot Television	408.9
Syndicated Television	123.9
Cable TV Networks	214.8
National Spot Radio	20.3
Grand Total	1,628.3

© Copyright 1997 Competitive Media Reporting and Publishers Information Bureau.

Marketing Expenditures: *House Party 2*

January – December '91

$(000)

Magazines	17.5
Sunday Magazines	37.2
Newspapers	505.1
Network Television	1,090.9
Spot Television	745.1
Syndicated Television	150.2
Cable TV Networks	135.7
National Spot Radio	423.6
Grand Total	3,106.0

© Copyright 1997 Competitive Media Reporting and Publishers Information Bureau.

Marketing Expenditures: *House Party 3*

January '93 – December '94

$(000)

Newspapers	1,068.1
Outdoor	7.2
Network Television	1,007.6
Spot Television	2.8
Syndicated Television	37.2
Cable TV Networks	37.1
National Spot Radio	728.1
Grand Total	2,888.1

© Copyright 1997 Competitive Media Reporting and Publishers Information Bureau.

Marketing Expenditures: *Waiting to Exhale*

January '95 – December '96

$(000)

Magazines	185.2
Sunday Magazines	0.1
Newspapers	7,360.7
National Newspapers	41.1
Outdoor	9.9
Network Television	7,225.3
Spot Television	1,868.7
Syndicated Television	993.8
Cable TV Networks	513.2
National Spot Radio	1,402.8
Grand Total	19,600.8

1. "Why Hollywood Keeps Blacks Waiting: A New Uproar Over the Film Industry's National Disgrace," Kim Masters, Jacqueline Trescott, *Washington Post*, March 24, 1996, p. G01.

2. "Second Time Around: Hughes Brothers Get a Chance to Improve on Their Debut," Marc Caro, *Chicago Tribune*, October 8, 1995, p. 7.

3. "Why Hollywood Keeps Blacks Waiting: A New Uproar Over the Film Industry's National Disgrace," Kim Masters, Jacqueline Trescott, *Washington Post*, March 24, 1996, p. G01.

4. Ibid.

5. "Marketing the Movies," Fred Pampel, Dan Frost, Sharon O'Reily, *American Demographics*, March 1994.

6. Ibid.

7. Ibid.

8. "Black Viewers Warm Up to Casting on WB, UPN," Stephen Battaglio, *Hollywood Reporter*, March 7, 1996, pp. 6, 143.

9. "Second Time Around: Hughes Brothers Get a Chance to Improve on Their Debut," Marc Caro, *Chicago Tribune*, October 8, 1995, p. 7.

10. "Nationwide Spread of L.A. Gangs Is Alarming, FBI Says," Robert L. Jackson, *Los Angeles Times*, April 24, 1997, p. B3.

11. *Menace II Society* press kit, New Line Cinema.

12. "*House Party*: If They Get Caught, It's All Over. If They Don't, It's Just the Beginning!", New Line Cinema Corp. press kit.

13. "New Line Cinema's *House Party 2* Completes Principal Photography," New Line Cinema Corp., on Business Wire, May 14, 1991.

14. "Film Information Council Votes 20th Century Fox's *Waiting to Exhale* Its Best Marketed Film Award for Month of December 1995," PR Newswire, January 19, 1996.

15. Ibid.

16. "*Waiting* to Start a Trend? Studios Are Anxious to See How Upcoming Black Films Will Fare," Elaine Dutka, *Los Angeles Times*, January 9, 1996, p. F1.

17. "Why Hollywood Keeps Blacks Waiting: A New Uproar Over the Film Industry's National Disgrace," Kim Masters, Jacqueline Trescott, *Washington Post*, March 24, 1996, p. G01.

18. "*Exhale*: The Right Film at the Right Time," Elaine Dutka, *Los Angeles Times*, December 28, 1995, p. F1.

19. "Tim Reid Fights to Get Word Out About his Film on Segregated South; Menace to Marketing?", Claudia Puig, *Los Angeles Times*, January 24, 1996, p. F1.

20. Ibid.

21. "A New Take on 'Colored' Life; Tim Reid Upsets Hollywood View of Being Black," Teresa Moore, *San Francisco Chronicle*, May 14, 1996, p. E1.

22. "Tim Reid Fights to Get Word Out About his Film on Segregated South; Menace to Marketing?", Claudia Puig, *Los Angeles Times*, January 24, 1996, p. F1.

23. Interview with Hughes Brothers that followed *Menace II Society* film on videotape, New Line Cinema.

11
MERCHANDISING AND PROMOTIONS

Plenty of hype preceded the opening of *Gone With the Wind*, but once fans saw the movie, that was the end of their purchase. The movie was the product, indeed the *only* product marketers were selling. While die-hard fans could obtain a copy of the poster for the movie, there were no *Gone With the Wind* baseball caps, T-shirts, ballgowns, tie-ins with fast-food franchises, home videos, etc. Today, movies can be much more than stories on celluloid. Many movies are positioned as "events," with numerous marketing opportunities associated with the opening and the duration of the run of the movie.

"Once you create value in a movie title, there's all kinds of other ways to cash in on it," says entertainment attorney Mark Litwak. "The theatrical release of a movie doesn't make a profit in many instances today, because it's expensive. But it builds public awareness of the title, which can become a valuable commodity and the basis for spinoff products, theme-park attractions, home video and cable TV sales, product-placement tie-ins, and soundtracks. These can generate enormous amounts of revenues."

"The real birth of the modern movie licensing business was the original *Star Wars* movie back in '77, and it caught a lot of people by surprise," says Martin Brochstein, editor of the industry trade publication *The Licensing Letter.* "That first Christmas, demand for *Star Wars* action figures so far outstripped supply that Kenner, who had the toy license for *Star Wars*, was forced to ship empty boxes to retail with IOU certificates in them so that people would at least have something to put under their tree. The certificates could be redeemed as supply caught up to demand. That really opened a lot of people's eyes as to what the possibilities were," recalls Brochstein. (Kenner, which is now owned by Hasbro, still has the license for *Star Wars*; Galoob also has a *Star Wars* license, for different merchandise.)

Star Wars was the first movie to show that merchandising revenues could rank right up there with ticket revenues. "*Star Wars* is a huge franchise that has done well over $3 billion in retail business over the years, and that has been one of the longer lasting ones in terms of that kind of property," says Brochstein. "There have been peaks and valleys over the years, and *Star Wars* merchandise has always sold. And obviously now, with the rerelease theatrically of the three movies, there's another big burst coming on. Check any magazine cover." For some movies—such as *Batman, Jurassic Park*, and *Star Wars*—merchandising revenues actually exceeded box-office revenues.[1]

"In the last ten years, merchandising has gone from being thought of as ancillary income to a very solid, well-researched budget line for the studios," says Brochstein. "In some cases it plays into the decision of whether a movie gets made or doesn't get made. It's not just this business on the side anymore. All the major studios have large consumer-products operations. Even the nomenclature of those divisions has changed. You now have Universal Studios Consumer Products and Disney Consumer Products. These are large, sophisticated operations, and they are growing in sophistication each year."

According to Brochstein, the filmed and TV entertainment/character licensing category accounted for approximately $16.7 billion of retail sales in 1996. This represents the largest segment of the total licensing industry, which Brochstein estimates to be $72.2 billion in retail sales in 1996. During the competitive summer feature season alone, industry experts estimate that corporate promotional partners funnel hundreds of millions of dollars into movie promotions. In the summer of 1995, for example, with promotions involving McDonald's (*Batman Forever* and *Mighty Morphin' Power Rangers*), Burger King (*Pocahontas*), and Pepsi/Pizza Hut (*Casper*), *Daily Variety* estimated that corporate tie-ins with movies totaled more than $200 million. Studios welcome these promotional tie-ins as maintenance advertising that kicks in once the studio has spent their big advertising dollars to open a film.

"Movies that offer the broadest opportunities in terms of merchandising are those that are aimed at juvenile audiences, because there you are dealing with parents who think something is cute and kids who want it bad," says Brochstein. "The types of products that are licensed has changed over the years, with more emphasis on adult merchandise, specifically, creating collectibles. For example, at a big sportswear-industry show, Disney put on a whole fashion show of adult clothing based on the *101 Dalmatians* theme. Movie character figurines are being sold at much higher price-points than in the past, obviously catering to an older, more affluent clientele.

"Disney has been commonly accepted as king of the merchandising hill," says Brochstein, "but they're being challenged by Warner and others. I think a lot of the studios have seen what a job Disney has done and want to replicate it, because there's a lot of money out there." Disney's biggest merchandising success has been *The Lion King*, which has generated more than $1.5 billion in retail sales of licensed merchandise; *Little Mermaid* merchandising chalked up $1 billion in retail sales. Of all the studios, Disney has been most successful at positioning itself as the "family brand" of filmed entertainment. Other companies, like Time Warner, are trying to compete with their own "brands." Time Warner's 1996 annual report has *Batman* on the cover with the message "Building Global Brands," which is repeated in the inside copy: "Brands build libraries, libraries build networks, networks build distribution, distribution builds brands."[2]

No one disputes Disney's pre-eminent position in the merchandising race. In 1995, twenty-one percent of Disney's revenue came from consumer products.[3] Disney had a head start on the merchandising competition, effectively opening its first studio store in 1955 with the opening of Disneyland. The first official Disney store opened in the Glendale (California) Galleria in March 1987; now Disney has 530 stores worldwide. Warner started playing catch-up in 1991, when it opened its own studio stores, and now has more than 150 worldwide. In May 1996, Disney opened its largest U.S. store in a 40,000-square-foot space at Fifth Avenue and 55th Street in New York; Warner Bros. opened their store, with 75,000 square feet, at Fifth Avenue and 57th just a few months later.

Warner Bros. is reportedly embarking on a new branding strategy for *Looney Tunes* that will involve creating a consistent identity and look for merchandise, home video, and studio store displays.

The Feature Animation Division's first full-length feature, *Space Jam*, which opened November 15, 1996, revives classic *Looney Tunes* characters in a live-action/animated film featuring NBA star Michael Jordan, and opens up a myriad of new merchandising possibilities. The movie combines live action and animation in a style similar to *Who Framed Roger Rabbit?*

Space Jam originated with television commercials featuring Bugs Bunny and basketball player Jordan. The story features Jordan and Looney Tunes characters playing a winner-take-all basketball game against players from outer space. Studio executives have been quoted saying that the budget for *Space Jam* is in the mid-$80 million range; industry speculation has placed it as high as $100 million. Its importance as a merchandising vehicle was emphasized by Time Warner chairman Gerald Levin when he reportedly told the *New York Times*, "*Space Jam* isn't a movie. It's a marketing event."[4]

In order to capitalize on their *Space Jam* investment, Warner Bros. has made merchandising deals with more than 200 licensees throughout the world to sell products ranging from apparel to greeting cards. Promotional partners include McDonald's, Jell-O, and Kraft. Despite the merchandising and promotional blitz, Warner Bros. executives try to keep their eyes on the prize. Says Robert Daly, Chairman and Co-Chief Executive Officer of Warner Bros.: "You don't do these movies just to sell merchandise. First, the movie has to be good, because all the merchandising doesn't mean anything if the movie isn't. The merchandising, as important as it is, is not going to be enough to justify the expense of making this movie."[5] *Looney Tunes* characters Bugs Bunny and his friends already generate $3 billion a year for Warner Bros. Some estimates place Warner's expectations for *Space Jam* at more than $1 billion in retail merchandise sales at the studio stores and at retail outlets such as Sears, Target, Wal-Mart, and Kmart.[6] If sales reach expectations, *Space Jam* merchandising profits would beat out Warner's *Batman Forever*, making it the most profitable merchandising effort for the studio thus far.

Competing at the box office with *Space Jam* in the fall of 1996 was Disney's *101 Dalmatians*. This live action remake of the 1961 animated classic starred Glenn Close, Jeff Daniels, and numerous puppies. Disney launched the most extensive merchandising campaign in their history for the *101 Dalmatians* opening. The studio made agreements with more than 130 companies licensed to sell *Dalmatians*-based products, which ranged from life-size stuffed dogs retailing for $200 to spotted roller skates, designer jewelry, silk scarves, luggage, and spotted Hush Puppies. Even Fido was included in this marketing blitz: Disney developed a line of expensive pet products as part of its merchandising effort. Disney, which now has an exclusive ten-year deal with McDonald's, launched its first major promotion with their fast-food promotional partner when *101 Dalmatians* was released. Other promotional partners included Dr. Pepper, Nestlé Corporation, Frito-Lay, and Alpo.

Brochstein estimates that movie property owners like Disney probably receive at least ten percent of the wholesale price as their share of profits; other industry observers estimate that licensers take can be as high as fifteen percent of wholesale. "Success in licensing efforts is a function not only of how much business it did, but also how much business you expected it to do," says Brochstein. "You're dealing with costs of manufacturing and inventory, so if you expected to do a billion dollars and you only did $700 million, that's going to disappoint an awful lot of people. For example, *Pocahontas* and *Hunchback of Notre Dame* did hundreds of millions of dollars, but there were expectations in the market that they would do better than that." Brochstein speculates that "*Hunchback* didn't do as well as *The Lion King* or *The Little Mermaid* because the nature of the characters and the story were not as clear-cut a warm-and-fuzzy children's property as some of the more successful Disney films."

Disney underestimated the appeal of *Toy Story*, leaving retailers empty-handed when children came looking for their Buzz Lightyear dolls. "From what I understand, Disney made a conscious decision not to stress licensing when they released *Toy Story*," says Brochstein. "What they were able to do was take advantage of the video launch of *Toy Story* in the fall of 1996 and do a much broader licensing job around that. It all comes down to people making decisions, even at a company like Disney. What's going to succeed? Not even Disney knows. You can have all the numbers in front of you that you want, but at a certain point, particularly in the entertainment business, it comes down to gut. *Pocahontas* was their big push. Even at Disney, they have limited resources. They made a judgment that *Toy Story* was going to be a nice movie, but it wasn't going to be a merchandising spectacular. There's an old story about the movie *E. T.: The Extraterrestrial.* Somebody at M&M Mars made the judgment that they didn't want to be involved with the movie. So all of a sudden, *E. T.* picked up Reese's Pieces along the way. People make judgments. Sometimes they screw up. Someone at M&M has probably made twenty other wonderful decisions along those lines, but sometimes you miss."

In order to avoid costly errors and cover all marketing bases, marketers have expanded to every available medium. "What has happened is that all the major studios are now integrated merchandising operations which tie in theme parks, movies, recorded music,

TV—they're multimedia operations, interactive entertainment," says Brochstein. "Take Internet-based marketing—the Internet has pretty much become an item on the checklist of things you do. Nobody knows if it really does anything for you, but it has become an item on the checklist: 'Oh, we must have a web site for his movie.' Most of the studios have their own web sites, and they have home pages on those web sites for specific movies."

One of the first providers of multimedia entertainment information to online services and the Internet was Hollywood Online, Inc. Its service is available on the Internet (http://www. hollywood.com) and through commercial online services such as America Online, CompuServe, Delphi, the Microsoft Network, Prodigy, and Japan's NIFTY-Serve Network. Hollywood Online is known for creating "Interactive Multimedia Kits," which are basically ads in the form of multimedia games. The service was started by Steven Katinsky and Stuart Halperin, marketing executives who lugged cumbersome computers to demonstrate the power of their new service to prospective clients when they were first launching their business.

Hollywood Online first appeared on American Online in July 1993 with interactive information for Columbia Pictures/Castle Rock Entertainment's *In the Line of Fire*. Since then, HOL has featured more than 100 major motion pictures in their entertainment areas, including *Forrest Gump, Species, Die Hard With a Vengeance, The Usual Suspects, Star Trek Generations, Dumb and Dumber, Little Women,* and *Judge Dredd*. The standard HOL interactive kit includes the usual elements of a press kit—cast biographies, storylines, photos—along with an interactive game. The *Forrest Gump* kit included a multiple-choice quiz on recent American history; for every correct answer, the player received a symbolic piece of chocolate from Gump's box of chocolates. Other elements in the kits can include online conferences with filmmakers, actors, and musicians; electronic shopping for movie merchandise and memorabilia; E-mail message exchange with people in the film industry; special games and contests and trailers. Internet users can download the information for no cost except the online service provider's fee.

For movie marketers, the demographics of web users are very attractive. Price Waterhouse estimates thirty to forty million people use the Internet worldwide; U.S. research shows that the majority of these users are thirty to forty years old, with one-third in the eighteen-to-twenty-nine age group, college-educated, with higher-than-average incomes.[7] The Internet audience has grown exponentially, with some observers estimating that the number of adult users of the worldwide web multiplies each year. Hollywood Online's Stuart Halperin says their research shows that Internet users are usually regular moviegoers, making them an ideal target audience for studios.

In the past, licensing and merchandising executives entered the filmmaking process late in the game, often after the film had completed development. Now they're entering the process far earlier, says Brochstein: "In some cases they are having an effect on characters, if not storyline. For example, one of the things that is stressed about next summer's *Batman* movie is that there are twice as many villains as there were before. That translates into twice as many villain figures and whatever goes with them. It's more merchandising opportunities. It's the same thing with *Jurassic II* [*The Lost World*]—there are twice as many dinosaurs. Certain decisions are made—if they're not driven by the merchandising, it's on people's minds."

Nowadays, licensing decisions are made as early as possible because the toy industry needs a lot of lead time. "Major retailers were having presentations made to them in the fall of '96, for holiday '97," says Brochstein, of the longer lead time. "Fox has an animated feature, *Anastasia*, coming out in the '97 holiday season, and they actually started some teaser marketing on television this past holiday, a year in advance."

Profits from licensing can add substantially to a movie's bottom line. *Jurassic Park* tie-ins generated more than $1 billion in sales. Universal Studios Consumer Products division, which coordinated the licensing efforts, is now gearing up for the merchandising of *The Lost World*, Steven Spielberg's sequel to *Jurassic Park*. Universal Studios' Hollywood's Jurassic Park: The Ride was launched in summer of 1996. Universal Merchandising President Jim Klein says that *The Lost World* sequel will involve fewer licensees than the first dino movie, but will involve a more extensive "fashion"[8] apparel line. Klein has estimated that the film's status as an "event" will help boost sales from twenty percent to twenty-five percent over the $1 billion in retail merchandise sales generated by *Jurassic Park*.

Perhaps the most ubiquitous promotional efforts for movies involve fast-food franchises. Taco Bell has signed up to promote Warner Bros.' *Batman and Robin*, Burger King will promote Amblin/ Universal's *Lost World*. From their track record, it appears that fast-food companies prefer to tie in with properties that have had some visibility and longevity in the marketplace. These tie-ins can prove lucrative to both promotional partners. When Burger King invested an estimated $45 million in ads and premiums in its *Toy Story* promotion, they saw a decisive return on their investment. During the first week of Burger King's *Toy Story* promotion, which began a week before the film's November 22, 1995, opening, the fast-food chain doubled its sales of Kid's Meals over the previous year's sales, when Burger King was promoting the re-release of *The Lion King*.[9] Burger King reportedly sold 6.4 million Kid's Meals that first week; they produced fifty million toys for the *Toy Story* promotions. In addition to Burger King, Disney's promotional partners on *Toy Story* included Nestlé and Minute Maid. Together, the promotional partners' investment expenditures came to $125 million, including $50 million in media, which complemented the $15 to $20 million the studio reportedly spent on its own advertising campaign.[10]

Until McDonald's signed an exclusive, ten-year tie-in deal with Disney, Burger King had a series of beneficial tie-ins with Disney movies, beginning with *Beauty and the Beast* in 1991. In the summer of 1995, Burger King ran an eight-week promotion tied in to *Pocahontas*, distributing eight action figures from the movie with their Kid's Club Meals. Burger King distributed fifty-five million of the *Pocahontas*-theme action figures. Industry experts speculated in the *Wall Street Journal* that the *Pocahontas* promotion cost Burger King $25 million.[11] According to Kim Miller, a spokeswoman for Burger King, the tie-in with movies is well worth it: "Between thirty and thirty-five percent of our business is comprised of families. . . . The *Pocahontas* movie and our tie-in with Disney offers superior family entertainment, so that buys in with our concept of appeal to the family . . . the movie is nonviolent and has equal boy-girl appeal."[12]

Many parents consider a "free" toy with a meal a deal. At Burger King, Kid's Club Meals cost $1.99 and up, for a hamburger, french fries, a drink, and a toy. Marketers believe the toy premiums represent value added to a meal, since the toys could cost from $2 to $5 if they were purchased in a store. On the other hand, no one has ever done a study on how many parents avoid fast-food franchises with toy giveaways, precisely because of the incessant nag factor—once you give children a toy, they'll nag you endlessly until you give them another one, with children ordering meals they have no interest in eating, just to get the toy. Many parents prefer abstinence to submission when it comes to fast-food-outlet toy promotions, but for the time being, no one knows how big a segment of the potential market they represent.

In the trenches of merchandising are the toy designers and manufacturers who work with fast-food clients to develop the positioning for movie premiums—those little toys kids receive with their Happy Meal at McDonald's or their Kid's Meal at Taco Bell and other fast-food restaurant chains. Bill Howard, one of the owners of the toymaker Playworks, is in the business of developing premiums for corporate partners of entertainment properties to give away with their product. Howard's company works exclusively with Pepsi World Trade, a division of Pepsi International that develops premiums for both internal and external customers, including the Pizza Hut and Taco Bell marketing groups. "Our involvement comes when they have selected a property and ask us to develop the product positioning, not for *Star Wars*—Mr. Lucas has a positioning for *Star Wars*—but for Taco Bell *Star Wars* premiums or for Pizza Hut *Star Wars* premiums," says Howard. "How should those premiums be positioned at the restaurant? What should be the strategy in terms of play value and what the toy is?"

Pizza Hut and Taco Bell have four companies, including Playworks, that are prequalified to make toy premiums for them. Although Playworks is considered an internal company, they still compete with the other three vendors for Pizza Hut and Taco Bell contracts, because the client wants the creativity that springs from competition among multiple vendors. The end product is like any inexpensive toy you might find at Toys R Us, but the development cycle for premium toys is much shorter than for retail. Toy manufacturers like producing premiums because they involve a one-time sale, without the vicissitudes of retail supply and demand and the headache of returns.

"The restaurants, the beverage producers, and the cereal companies want to borrow interest from what's considered exciting and is going to be talked about among their target audience," says Howard. "They tie into entertainment properties like *Batman* or *Star Wars* because they're exciting and they have high awareness and high interest among their target audience. People who are considering licensing the entertainment property to make merchandise look carefully to determine if this license has ready product application for the kind of product they do on the kid meal side.

"Taco Bell was very successful this past year with *The Tick* program," says Howard. "*The Tick* has a good following and it is sort of an edgy cartoon that fits in with Taco Bell's little bit hipper, little bit edgier position in the market place with six-to-eight-year-olds. The fact that there isn't a lot of shelf space devoted to *Tick* merchandising in the toy area made the merchandise that was given away by Taco Bell that much more exciting to consumers."

The process of developing a toy premium involves close collaboration between the film studio and the toymaker. Howard worked on the creation of a toy premium for *Flipper* with promotional partners MCA Universal and Pizza Hut. "We met with Pizza Hut and with MCA/Universal, and they talked about what the movie was going to be and how they were positioning the movie.

Their people were really terrific at getting across the essence of the film, as well as the personality of Flipper and what Flipper was all about as part of this film. One of our first processes was to ask ourselves, 'Why do kids care about Flipper' and 'Why are kids going to care about our Flipper toys?' Well, Flipper is your friend. Flipper is like your dog in the water. He's your buddy. But why is he your buddy? Why is he fun to be with? Well, he's kind of clever and he's a little bit witty. He's your clever and witty friend in a water/summer kind of environment. Then every concept that the creative group came up with was looked at in terms of 'Hey, does that look like a cool toy? Is it the kind of thing that you're going to take and show to your friends? Does it meet the requirements for product strategy and extended play values that we're looking for? Does it also represent Flipper as a clever and witty friend of the water who you can play with and who will give you a smile?'"

Given the turnaround time required to manufacture toy premiums, toymakers like Howard usually begin the design and manufacturing process several months before the movie itself is completed. "A lot of the premiums that we do are injection plastic, which takes a couple of months in sculpting, tooling, and reproduction," says Howard. "The premium is produced in the Orient, shipped over here, then needs to work its way through a distribution system to get to the restaurant. We're usually somewhere between six and nine months ahead of the movie, so what they'll show us is selected pieces of the movie—enough to give us a flavor. In the case of *Flipper*, they had some footage that E! Entertainment had done and a sizzle piece MCA Universal had put together to try to sell licenses and get retailers excited, a piece to show to people who needed to have the enthusiasm to make that commitment up front. When we worked on *Dragonheart*, the director put together a special ten-minute screening of the movie for us. The dragon wasn't in there yet, so he was taking a risk that people would be able to make the creative jump from where he was to a finished product."

Frequently, the toy design involves a combination of the old and the new, classic toys with contemporary characters. The *Flipper* premium was based on a timeless toy design. Howard describes its genesis: "One of the guys regularly goes to the flea market and sometimes he'll pick up an old toy, a collectible. He'll find a way of making it in new materials, contemporizing it in terms of its materials and its play value and design. In this case, he came back with a wooden clown on two sticks that you could make jump and do some acrobatics on two little strings when you squeezed the two wooden sticks. The engineers started working with that, using different kinds of plastic. The *Flipper* toy they designed is made of ABS plastic and polypropylene and it's actually a little bit of a hand-skill game. You need to give it a little toss to keep it going. They gave two million of these away when people bought a certain pizza and soft drink combination. Then another company made a *Flipper* hand puppet that could squirt at you—you might have seen it advertised—and they sold those for a buck sixty-nine. The hand puppet had a ball inside that you squeezed and it squirted out water. We made the free giveaway, and one of the other companies in the vendor pool made the item that was sold."

Coordinating the promotional effort with the release of the movie is essential for both promotional partners to get maximum bang for their buck. Howard first learned the importance of timing in promotions when he worked for ad agency Ogilvy & Mather on their Paramount Studio business. "At Ogilvy & Mather, I was on the other side of some of these deals, attracting corporate partners to tie in with the movie property. Ideally, we wanted people three weeks ahead of the movie—you didn't want it too far ahead. It is really the same place that the studio puts all of its money. You want it close enough to when people are going to make a purchase decision. The job of the marketing people is to open that picture opening weekend and give it legs—but it's really about 'Can you open?' If you open with five million, you're not going to turn around and get ten or fifteen million the following weekend. It is generally one of two directions from there: it is stable to a slight decline, or it starts falling off then, depending on how the picture plays and how good the word-of-mouth is. So, the studio wants the promotional effort up front, so they can get enough people there with word-of-mouth on opening weekend to get the number-one box-office position, which has publicity value. The studio wants as much media weight from the promotional partner as possible. They are certainly going to want the creative to fit the position of the film, but they want to have the media weight. So the more dollars they have, the more targeted and properly positioned impressions the promotional partner can deliver, the better for the property. They're not going to want you out there, and you're not going to want to be out there ten or seven weeks before the film opens. As the partner, part of what you're buying into is the heat, the awareness, and the buzz, and that's not there ten weeks out. The studio's money isn't really kicking in until the last couple weeks. So it's in both the partner's interest and the studio's interest to have the media dollars spent two to three weeks prior to the film's opening and going through the opening. For example, if the film is opening on Friday, July 14, ideally you want most of the media dollars spent for those first weeks.

They'll take it as long as they can get it, but the reality is, there is usually a window that works for the corporate partner. I haven't seen things stretch for too much more than three to four weeks of pumping in media."

Financial arrangements between promotional partners vary with each studio. Howard points out that studios such as Universal and Fox have their theatrical promotions person within the licensing division while other companies, such as Paramount, Disney, and MGM have their promotions people report directly to theatrical marketing, not to the licensing division. "Some arrangements involve a licensing fee and others are purely about the studio getting the exposure and the media dollars. Both arrangements have a value. The studios may vary from project to project in terms of what they are looking for. I would say for the most part, the studios are very conscientious in having that big media push to help on the awareness side. From the studio side, they would love to have a promotional partner bring in three, four, five hundred television ratings points a week, but they'll take a hundred points a week, too."

The contribution of a promotional partner is measured by rating points as well as the total media value a studio gets from a corporate partner. "A good-size partner might involve bringing six to ten million dollars in media spending," says Howard. "Of course, whenever the studios talk about their big films, they inevitably say they have a hundred million dollars of promotional support from corporate partners. They like the sound of that rule of thumb. I think the numbers all get a little bit inflated when people are trying to make it seem exciting." The small premium toys given away in the first-tier restaurants cost from twenty-five cents to fifty cents each. Many fast-food restaurant promotions involve the give-away of millions of these premiums.

Howard segued into entertainment marketing after working in the advertising business in packaged-goods products for clients such as General Mills and General Foods. He received a B.A. in History and Art History from the University of Pennsylvania, and became interested in communications after editing a literary magazine in college. He was attracted to advertising because he thought it offered him the opportunity to be involved in "creative collaboration, business analysis, and a diversity of problem-solving situations." He spent two-and-a-half years as vice president of advertising at the Universal Studios theme park in Florida, handling the development of all the initial advertising for point-of-purchase (that is, the advertising you see at the location where you purchase the product). Then he moved to Los Angeles, where he joined Ogilvy & Mather, managing the Paramount Pictures account, working on both advertising and promotions. At Ogilvy & Mather, Howard worked on films such as *Days of Thunder*, *The Addams Family*, and *Wayne's World*. "At that point, I was working from the studio perspective, calling on the Subway Sandwiches and Pizza Huts of the world, trying to get them to take on our property. We were not license-dollars focused, we were media-dollars focused. We wanted to have them help bring awareness to our pictures. In addition to our corporate partners, we were looking at the cable networks where we spent advertising dollars. We would try to leverage our advertising dollars on cable and exercise some creativity to get them to do promotions that would create excitement for their network and at the same time benefit the corporate partner. Howard cites the example of a cross promotion that involved *All I Want for Christmas* (a Paramount family movie), Lifetime Cable Network, and Macy's department store. The promotion involved a contest with a prize of a trip to New York and a chance to be in the Macy's Thanksgiving Day Parade. Lifetime advertised the contest and encouraged viewers to enter the contest at Macy's; Macy's ran video trailers for the movie in their stores, and also supplied the contest winner with the payoff of being in the Macy's Thanksgiving Day Parade.

Howard was often involved in agency advertising shoots, such as the promotional spot for *The Addams Family* movie, which involved M.C. Hammer, who did some of the music for the movie. On this shoot, which was for an MTV spot, Howard was concerned about overtime, as always. "I've done a lot of advertising shoots and you really want your shoot to come in on budget, you try to avoid overtime situations. I went on the MTV shoot to represent Paramount's interest and we're sitting around there for six hours. M.C. Hammer shows up six hours late. He shows up with fifteen people and a couple of big limos, and goes off into the trailer where he's going to change, and we don't see him for another couple of hours. By the time they started shooting the spot, it was an overtime situation. Big stars." Despite occasional glitches, Howard really likes his work: "Like the advertising business, it has both a creative collaboration process and a more analytical problem-solving process."

In the toy-premium business, the biggest obstacles toymakers face is often the short turnaround time they are given to design, produce, and ship the toys. When Playworks produced eight figurines based on *The Hunchback of Notre Dame*, characters that were scheduled to go into Kellogg's cereal boxes in Latin America, the job involved the production of millions of figurines. They got the job when the company who had originally been awarded the bid couldn't deliver. The biggest problem they faced was meeting the client's deadlines. "Often we're faced with timing that makes it very difficult to manage your product," says Howard. "It just puts you in the high-risk situation that you might not be able to deliver. If you can't deliver, you can be looking at large consequential damages lawsuits. We do a careful risk evaluation at the beginning, but we're often pushing the envelope. Because our engineers and our designers are so integrated and we have very good factory management people, we're probably able to take some risks that other companies wouldn't."

Ultimately, the success of a movie depends on the story, and the story depends on the writer. Merchandising is an extension of the success or failure of the story, but also a function of the forces put behind products in the marketplace. Given the profitability of merchandising when it is successful, we're likely to see a greater proliferation of ancillary products and experiences as the studios compete to produce the next blockbuster movie/marketing event. After all, look at *Star Wars*. The trilogy has been with us for more than twenty years now, and we've been inundated with videocassette versions, fan clubs, action figures, costumes, collectibles, 963 sites on the world wide web, all garnering an amazing $4 billion in merchandising sales. The first *Star Wars* movie itself brought in $323 million domestically, putting it fourth on the all-time box-office hit list, behind *E.T.*, *Jurassic Park*, and *Forrest Gump*. Worldwide ticket sales for the entire trilogy were $1.3 billion the first time around. The merchandising sales were triple that figure. *Star Wars* is the most profitable "brand" in Hollywood, and director George Lucas owns it because his original *Star Wars* contract gave him sequel and licensing rights in exchange for a reduced directing fee.

No question, *Star Wars* changed the fiscal dynamics of Hollywood forever, and not necessarily for the better. A recent *Wall Street*

Journal article reported that two of today's three best-selling children's books are spinoffs of movies—a development certain to distress lovers of children's *literature*. The bestsellers were *Pocahontas, Math Curse* by Jon Scieszka, and *The Lion King*.[13] Nonetheless, questions of value rarely torment the most profit-obsessed in Hollywood, convinced as they are that moviemaking is first and foremost show *business*. Unwittingly, *Star Wars* changed the face of that business, ushering in the era of the mindless, big-budget, special-effects-laden, merchandising-obsessed blockbuster—the staple of studio production today. Mercifully, the forces of good and evil continue to fight it out in the marketplace, guaranteeing an audience for not only the inane and the lowest common denominator, but also the inspired and the finest artistic achievement.

1. "101 Movie Tie-Ins; With Merchandising Money Rivaling Its Box-Office Take, Hollywood Is Saying, 'Attention Shoppers!'" Bruce Handy, with reporting by Georgia Harbison (New York) and Jeffrey Ressner (Los Angeles), *Time*, December 2, 1996, p. 78.

2. "This Year, the Entertainment Industry Has a Brand-New Angle," James Bates, *Los Angeles Times*, July 30, 1996, p. D6.

3. "Hollywood's New Toy Story," Marla Matzer, *Los Angeles Times*, November 13, 1996.

4. "101 Movie Tie-Ins; With Merchandising Money Rivaling Its Box-Office Take, Hollywood Is Saying, 'Attention Shoppers!'" Bruce Handy, with reporting by Georgia Harbison (New York) and Jeffrey Ressner (Los Angeles), *Time*, December 2, 1996, p. 78.

5. "Merchandising Mania," *Los Angeles Times* "Calendar," October 17, 1996, p. F13.

6. "Hollywood's New Toy Story," Marla Matzer, *Los Angeles Times*, November 13, 1996.

7. "The Internet as Film Marketing Tool," John Adair, *Film Marketing International*. [Taken off the Moving Pictures International web site at http://www.filmfestivals.com/mpnews/mpn1509.htm]

8. Ibid. [*Variety*, June 24, 1996. p. 14.]

9. "Toying with Success: Tie-Ins Tap Big $: *Toy Story*," Gary Levin, *Daily Variety*, December 15, 1995, p. 18.

10. Ibid.

11. "Burger King Scores TKO with *Pocahontas* Tie-In," Don Ruggless, *Nation's Restaurant News*, July 17, 1995, p. 14.

12. Ibid.

13. "That Was Then, This Is Now . . . At Age 5, Reading, Writing, and Rushing," *Wall Street Journal*, February 4, 1997, p. B1. [Sources cited for bestseller statistics are *Publisher's Weekly* and The New York Public Library. The three bestselling children's books in the 1960s were *Green Eggs and Ham* by Dr. Seuss, *Richard Scarry's Best Word Book Ever*, and *Where the Wild Things Are* by Maurice Sendak.]